$11.00

DATE DUE

AUG 1 7 1983	SEP 1 3 1991
OCT 1 6 1983	
	SEP 2 8 1991
FEB 4 1984	NOV 25 1991
JUL 3 1 1984	AUG 25 1993 R
AUG 20 1986	Sept 20
AUG 20 1987	DEC 3 1 1991
NOV 9 1987	JAN 3 1 1992
JUL 5 1988	
JUL 2 6 1989	JUL 27 1992
	JUL 3 0 1992
MAR 1 1 1990	MAY 2 2 1993
OCT 2 '90	JUN 1 9 1993 R
	DEC 2 7 1993
JUL 1 6 1991	JAN 31 1994

261-2500

Printed in USA

Going Vegetarian

A Guide for Teen-agers

by **Sada Fretz**

illustrated by Eric Fretz

William Morrow and Company
New York 1983

I would like to thank Kathleen Carpenter, M.S., R.D., doctoral candidate at Columbia University's School of Public Health, instructor in community nutrition and nutrition education at New York University, and editor of *Environmental Nutrition,* for reading the manuscript. Special thanks also to Bruce Kramer, currently a student at the New Jersey School of Medicine, for weekly loaves of sustaining bread, hours of nutrition conversation, reading chapters in progress, and off-duty service on the Science Hot Line. Any errors in fact or interpretation are entirely my own.

Library of Congress Cataloging in Publication Data
Fretz, Sada.   Going vegetarian.
Bibliography: p.
Includes index. Summary: Explains philosophical, practical, and nutritional aspects of vegetarianism, a term which had nothing to do with vegetables when coined in the 1840's. Includes more than 50 meatless recipes.
    1. Vegetarianism—Juvenile literature. 2. Vegetarian cookery—Juvenile literature. 3. Youth—Nutrition—Juvenile literature. [1. Vegetarianism. 2. Vegetarian cookery. 3. Nutrition] I. Fretz, Eric, ill. II. Title.   TX392.F83   1982   641.5'636
82-14230
ISBN 0-688-01713-4

Contents

List of Recipes

Foreword

More and more young people are adopting a vegetarian lifestyle these days. For some, vegetarianism is a temporary way of life while they experiment with making independent choices in preparation for adulthood. For others, however, a vegetarian diet represents concern with environmental, health, and religious and philosophical issues, and may signal the beginning of a lifelong commitment.

In light of recent research, vegetarianism is now seen as a viable alternative to a meat-based diet. Enough evidence has accumulated to suggest that the high fiber and carbohydrate and lower fat and cholesterol levels of the vegetarian diet have definite health benefits.

Like all diets, however, vegetarian menus depend on moderation and variety for nutritional adequacy. For young people who are still growing and developing, the question of nutritional adequacy has special importance. Because most aspiring young vegetarians come from meat-eating families, they cannot rely on the "folk wisdom" they grew up with to tell them what to eat and how much. The good news, though, is that thousands of American young people have reached a healthy adulthood on vegetarian diets. The key is information.

In her book, Sada Fretz covers the health and nutritional concerns of the vegetarian accurately and completely. The recipes and menus provide invaluable assistance in meal planning and encourage self-reliance on the part of the teen-age vegetarian. Her book encourages moderation and warns against extremes. This book will be a welcome resource for aspiring young vegetarians.

Kathleen Oliver Carpenter, M.S., R.D.
Editor, *Environmental Nutrition Newsletter*

PART 1

The Case Against Meat

CHAPTER
1

The Age of
Asparagus

Not long ago, any American who admitted to being a vegetarian was considered a crackpot, a counterculture faddist, or possibly a member of some weird religion. Most people's picture of a typical vegetarian was either a little old lady with constipation anxieties or a feeble young hippie wasting away on brown rice, seaweed, and far-out philosophy.

Today, it seems that almost every family has one. By 1979 so many American teen-agers had gone vegetarian that *Time* magazine was offering parents wry advice on dealing with their righteous offspring. College cafeterias were offering a choice between veggie and nonveggie lines; and the food-service director at Smith College called the trend to vegetarianism "the most drastic and widespread change in student eating habits" he had seen in twenty years on the job.

Now, people who choose not to eat meat can sign up for vegetarian cruises, attend meatless potluck suppers at their churches, and find recipes for turkeyless Thanksgiving dinners in supermarket magazines. They also can drive across the United States sporting vegetarian bumper stickers, stopping off at restaurants recommended by national guides to vegetarian dining.

A 1978 Roper poll found 7 million adult vegetarians in the United States. With teen-agers added in, the Vegetarian Information Service estimated the total number of American vegetarians at over 9 million. Another 37.5 million were being "careful" about how much meat they ate. An impressive 78 percent of all the people polled agreed that there were good reasons for being vegetarian. Yet the thought of going without meat still strikes the average American as grim. The comedian Dick Gregory says that when he first became a vegetarian in 1965, he had the idea that he would have to survive on "side orders." At the time, he couldn't think of dinner as anything but meat or fish, with vegetables on the side.

A lot of Americans still think of dinner that way. Though beef consumption began to decline in the late 1970s, the vast majority of Americans are still heavy meat eaters. We still consume twice as much beef and less than half as much grain per person as our grandparents did seventy years ago. As a consequence, many have forgotten what goes into a meatless meal. Ask what vegetarians eat and the answer will probably be "Vegetables, of course."

Actually, most vegetarians base their diets on grains, which they eat in greater abundance and variety than many meat eaters know. According to the British Vegetarian Society, which coined the term back in the 1840s, the word *vegetarian* has nothing to do with vegetables. The society's founders based their name on the Latin word *vegetus,* meaning active, lively, or vigorous. At the time, the word *veget* was used in England to describe a robust, healthy person. According to the society, the diet most conducive to a healthy, vigorous life was a meat-less one.

Vegetarians do eat vegetables every day, just as meat eaters do; but those who take an interest in cooking and eating use a greater variety of vegetables, prepared in more interesting ways, than the canned or frozen peas and carrots that most meat eaters use as side dishes. Instead of the so-called standard American dinner of meat and potatoes, vegetarians choose from other traditional foods. Instead of the daily burger or chicken breast, they might get their protein from Mexican re-fried beans and tortillas, Indian chick peas and rice, lentils and bulgur wheat from the Middle East, or the Oriental soybean cake called tofu. Or they might stick with more familiar fare such as pizza or spaghetti and cheese, or even good old peanut-butter sandwiches. Nutritionists now recognize that these foods can keep you at least as vigorous and robust as meat does.

Of course, not all meatless diets are healthy. And if meat eaters have a kooky image of vegetarians, there are always plenty of kooks around to live up to it. One Indian swami now in New York goes on "mono diets," eating only one food for a long period of time. He bases this practice on "common sense," which he says tells him that every natural food is well balanced by itself. As proof he points to the cow, who "eats only grass yet brings forth milk that contains all the nutrients." Apparently common sense doesn't remind him that cows' digestive systems are totally different from ours—or that milk does not contain "all the nutrients."

Most vegetarians don't support mono diets, but many have claims for their diet that are just as hard to prove. For example, ever since vegetarianism has been a movement, there have been enthusiasts who link meat eating with beastlike behavior. In the buttoned-up Victorian days, British vegetarians warned their carnivorous countrymen that eating meat could stimulate lewd appetites and animal passions. Today, when nuclear war and violent crime are among our major worries, some vegetarians blame meat for making people warlike and vicious. The general idea seems to be that one violent act leads to another, and eating meat depends on the violent act of killing. As one vegetarian said, "I eat everything that nature voluntarily gives: fruits, vegetables, and the products of plants. But I ask you to spare me what animals are forced to surrender."

Many young people who give up meat announce that they feel more "gentle" as a result. After all, some will argue, who could be more gentle than Mahatma Gandhi, the great Indian leader who helped his people win independence by waging a campaign of nonviolent resistance to British rule? Gandhi was a fervent vegetarian, and his strong views against meat eating were an integral part of his nonviolent philosophy. But Adolf Hitler, the madman responsible for the murder of millions and the biggest war in history, was also a faithful vegetarian—and the Reverend Martin Luther King, who applied Gandhi's nonviolent philosophy to the American civil-rights movement, was not. And that gentle statement I just quoted about nature's voluntary gifts was made by Adolf Hitler.

The meat-and-violence theory doesn't hold up any better when applied to whole populations than it does with individu-

5

als. There are some peace-loving groups who eat very little meat. But the Eskimos eat almost nothing but meat and fish, and they have been among the most peaceful and friendly people on earth.

If it is impossible to prove that meat eating makes people violent, it is just as hard to generalize about the life-styles of today's vegetarians. Many new vegetarians are, in fact, gentle folk, committed to living a simple, harmless life, in harmony with nature and as far removed as possible from what they see as our energy-guzzling, overconsuming society. Some hope that by living this way they are setting the example for a new age of peace and sanity. Their models might be Helen and Scott Nearing, who left a comfortable life as a concert violinist and an economics professor for one of self-sufficient home-steading in Maine. The Nearings built their own stone house and other farm buildings by hand. Their fuel is the firewood they chop by hand, and they grow 85 percent of their food. As for the healthfulness of their simple and meatless life, neither Nearing has seen a doctor since they took it up fifty years ago. Helen is now in her late seventies and Scott in his late nineties.

There's a world of difference between the New Age life-style of the Nearings' admirers and the New Wave life that hits its peak at two A.M. in New York's punk clubs. But if the two groups should happen to pass at dawn, they might find themselves trading recipes. Seeing the tacky fashions and hearing the avant-garde dance rhythms of the B-52s, you wouldn't peg them as zucchini-bread-with-tomato-sauce types. But that's what Kate Pierson, the group's female vocalist, says they like to cook at home. Male vocalist Fred Schneider gave up meat in 1975, out of concern for animals and his own nutrition. Now three of the group's five members are committed vegetarians.

The vegetarians of the past have been just as independent and unpredictable. One group that reinforced the meatless diet's kook image in western Canada was the Doukhobors, a band of Christian pacifists who migrated from Russia around the turn of the century. One particular set of Doukhobors, calling themselves the Sons of Freedom, soon became notori-ous for their meatless, raw-food diet, their nude protest marches, and their habit of throwing incendiary bombs to make their pacifist points. In the early 1900s, the Sons of Freedom made colorful news copy, but they were hardly typical vegetarians. And the many other religious groups who abstain from meat are as mixed a lot as those who eat it.

For the Jains, members of an ancient sect in India, vegetarianism follows necessarily from their reverence for all life and their strong principles against killing any creature, even a mosquito. In this country, the Seventh-day Adventists refrain from eating meat—not for the animals' sake but because they believe that it pollutes the human body, which they view as a temple of God. John Wesley, who founded the Methodist Church, was a vegetarian, though most present-day Methodists are not. The silent, retiring Trappist monks, who are Catholic, do not eat meat, nor do those chanting, saffron-robed, Easternized Americans popularily known as the Hare Krishnas.

With all this diversity, about the only generalization we can make about vegetarians is that they do not eat meat. But even this rule is interpreted differently by different vegetarians.

At one end of the vegetarian spectrum are people who are simply eating less meat than they used to and calling themselves "partial" vegetarians. More committed, or at least more consistent, vegetarians will eat fish, or fish and fowl (such as chicken), but not red meat, such as beef, lamb, or pork. *Lacto-ovo-vegetarians* will eat milk and dairy products and eggs, but won't touch red meat, fowl, or fish. (Lacto and ovo come from the Latin words for milk and eggs.) *Lacto-vegetarians* take milk and dairy products but not eggs, meat, or fish. *Total vegetarians,* also called strict vegetarians or *vegans,* take no animal products whatever, not meat or fish or eggs or milk. Stricter yet are the *fruitarians,* who eat only fruit. This is not as extreme as it sounds, because to them, seeds, grains, and vegetables that have seeds in them are considered "fruits of the earth."

Going several steps further, there are scrupulous souls who say they feel guilty about eating anything at all that was once alive, plant or animal. Some of these people point to reports of experiments on laboratory plants that were publicized on TV in the 1960s. The experimenters recorded electrical signals from plants and interpreted the signals as expressions of feelings, such as fear, anger, and pain. Their ideas lost a few believers when some of the same scientists later announced that yogurt, too, had feelings. They lost more credibility when scientists in other laboratories tried the same experiments without detecting any responses.

At the far end of the vegetarian rainbow is Dick Gregory, the former omnivore, who wrote a book about his food philosophy in 1973. At that time Gregory had been on a liquid diet for over a year, and he declared that his ultimate goal was to be a "breathatarian," living on nothing but air and sunshine. Gregory, now a fruitarian, seems to have given up that goal, but he is still coming up with original ideas about nutrition. He once told an interviewer that fruit is the best food for people because it comes closest to body chemistry. "The human body is 97 percent water," said Gregory, "and fruit tends to have more water in it than anything else." But nutritionists tell us that the human body is about 70 percent water, not 97 percent. Obviously, too, not all fruit has the same water content. (Think about watermelons and bananas.) And it would be just as sensible to say that we should all eat meat, preferably human flesh, because it comes closest to our body chemistry.

Gregory's ideas about nutrition are entertaining, and his wide influence as an apostle for concerned eating and living has been all to the good. But there must be a better basis for determining what foods the human body does and does not need.

A lot of nonsense has been written about vegetarianism, for and against, based on ideas the writers believe to be logical. This book will look instead at the nutrition standards set by professionally qualified specialists who are recognized as authorities by their peers. These experts review a wide range of laboratory studies and other evidence before making their decisions. How well do vegetarian diets live up to these established standards? And how can vegetarians plan their diets in order to get all the nutrients they need? (The word "diet," to nutritionists, simply means a way of eating, not necessarily a way of eating to lose weight.)

Until recently many Americans, practicing doctors among them, have considered vegetarianism a fad diet, loaded with hazards for the nutritionally unsophisticated. By the 1970s, however, there was so much public and professional interest in the subject that nutrition experts felt called upon to correct such misinformation.

In 1974, the National Research Council's Food and Nutrition Board, which sets the standards for American nutritionists and government groups, stated officially that a well-planned vegetarian diet could be entirely adequate for people of all ages. The eminent nutritionist Dr. Jean Mayer, then a Harvard professor, brought the message to a wider audience. In his best-selling book, *A Diet for Living,* Dr. Mayer assured American parents that their teen-agers could be perfectly healthy without eating meat. Finally, in 1981, after a string of health officials had advised Americans to cut down on meat consumption, the American Dietetic Association issued a paper stating that plant-based diets could be not only adequate but even superior to the traditional American meat-based diet. At present, no recognized authorities maintain that humans need meat for health.

Both the Food and Nutrition Board and the American Dietetic Association state that a vegetarian diet, like any diet, should be "well planned." This is not difficult or complicated, but as most Americans are used to planning meat-centered meals, making the switch requires a conscious effort at first. How to plan vegetarian diets to meet the experts' standards will be considered in the nutrition section of this book. But before going into *how* vegetarians should eat, we will look at the various reasons people give for becoming vegetarian.

On the subject of health and nutrition, we will look at the evidence behind the current opinion that Americans eat too much meat for their own good. We will also look into the question of whether the human body was designed for a meat or a plant diet. The economic costs of meat are another consideration, and these include not only supermarket price stickers but also the "hidden" costs to consumers, taxpayers, and society in general.

Some people give up meat because it is a wasteful use of world resources. They can demonstrate that meat eaters use up much more grain, land, and energy than do people who eat only plants. What would happen if more of us gave up meat, though, is another question. Would there be more grain to feed hungry people, or would farmers grow less grain? Does it do a starving Indian any good for an overfed American to go vegetarian? These questions are not easy to answer.

Many young people become vegetarian out of sympathy for the animals used for meat. Some have loved pets and animals from childhood and refuse to eat them out of simple fellow feeling. Others believe it is morally wrong to kill for food, or to treat any creature the way today's factory farmers treat their animals.

I first began to study vegetarian nutrition because my daughter, Deirdre, had given up meat and I wanted to make sure that she was eating adequately. I have never shed a tear over the death of a pet, or had any particularly tender feelings for animals. However, after looking into the way meat animals are raised, I began to question whether people have the right to inflict on them the unnecessary and unnatural suffering you'll read about in the next chapter.

Most vegetarians, I have found, have more than one reason for their choice. Some give up meat for one reason and that starts them thinking about the others. The one ultimate reason that can never be either proven or disputed was given by the British playwright George Bernard Shaw, who died in 1950 at the age of ninety-four. Shaw became a vegetarian in his early twenties, and through his long life he came up with a number of original replies when people asked him to explain his unconventional diet. But the one I like best is his statement that he simply did not care to dine on corpses.

Whatever their original reasons, many vegetarians come to feel the same way. When our family started eating vegetarian meals, Deirdre was the only committed vegetarian. When she was not home for dinner, we would buy steak with some of the money we saved on meatless nights. But the third time this happened, half the steak sat on the platter uneaten. Tastes are easily influenced by suggestion, and very possibly our new interest in vegetarian issues made this slab of flesh seem gross to our senses. But whether it was suggestion or the sheer force of new habits, we realized then that we no longer cared to eat corpses.

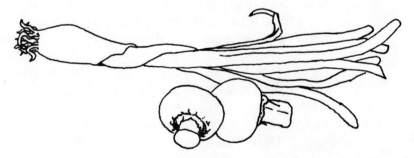

2

Animal Rights

One of the first books a typical child encounters is a simple little picture story about farm animals. There are many such books, but all are likely to show sun-drenched meadows and barnyards occupied by free-roaming, contented creatures. In these harmonious settings, the cow says moo, the pig says oink, the lamb goes baa, and a little chick wanders around looking for its mother. If the farmer appears, it is as a kindly provider of food, which the animals eagerly gobble up. If there's a villain in any of the books, it's an intruding fox, which the protective farmer and his smart dog soon dispatch. The ultimate fate of most of these animals is ignored. Presumably, the farmer keeps them around solely for their eggs, milk, wool, and perhaps companionship.

The children who learn their animals from books like this might later see some real chicks and lambs at a children's zoo, or they might pass browsing cows in fields near a highway. The animals are more real to them now, but they are still imagined with the humanlike personalities and carefree lives first met in baby picture books.

And then, some evening at the dinner table, the connection is made. That hamburger or steak or stew meat, all forms of something called beef, is really the flesh of an animal much like the motherly moo-cow. The bacon on the breakfast table was cut from the side of one of those curly-tailed little pigs. And the chicken parts—well, that's obvious.

It's no wonder that many children throw down their forks at this point. But then the parents reason with them. They explain that everyone needs meat to stay healthy and to grow big and strong. They argue that the meat animals wouldn't even be alive if they weren't being raised for people to eat. They point out that animals eat other animals, so when we eat them we're only taking part in the natural order of things. (The children are usually too young to know that cows, lambs, and pigs, the animals we use for meat, don't eat other animals.)

When you think about it, it's an odd way for parents to behave. First they encourage their children to know and love farm animals, then they encourage them to eat them. But at this stage parents are the people with the answers, and so the children eventually come round—at least until they are ready to make decisions of their own and question some of their parents' arguments. For now, they go back to thinking of their meat as bacon or pork instead of pig, and hamburger or steak instead of cow muscle. Chicken legs might or might not become "drumsticks." (People don't seem as compelled to cover up the identity of chickens with new names, perhaps because chickens are not mammals like pigs and cows and humans.)

The children who are shocked at the idea of eating animals might be even more upset if they knew how the animals are treated on today's big farms. In recent years proponents of animal rights have been trying to make people aware of the conditions on these farms. In *Animal Factories,* written in 1980, philosopher Peter Singer and coauthor Jim Mason argue that today's mechanized, mass-produced animal farming abuses the environment, the economy, and above all the animals.

On these factory farms, machines are used for many of the jobs that farmers used to do, and farmers are encouraged to think of the animals as "biomachines" for producing meat. Instead of roaming freely, animals are packed into pens or cages so small they can't turn around. To get the most money from land and equipment, farmers crowd the animals as tightly as they can without killing off so many that they start losing money. Animals are kept indoors, sometimes in total darkness. They are stuffed with food to hasten their growth, and slaughtered young to make room for the next generation.

LIFE IN AN EGG FACTORY

In the picture books, the little lost chick eventually finds its mother. On a real factory farm, it hasn't a chance. In fact, it never sees its mother. If the mother hen is used to breed egg-laying chickens, her own eggs are taken away and hatched in an incubator. If a hatchling happens to be a male, he is killed on the spot. Male chicks are of no use to egg producers because males don't lay eggs. They aren't used for meat either, because they haven't been designed for that purpose. In today's specialized poultry factories, one type of chicken is selectively bred to produce ample, tender flesh. Another type has been developed to lay as many eggs as possible. Mason and Singer report seeing these useless male hatchlings gathered up, dumped into plastic bags, and left to suffocate.

Life for the female chicks begins with a shock when their beaks are cut off. This will prevent them from pecking each other to death. In the barnyard, chickens keep order among themselves by establishing a social hierarchy. Rank is enforced by pecking, with each chick free to peck those who fall below her in rank. But in modern egg factories, chicks are crowded together in cages. Without the chance to move about or establish their own social order, their pecking instincts go haywire.

When they are old enough to lay eggs, the birds are de-beaked again and packed into the wire cages where they will spend their lives. The floors of the cages are also wire, which allows the birds' droppings to fall through and collect in a pit underneath. The wire floors can also injure the animals' toes and entangle them in the mesh. Crowding in the cages induces fighting and jostling among the birds, and so, to keep them quiet, the farmers keep them in the dark. The cages are lined up in windowless buildings, where the only light the chickens see is the artificial light turned on at feeding time.

Magazines for egg farmers speak matter-of-factly of keeping as many as five birds in a cage, each cage with a floor space measuring about twelve by eighteen inches. That would not be enough room for even one bird to spread her wings. The cages are piled on top of each other and lined up in endless rows, so that as many as ninety thousand hens might be jammed into one building. No friendly farmer comes in to feed ninety thousand or even twenty thousand birds. Instead, mechanical conveyer belts supply the hens with food and remove their eggs.

One task the farmers do have to perform is to remove the birds that die off each day, mostly from the effects of distress and crowding. This weeding job is kept up for the first year and a half or two years of the hens' lives, until the overall egg production begins to drop. After this point it would not pay to weed out only the less productive birds, so the whole batch is sent off to be made into chicken soup. A hen's natural life span is more like fifteen to twenty years, but few hens today lead natural lives. About 90 percent of our yearly sixty-five billion eggs are produced on factory farms. To get eggs from hens raised in the traditional way, you have to seek out a small, natural farmer or a natural-food store that deals with such farmers.

ASSEMBLY-LINE CHICKEN

About 98 percent of our eating chickens, more than three billion a year, are also raised in factories that are owned or controlled by large corporations. They, too, are debeaked, fed by machines, and crowded into cages in windowless buildings. After eight or nine weeks of life they are hung by their feet from a mechanical conveyer belt that moves them along to the butcher's knife.

RAISING A SAUSAGE MACHINE

Now that chickens have been turned into machines for mass-producing eggs and meat, economic pressures are encouraging hog farmers to expand and mechanize. "Forget the pig is an animal," one magazine for hog farmers advises. "Treat him like a machine in a factory."

On more and more large hog farms, pigs are now confined in indoor pens. The floors are sometimes cement, sometimes slatted so the pigs' manure can drop through to pits below. Like chickens, pigs suffer deformed and damaged feet from these floors; but the hog farmers find the slats cut down the costs of cleaning out the pens. Also like chickens, pigs are bored and unhappy in pens, where they don't have room to turn around. Some take to biting each other's tails—or they did, until hog farmers took a cue from chicken raisers and began cutting off the young pigs' tails.

14

Just as there are hens whose only function is to produce more of their kind for eating or laying, there are sows who do nothing but produce piglets. These animals spend their lives pregnant, giving birth, having their babies taken away from them, and then starting the whole cycle over again. According to another hog-farmers' magazine, "The breeding sow should be thought of and treated as a valuable piece of machinery whose function is to pump out baby pigs like a sausage machine."

LIFE AND DEATH OF A STEER

Compared to pigs, the cattle raised for beef begin life with a normal childhood, moving freely and grazing on grasses. On some farms and ranches, they may graze for a year or two. On others they are rounded up within months and taken to centers called feedlots. Either way, most end their lives in feedlots, where they are confined in pens and fattened on grain, soybeans, drugs, hormones, and whatever else will bring them rapidly to market weight.

Free ranging or not, beef cattle undergo several operations that animal defenders consider unnecessarily painful. Because castration makes for fatter and more docile animals, most quality beef comes from males that have had their testicles cut off early in life. (This is what turns a bull into the animal cattle-raisers call a steer.) Their horns are also removed, so that they won't injure each other when they are crowded together during roundups, or on trucks or feedlots. Like the removal of chickens' beaks and pigs' tails, these operations are performed without anesthetic. On the way to feedlots and slaughterhouses, the steers are sometimes crowded for days, without food or water, in overheated or unheated trucks. It is taken for granted that some will die on the way.

Once in the slaughterhouse, cattle might be subjected to further distress. One practice that disturbs many humanitarians, including some who eat beef, is the pretreatment associated with kosher ritual slaughter. The problem arises from the need to follow the requirements of two different authorities. According to the ancient kosher law observed by Orthodox Jews, animals must be conscious at the time of slaughter. This is not a problem in itself; when the animals are killed with a sharp, swift cut to the throat, death is almost instantaneous. But U.S. sanitary law requires that the animals be off the floor when killed. In humane slaughterhouses, they are stunned first, then hoisted up on a conveyer belt to hang upside down by one leg while awaiting the knife. If the stunning is done properly, the cattle are immediately rendered unconscious. But preslaughter stunning is forbidden in ritual slaughter, so the steers must hang there fully conscious, twisting in agony. Often a leg or a pelvic bone breaks, or a leg is torn from its socket, as the animal struggles to get free.

Ritual slaughter methods are not confined to beef. Lambs and goats are killed in the same way. Nor is ritual slaughter limited to the meat that ends up with kosher labels. Usually only part of the animal is prepared in the kosher manner after slaughter. The rest is sold to the general public without the label. According to Peter Singer, over 90 percent of the beef sold in New Jersey and New York City comes from animals killed by ritual slaughter.

MILK PRODUCTION

Many vegetarians question the whole concept of humane slaughter. In their view, once we assume the right to kill other animals for our own dining pleasure, we are not likely to give the victims' feelings and well-being top consideration. But most people who become vegetarians from compassion for animals continue to drink milk, because cows do not have to be killed or mistreated to obtain it. Farmers have always believed that if a cow is too upset she will not "let down" her milk. Today they know that this process involves a hormone, which does not function properly if the cow is frightened or in pain. Still, the lives of the cows in today's large milk factories are not much like those shown in picture books.

High milk production is literally a matter of life or death to milk-factory cows, who will not be kept on if they do not produce. The level of production deemed acceptable has more than doubled since 1950, when the average cow produced about 5,000 pounds of milk a year. In 1975 one Indiana Holstein made history by producing 55,660 pounds. "A farmer can't be fussing around with a lazy old cow that only produces 10,000 pounds a year," bragged a dairy association official.

16

Because a cow's milk tends to dry up about ten months after her last calf's birth, dairy cows are made pregnant regularly to keep the milk running. This way the cows give birth once a year, giving them about a two-month rest each year. During dry periods the cows can browse in meadows as before. But while "in milk," they are fed a high-calorie grain mixture to supplement the grasses their intestinal systems were made to handle. If the farmer does not mix in enough hay or other roughage, the unnatural low-fiber diets can cause disabling stomach problems. According to a 1980 textbook, *Dairy Farm Management*, 15 to 20 percent of the cows in a herd may suffer from a displaced abomasum, the fourth and most essential of the cow's four stomachs. Feedlot bloat, a "gassy" condition that can be fatal, is also attributed to a diet too high in concentrates.

Whatever the diet, the dairy cow's unnaturally heavy milk production uses up so many nutrients that the cow might not get enough for herself. The same textbook warns that milk fever, a result of calcium deficiency, is common among high-producing cows. Without treatment most will die. With treatment one in four victims still die. High-producing cows are also more susceptible to rickets, a result of vitamin-D deficiency, and to a chemical imbalance called ketosis.

In the interest of milking efficiency, more and more cows spend much of their time indoors in barns, where they are fed in troughs. Unlike some farm animals, most cows are allowed to wander about within the barns. But unless the farmers provide expensive rubber mats, the animals can develop foot and leg problems from the barns' hard cement floors. The cows are milked by machines, and careless handling of the machines can cause a painful udder inflammation called mastitis.

Good dairy-farm managers take steps to prevent all these problems and treat them when they do occur, if only because healthy cows are more profitable than sick ones. But in most cases it is the unnatural pressures of the factory farm that cause the problems in the first place.

Under more natural conditions, a dairy cow might live for twenty years, and her milk production will peak when she is about ten or twelve. Under factory-farm conditions, most cows' production starts to fall off after about four or five years. Soon afterward they are sent off to market, to be made into canned soups or stews or fast-food hamburgers.

Like other textbooks, *Dairy Farm Management* advises farmers to make a regular practice of "culling the herd." A cow should be "culled," or weeded out, if she has a serious disease or disability which is unlikely to clear up. She may not be worth keeping if her milk dries up early, if she has not become pregnant on schedule, or if she falls within the lowest 20 percent of the herd in milk production. Finally, those cows may be culled who "are slow milkers and therefore do not fit into the daily chore routine."

Dairy farmers and other farmers have always culled their herds. But now that animals are treated like machines, more are becoming disabled and fewer disabilities are tolerated. To the owners of large dairy farms this situation is justified if it results in higher milk production. But we will see in chapter 6 that American dairy farms already produce more milk than they can sell on the open market.

THE PRICE OF VEAL

If a cow's life is not pure contentment, what happens to the calves who are cranked out on schedule, essentially as by-products of their mothers' milk? These animals' normal childhood lasts for perhaps three days. Then they are removed from the mothers so that they won't drink too much of the milk that is intended for sale. Females might be kept on the farm as future dairy cows. Some males are killed and sent off to market right away, to end up, as their mothers will, in canned soups or pet foods or other low-quality meat products. They will not be raised for beef, because high-grade beef comes from a different breed of cattle. Like chicken breeders, cattle breeders have developed different types of animals for different purposes: one kind of cattle for maximum milk production and another for maximum beef production. But some male calves are sold off to veal producers, who provide the tender, light-colored meat that gourmets prize.

In the past, veal was made from very young calves who were still eating nothing but their mothers' milk. The all-milk diet left their flesh a light pink color, a sign to shoppers and diners that the veal is really young and tender. The meat was expensive because of the small amount obtainable from one hundred-pound carcass. (A beef steer's market weight might be a thousand pounds.) After about three weeks, calves normally begin to graze on grasses, which give them nutrients such as iron that aren't present in milk. At this point their flesh turns darker from the iron in the grasses and tougher from the exercise they are getting, and they lose their gourmet appeal.

Now, however, veal producers have found a way to get more meat per calf and still keep the flesh light and tender. The calves are taken from their mothers the day after they are born, and fed a liquid mix of dried skim milk, fat, and sugar for about fifteen weeks. By then they weigh about three hundred pounds and are ready for market. The reason that they aren't fattened to a more profitable weight is that after fifteen weeks or so they begin to die off from anemia. This could be prevented if they had iron in their diets; but iron would darken their flesh and reduce its market value. As it is, calves spend their last weeks growing progressively weaker and sicker. Some die of diarrhea caused by their liquid diets, some of infectious diseases brought on by their poor nutrition and unhealthy living conditions.

During their entire fifteen weeks, veal calves are confined indoors in pens four feet six inches long and one foot ten inches wide. Often they are tied by chains around their necks to keep them from moving around. (The less the muscles exercise, the more tender is the flesh.) The chains are removed after they have grown to the point where they can't turn around in the pens anyway. The buildings are kept dark except at feeding time. The floors of the stalls are slatted, with concrete below, and the calves get no straw bedding to lie down on. If they did, they would probably eat it to satisfy their need for solid food and iron.

Like all mammals, calves are born with a strong desire to suck. Their sucking needs may be satisfied when they are fed from bottles with plastic nipples. But many veal producers don't want the expense of washing and changing nipples, so calves are often fed from open buckets. Visitors report that the calves reach out to suck their fingers or clothing, in a desperate attempt to satisfy a frustrated sucking instinct.

TENDER MEAT OR TENDER FEELINGS?

How does it happen that otherwise decent people end up mistreating baby animals just for soft, pale flesh? How can veal

19

eaters enjoy their dinners when they know how the meat was produced? Why are meat factories allowed to abuse chickens and calves when a pet owner can be arrested for abandoning a kitten?

Many vegetarians have said that if we all had to kill our own meat, we would all be vegetarians. Obviously this isn't true, because the people who do kill meat also eat it. In the past, a large proportion of Americans lived on farms and did kill their own meat. It is probably true that many meat eaters would be shocked to see how their meat is produced today. But then, out of long habit, they would tell themselves that these methods are necessary in order to provide a large population with enough meat for good nutrition. (Americans are just beginning to learn that the amount of meat most of us eat goes far beyond the requirements of good nutrition.)

Some meat eaters have sworn never to eat veal after they learn how veal calves are treated. Somehow a sorrowful calf is easier to pity than a pig or a chicken. But for the most part, meat eaters would rather just not think about where their meat comes from. They have learned over the years to think of cows and pigs and chickens as objects and not as fellow creatures. They know that animals have feelings, but, as one young animal-rights defender put it, they don't really feel that knowledge.

As for the farmers, most cannot afford to consider their animals' comfort. A few, however, are disturbed by the growing attitude that animals are only egg or meat machines. One large pig farmer with two sons told an interviewer: "It's true, you can train yourself not to think of the pigs as animals with feelings. I can do that. But I worry about my kids. If they grow up to think of animals as machines, how will they end up thinking about people? If they take over the farm and hire help, how will they think of their employees? How will they think about their own wives and kids?"

SPECIESISM AND ANIMAL RIGHTS

Most farmers and consumers are sure they can draw the line between pigs and people. But some defenders of animal rights say there shouldn't be a line. What gives us the right, they ask, to treat animals in ways that we would not treat people?

The most common answer to their question is that we are intelligent beings and pigs aren't. As we are capable of deeper experience and higher achievements, our lives are worth more. Therefore, this argument goes, we have the right to use inferior animals for our purposes. But defenders of animal rights do not believe that superior intelligence gives one creature the right to inflict harm on another. Certainly most people would not approve of a genius treating a retarded person in the way that factory farmers treat pigs and chickens. Nor would most people condone killing a retarded person, even if it meant that smarter people could somehow derive benefit from the corpse.

The British philosopher Jeremy Bentham put forth this argument for animal rights almost two hundred years ago. Bentham noted that many animals can think and communicate on a higher level than a newborn human infant can. But, said Bentham, their intelligence is not the real issue. "The question is not, can they *reason?* nor can they *talk?* but, *can they suffer?*" The answer to this last question must be yes. There is no real doubt that the mammals, birds, and even fish that humans use for food can and do feel pain. By any common definition, the mammals, at least, can suffer emotional distress as well.

Most ethical philosophers in our society concern themselves only with how we should behave toward other people. But Peter Singer is one contemporary philosopher who shares Bentham's concern for animal rights. To Singer, the attitude that allows other animals to be used for human purposes is a form of discrimination just as wrong as racism and sexism. In his book *Animal Liberation,* Singer coined the term "speciesism" to describe this common attitude toward all species but our own. Singer does not argue that animals should be given human rights such as the right to vote, for example. Obviously, they would not be able to exercise such a right. But he does believe that the interests of animals should be given equal consideration with humans' interests.

To illustrate how this consideration should work, Singer imagines a situation where a human and an animal are both in pain and there is only enough painkiller to help one of them. As animals are just as capable of feeling pain as humans are, Singer thinks their relief should get equal consideration. Therefore, if the animal is in greater pain, the animal should get the painkiller. Most people would not go along with Singer's argu-

21

ment on that point. But that, Singer would say, is because most people are speciesists.

To Singer, the principle of equal consideration does not mean that all lives are of equal value. If we had to choose between killing a pig and killing a normal human being, almost any of us would choose to kill the pig. This time Singer would agree, because the human's superior intelligence and other qualities probably do make the human life worth more than the pig's. But meat eating does not involve that drastic a choice unless people need to eat animals in order to live. Singer and other vegetarians say we don't, and nutritionists have come to agree.

WHERE TO DRAW THE LINE

If the children who rebelled against meat eating knew how factory-farm animals are raised, they might be able to answer some of their parents' arguments. One argument, you'll remember, is that animals kill and eat each other in nature, and we are only taking part in nature when we do the same. But there is nothing natural about the lives or deaths of factory-farm animals. It is true, as parents like to point out, that if we weren't raising pigs and chickens and cattle for meat, the animals would not exist at all. But it's hard to pretend that we are doing the animals a favor by giving them such a short, unnatural, painful existence.

If we could raise and kill the animals without causing them pain and misery, the answer might not be so easy. But Singer believes that any way of raising and killing animals for our own ends is bound to cause them pain. Singer also disapproves of eating fish, even though few fish are factory reared, because we cause them pain when we catch them. But another class of sea animals, the mollusks, are more primitive animals, without well-developed nervous systems. Singer believes that it isn't wrong to eat this group, which includes oysters, clams, mussels, and scallops, because they probably are not equipped to feel pain. "Somewhere between a shrimp and an oyster seems as good a place as any to draw the line, and better than most," Singer says in *Animal Liberation*.

Singer also eats eggs from free-ranging hens, because the hens are not harmed in the process, and he eats dairy products.

In an ideal world, says Singer, we would not exploit dairy cows for milk either. But giving up all animal products is difficult for many reasons, and it is more important to stop the worst abuses by avoiding meat and factory-farm eggs.

In *Animal Factories,* Mason and Singer speak to people who might not be ready to become actual vegetarians. Mason and Singer urge all consumers to stop eating the meat, poultry, eggs, and milk produced on factory farms. As most supermarket products fall into this category, they suggest shopping in natural-food stores that carry alternatives. The prices will be higher, but you can make up the difference in cost by eating less meat. Mason and Singer don't tell us, though, how to find such stores and verify their claims. As we'll see in Chapter 19, this can be difficult. They do counsel readers not to be so rigid that they refuse an omelet in a restaurant or a birthday cake made with eggs. The idea is simply to use your buying power to discourage factory farming.

If enough people cut back this way, Mason and Singer believe, high-output factory-farm methods would no longer pay off. To any objective analyst, such a prospect must seem unlikely. But Mason and Singer feel that even without such an outcome, individual consumers can at least be satisfied that every meat meal they pass up means that much less animal suffering.

In his various writings, Singer has worked out a persuasive argument for animal rights and vegetarianism. Still, not all vegetarians would draw the same line or give the same reason for sparing animals. Some question Singer's assumption that oysters do not feel pain. Some, like the members of the Jain religion in India, believe that all life is sacred. To the Jains, all forms of life, including human life, are only stages in the transmigration of souls, which must be reborn many times in different bodies. The Jains are among the strictest of the world's vegetarians, so careful that they avoid eating after sundown for fear of accidentally taking in an insect with their food. Their vegetarianism is based on the principle of *ahimsa,* a reverence for life that precludes killing or injuring even the tiniest of creatures.

Between the Jain principle of *ahimsa* and the boycotting of factory-raised veal, consideration for animals has given rise to a wide variety of eating practices. The Jains themselves drink milk and eat other dairy products, because this does not involve killing. But vegans, who refuse all food obtained from animals, feel that we shouldn't exploit other creatures for our purposes whether we kill them or not. Vegans maintain that it is hypocritical to boycott veal and drink milk, as the veal industry is essentially a by-product of the dairy industry. Some milk-drinking vegetarians, who oppose only killing, join vegans in refusing to wear leather shoes or belts because these are made from the hides of dead animals. Some vegetarians who eat cheese shop at natural-food stores for special rennetless cheese. Traditionally, cheese has been made with a small amount of rennet, an enzyme-rich substance that is taken from the lining of a dead calf's fourth stomach. Enzymes in the rennet help thicken the milk into curds, a necessary step in cheese making but one that can be accomplished without rennet. Today, in fact, commercial cheese makers are turning to other, less expensive sources of enzymes.

To most of us, debates about rennetless cheese and oysters' nervous systems may seem like nit picking. And to the children who are shocked to discover that they've been eating dead animals, the logic of animal rights means nothing. The children's response is a matter of feeling, mostly simple fellow feeling for the animals in question. They might not understand the fine points of Singer's arguments, but they do understand the meat pudding's question to Alice in *Through the Looking Glass:* How would you like it if someone took a slice of you? Mixed in with children's compassion for fellow creatures might be something like the horror most of us would feel to discover we'd been dining on human flesh. Many children feel more kinship with animals than they do, say, with the doctors who give them shots or the world leaders they see on TV.

In a world where practical considerations are honored above inconvenient tender feelings, most of us lose that sense of kinship in the process of growing up. At the same time, we learn to like the taste and even the idea of meat. Without any pressure from the victims, it is hard to imagine that a majority of people will ever take it upon themselves to give this up. And unless high prices make it for them, the decision to give up meat is one consumers have to take upon themselves. Unlike blacks, women, and workers who have found themselves exploited by those in power, animals cannot organize to protest and resist injustice.

To defenders of animal rights, the fact that animals can't speak up for themselves is all the more reason why we should act in their interests. Unlike other animals, these compassionate humans remind us, people are capable of considering the consequences of our actions. We can recognize the connection between plastic-wrapped steaks or sausage or chicken parts and the suffering of crowded, injured, sick, and unnaturally raised animals. Unlike the wild animals who kill other animals for food, we can make decisions based on those connections. Ethical vegetarians, as such abstainers are called, differ among themselves as to what can be eaten with a good conscience, but they agree that the animals raised for our tables have a claim on our conscience.

Concern for animals may be all very well, but what about our own animal nature? Many people who wouldn't hurt a pet or wear a coat made out of clobbered seals still eat meat, because they believe that it's a "natural" food of man. Our bodies are built for it, they say, which proves that vegetarianism is an abnormal way to live. We will deal with that question in the next two chapters, when we look into how people have eaten throughout human history, and what kind of diets our bodies seem built for.

Human Nature

Wherever vegetarianism is debated, one question always seems to come up: Are humans meat eaters by nature? Those who believe we are point out that humans are endowed with two pointed dogteeth, or canines, in our upper jaws. These teeth are characteristic of meat-eating animals, who use them to tear the flesh from their prey. It is often said that early men were wandering hunters, and so the human race developed with a need for meat.

Vegetarians, on their part, have long argued that our bodies have more in common with plant-eating animals than with meat eaters. In 1813, the English poet Percy Bysshe Shelley wrote a pamphlet arguing that people were not designed to eat meat. Shelley said that human anatomy resembled that of fruit-eating animals more than it did that of carnivores. Not long afterward, an American minister named Sylvester Graham became interested in the subject of health and diet. Graham became a vegetarian and published a health journal, where he compared the human body with the orangutan's and concluded that a vegetable diet was "natural" for both. (Graham also invented a successful health-food biscuit that made him famous. Graham crackers still sell today, but the product hasn't much to do with Graham's original recipe.)

Nathaniel Altman, a contemporary vegetarian writer, sums

up the case for our vegetarian makeup in his book, *Eating for Life*. Like others before him, Altman divides animals into four categories, according to their diets. Carnivores live mostly on meat; herbivores eat grass and leaves; frugivores live on fruit, nuts, and grain; and omnivores eat both animals and plants. Altman points out that a real carnivore, such as a lion, dog, or cat, has a simple digestive system, about three times the length of its body. This makes for fast digestion, an advantage with meat, which decays rapidly. Carnivores have strong claws and powerful jaws for catching their prey. They have long, sharp canine teeth to tear the flesh from their victims, and they do not have molar teeth as we do.

Herbivores such as cows, sheep, and elephants do have molar teeth, which they use to grind their food, and their canine teeth are very small. Herbivores have sweat glands, as we do, but carnivores pant with their tongues when overheated. (Carnivores don't need sweat glands, Altman says, because they hunt at night and rest in the heat of the day.) Altman even goes into the differences in how the animals drink water. Herbivores, he notes, suck up their water as we do, whereas carnivores lap it up with their tongues.

Herbivores' saliva contains an enzyme for digesting starch, which carnivores don't need. Human saliva contains the same enzyme. Herbivores' intestines are long and winding like ours, stretching to about twelve times their body length. This is useful in digesting bulky, fibrous, vegetarian diets. But unlike us, these animals also have several stomachs to help with the job of digestion.

It might seem sensible to class humans as omnivores, capable of digesting both meat and plants. But Altman puts people in the frugivore category with our closest relatives, the anthropoid apes. Like humans, apes such as gorillas, chimpanzees, and baboons share many characteristics with the herbivores. Like us, they have intestines about twelve times their body length; and like ours, their canine teeth are small and dull compared to those of carnivores. Their natural diet is fruit and seeds.

But early humans and their nonhuman cousins can't be lumped together. Anthropologist Alan Walker has studied primates much closer to our species than gorillas and chimps. Dr. Walker has been able to determine what foods animals have eaten from the kinds of scratches he finds on their teeth. From the almost-human *Australopithecus* and *Homo habilis,* all the teeth Dr. Walker examined showed that these species were fruit eaters, not omnivores. But the same tooth analysis shows that our own species, *Homo sapiens,* has been omnivorous from the beginning. All the teeth of *Homo sapiens,* and of our immediate ancestor, *Homo erectus,* showed the coarse kind of scratches that result from eating meat.

Scientists have also come to realize that the apes aren't always faithful to their nonviolent diet. Gorillas, chimpanzees, and baboons do live mostly on fruits and nuts; but they also eat some insects. Jane Goodall, who is well known for her observations of African chimpanzees in the wild, saw them kill and eat other primates on occasion. By now, both baboons and chimpanzees have been seen to ignore their vegetarian foods when insects or rodents were easy to come by. Gorillas in zoos follow the same pattern.

Most likely, prehistoric humans ate more meat than African chimps do, if only because their brain development allowed for more effective hunting methods. But they ate far less meat than Americans do today. Despite the romantic macho image of man the hunter, today's anthropologists believe that the first humans got most of their food from fruit, nuts, seeds, and probably some insects. In the warm climate where humans originated, plant gathering was a more efficient activity than hunting, expending far less time and energy per calorie obtained. Large animals were hard to kill with early weapons and harder still to drag home to nonhunters. And as the stay-at-homes would include small children and the women who cared for them, the human race would have died out if large animals had been the chief food.

The belief that early humans lived on meat was based on discoveries of stone hunting weapons and of animal bones left behind at cooking sites. Now it is recognized that scraps from vegetable meals and sticks for digging up plants just don't remain intact for later discovery. More sophisticated analysis has turned up evidence of grain and seed meals, and anthropologists now believe that meat was more a treat than a mainstay.

Should it matter to us what kind of food our prehistoric ancestors ate? Perhaps not. We know that different people have had different diets, depending largely on what was available where they lived. In America, Pueblo Indians of the Southwest lived mostly on corn and beans. The Eskimos, who burn off large numbers of calories just to keep warm, can handle a high-fat diet of fish and meat in a land where plants are not abundant. No doubt our own way of life and our own physical makeup, not prehistoric teeth, are the best bases for deciding what is good for us.

Nevertheless, it is interesting that the recent findings about early humans conform with what we are finding out about our own nutritional needs. Unlike herbivores, people seem to need small amounts of vitamin B_{12} in their diets. As we'll see in the chapter on vitamins, B_{12} is present in meat, eggs, fish, and dairy products, but virtually nonexistent in plants. Most "vegetarian" cultures get their B_{12} from insects, if not from milk or fish. In this light, total vegetarianism does not appear to be "natural" for humans. On the other hand, most specialists believe that the large amounts of animal products in the typical American diet contribute to our high rate of heart disease, and possibly to the high incidence of certain cancers as well. The typical prehistoric diet, which was mostly vegetarian with small amounts of animal products, is closer to what doctors are currently advising for us.

CHAPTER
4

Why Eating Meat May Be Hazardous to Your Health

Until recently, eating for health was thought to be a matter of getting enough of the right foods. In school, health textbooks emphasized eating meat for protein and drinking milk for calcium. They talked about deficiency diseases such as rickets and pellagra, and told how the modern practice of adding vitamin D to milk and adding B vitamins to bread and cereal had eliminated these diseases.

Protein, vitamins, and calcium are still important, but we now know that we don't need meat for protein. We also know that vitamin-enriched white bread and breakfast food are not the best sources of B vitamins. And, as we'll see, the milk that gives us calcium has come under fire for its fat. Today, the major diseases associated with the way we eat are not caused by a lack of vitamins or any other nutrient. Instead, Americans are starting to worry about getting too much of the wrong food.

Too much food altogether makes people overweight, and overweight people, on the average, have shorter lives. Too much sugar causes tooth decay and possibly other diseases. Too much salt can contribute to high blood pressure. And too much meat, most authorities now believe, can increase our risk of heart disease and certain kinds of cancer. Too much meat can also contribute to our weight problems. The average American meat eater is twelve to fifteen pounds overweight according to medical charts, while American total vegetarians weigh an average of twenty pounds less than their meat-eating counterparts.

If today's anthropologists are right, our earliest human ancestors lived mostly on plants. Contemporary researchers have been able to study similar diets among the !Kung people of the Kalahari desert in Africa. The !Kung, a hunting-gathering people who still live much like prehistoric humans, enjoy good health and do not suffer from our leading killer, coronary heart disease. And as long as food from plants is abundant, they get all the protein and vitamins they need.

We don't have to go back to a prehistoric life-style, however, to discover how whole populations get along with little or no meat. In most parts of the world, people still eat far less meat than we do; and even traditional meat-eating countries have gone through periods of enforced vegetarianism. One experiment in changing diets occurred in Denmark during World War I, when the Allies set up a blockade to cut off supplies to Germany. Without American corn coming in, the Germans did not have enough grain to feed their people and their pigs. As the Allies intended, people went hungry.

But Denmark was also cut off by the blockade, and here the results were surprising. Authorities in Denmark decided to feed their grain to the people and do without the meat. During the blockade the Danes ate cereal, potatoes, green vegetables, milk, and small amounts of butter. And between October 1917 and October 1918, their death rate from noninfectious diseases dropped by a third. During this period the Danes also had less alcohol and probably got more exercise than before, so we can't automatically give all the credit to the change in diet. But the experience did prove that the people could get along without meat, and it suggested that low-meat diets rated consideration.

Then, during World War II, Norway was occupied by the Germans. Norwegians had to do with far less than their accustomed amounts of meat, eggs, cheese, and cream. Although the death rate from heart disease had been climbing in Norway before the war, it fell during the occupation. After the war, consumption of meat, eggs, and milk fat went back up. So did the death rate from heart disease. The British were also very short of meat during World War II, and their death rate from heart disease also fell. There, too, both meat eating and the coronary death rate went back up after the war.

Since World War II, a number of studies have compared heart-disease death rates worldwide. They have found that heart attacks are rare in countries where the people eat little or no meat. Wherever heart-disease rates are high, so is meat consumption. In the United States, where beef eating is a way of life, heart disease is the leading cause of death. We do know of one area where people live on cattle, yet heart attacks are practically unknown. This is East Africa, where the Masai people herd cattle and live largely on the blood and milk of their herds, with some meat. Some heart specialists attribute the Masai people's good health to the fact that they walk about twenty-five miles a day while herding their cattle. Studies conducted in this country have found that people who don't exercise vigorously are more likely to suffer from heart attacks than are people who lead an active life or make a point of regular exercise. One doctor who studied the Masai believes that they are protected from heart disease by some as yet unknown substance in the fermented milk they drink. His subsequent experiments with Americans suggest that yogurt may have the same effect—an interesting idea that has not yet been widely tested.

When the geographical differences in heart-attack rates were first discovered, one theory held that they might be genetic. Perhaps, it was suggested, certain races have an inborn immunity to heart disease. But it has since been found that the same people increase their risk of heart attack when they switch from a meatless to a high-meat diet. Coronary heart disease was rare in Japan until after World War II, when the Japanese began eating meat and milk. Now it is becoming common. When Japanese move to America and take up our eating habits, their heart-disease rate goes up. So does their rate of breast cancer and colon cancer. Like heart disease, cancer of the breast and large intestine (usually called the colon) are most common in countries where people eat the most meat. According to one study of twenty-eight countries, the more meat eaten per person, the higher that country's rate of colon cancer.

Of course, meat-eating countries probably have a lot of other things in common. The statistics don't prove that meat is to blame for heart attacks and colon cancer. But one series of studies in this country indicates that meat eating may increase the risk. These studies, begun in 1958, have been done on 100,000 Californians who are members of the Seventh-day Adventist Church.

The Seventh-day Adventists are a remarkably healthy group, with death rates from all causes well below the rates for Californians as a whole. They have less than half the cancer rate of other Americans and only 60 percent of the death rate from heart disease. When Adventist men do have heart attacks, they occur about ten years later than the average for all American men. The Seventh-day Adventists do not drink alcohol or coffee or smoke tobacco. About half of them are lacto-ovo-vegetarians.

Clearly, the Seventh-day Adventists' good health is not entirely due to their meatless diet. But again, studies within the Adventist community found some connection between meat eating and disease. Among Adventist men, vegetarians were significantly less likely to die from heart attacks than were nonvegetarians. Male vegans' heart-attack death rate was only one fourth that of the meat eaters. Among women, though, the difference between meat eaters and lacto-vegetarians was much less. This might be partly explained by the fact that middle-aged women in general have fewer heart attacks than men. Their female hormones seem to protect them until they reach menopause, around age fifty. However, one unexpected finding in the Seventh-day Adventist study was that the total-vegetarian women had higher heart-disease death rates than did the lacto-vegetarian or meat-eating Adventist women. This inconsistency has yet to be explained. With colon cancer, total vegetarians and lacto-vegetarians of both sexes had lower rates than meat eaters. When eaten over a twenty-year period, meat, fish, cheese (but not milk), and other high-fat foods all seemed to increase the risk.

ANIMAL FAT

Just what is it in meat that makes heart disease and bowel cancer more likely? In both cases, research attention has centered on the fat. With colon cancer, it's clear that diet is only one of many factors in a disease still little understood. But some studies indicate that high-fat diets increase the risk, whether the fat is from animals or from vegetable sources, such as salad oil. Other studies have found that meat eaters' intestines are higher than vegetarians' in certain substances that are also high in the intestines of colon-cancer patients. These include both the bile acids produced in the liver to help digest fat and the bacteria that can break these acids down into possible cancer agents.

Yet again, some doctors believe that the risk factor is not meat or fat as such but the absence of other foods that are under-consumed in modern meat-centered cultures. As Britain's Dr. Denis Burkitt first proposed, the indigestible fiber found in whole grains might protect against bowel cancer by moving waste material through the intestinal tract. But whatever the ultimate explanation, bowel cancer rates are higher among people on high-fat, low-fiber diets. And fiber does not seem to explain the association between dietary fat and breast cancer.

With heart disease, suspicion has centered more specifically on the fat in meat and other animal products. As with cancer, diet is not the only risk factor. Smoking, insufficient exercise, and possibly a driven personality all increase a person's chance of having a heart attack. But so, it seems, does eating saturated fat and cholesterol. Saturated fat is found almost entirely in animals, especially in cattle and other animals that give us red meat. It is present in dairy products as well as in meat. Cholesterol is a waxy substance found only in animal fat. It is especially high in egg yolks, and nonexistent in plants.

Doctors believe that animal fat can induce heart attacks by clogging up our blood vessels with cholesterol. Cholesterol is an essential chemical in human cells, but the body itself makes all the cholesterol it needs. When there is too much in the bloodstream, it tends to build up on the inside walls of our blood vessels, causing the condition known as atherosclerosis. The blood has trouble getting through the narrowed passageways, and blood clots can block them altogether. When this happens in an artery leading to the heart, the result is a coronary heart attack. If a brain artery is clogged, a stroke results.

For clues to how and why blood cholesterol builds up, researchers have been studying lipoproteins, substances in the blood that carry cholesterol through the body. There are two main types of lipoproteins. One type, called high-density lipoproteins (or HDLs), carries extra cholesterol out of the blood vessels. This cholesterol is eventually flushed from the body. Others, the low-density lipoproteins (LDLs), allow cholesterol to accumulate on the artery walls. Blood tests show that pre-menopausal women and men who exercise vigorously have high levels of HDLs in their blood. But smoking and eating foods high in saturated fat increase the levels of LDLs, and with them the buildup of arterial cholesterol.

Like cancer, heart attacks and strokes usually come late in life. But cholesterol starts to build up during the teen years. In the 1950s, a study was done on several hundred soldiers killed in the Korean War. At an average age of twenty-two, a majority of Americans examined already had significant buildups of cholesterol in their arteries. The Korean soldiers, who ate little or no meat, were free of cholesterol deposits.

Since it is hard to study the insides of living people's arteries, doctors often take blood tests to determine the amount of cholesterol circulating through the blood vessels. According to a classic long-term study of the residents of Framingham, Massachusetts, a high blood cholesterol level was the most common characteristic of people who eventually had heart attacks. This, too, begins to build up early, as the American Health Foundation confirmed with a study of fifteen thousand children in sixteen countries: The more meat and milk fat consumed in a country, the higher the children's blood cholesterol levels.

In Massachusetts, a Harvard University researcher was able to control male teen-agers' cholesterol levels by changing the menus in their boarding schools. (Only boys' schools were studied.) The students were fed fewer eggs, margarine instead of butter, fish and poultry in place of some of their usual meat, and leaner meat when meat was served. Health authorities now feel that these modest changes should be made in all schools. According to the American Heart Association, cutting down on saturated fat early in life can protect you from heart disease later.

U.S. DIETARY GOALS

Understandably, the meat, egg, and dairy industries were unhappy with the evidence against saturated fat and cholesterol. Their representatives pointed out that the different health records in different countries might have other explanations. For a long time the government agencies concerned with food and nutrition also disregarded the findings. For decades, the U.S. Department of Agriculture had published a daily food guide advising people to eat several servings of both meat and milk every day. Fat, the USDA booklets told consumers, is a necessary component of a tasty and filling meal. And that's all it told about fat. The trouble is that the USDA's main job is to help food producers, not consumers. At least that is how the department's officials have traditionally viewed their job. Earl Butz, who was Secretary of Agriculture under Richard Nixon, worked closely with large livestock producers and spoke out openly against consumerism.

Meanwhile, though, some U.S. senators decided to look into the scientific evidence against the modern American diet. The Senate committee on Nutrition and Human Needs heard testimony from a wide range of medical and nutrition experts. Dr. Mark Hegsted, then a Harvard professor of nutrition, helped draft the committee's final recommendations to the public. After many hearings and much deliberation, the committee concluded that Americans would be healthier if we made certain changes in our diets. The committee recommended cutting down on red meat, whole milk, and eggs. They advised eating less fat altogether, and especially less animal fat. In addition the committee recommended eating more fruit, vegetables, and whole grains and less sugar and salt.

When the Senate report was released, the meat, egg, and dairy industries protested that the government had no right to tell people what to eat. (They hadn't objected, however, when the Department of Agriculture told people they should eat meat, milk, and eggs.) The publication was quickly recalled and reconsidered. Two senators on the committee were persuaded by farm groups in their states to qualify their support for the Dietary Goals, as the recommendations were called. However, the committee's chairman, Senator George McGovern, held to the experts' recommendations, and the revised version that finally came out contained the same basic advice. (For a list of the Dietary Goals, see the Appendix.)

The Senate's recommendations were not new to doctors or their patients. The American Heart Association had come out years earlier with similar advice about saturated fat and cholesterol. So had the governments of eight other nations, including Canada. A Norwegian poll of 214 leading heart-disease researchers in twenty-three countries found 92 percent in favor of such recommendations. By the time the Dietary Goals were published, Americans had already begun to cut down on animal fat, especially in the form of eggs and butter.

After the Senate broke the political barrier, the U.S. Surgeon General's Office, and then the National Cancer Institute, endorsed the new goals. In 1980, despite charges of consumerism from former Secretary Butz, President Carter's Department of Agriculture issued a softer version of the goals, called *Dietary Guidelines.* This guide was cosponsored by the Department of Health, Education, and Welfare (now Health and Human Services). By 1981, according to Jane Brody of the *New York Times,* over eighteen government agencies and major health organizations in the United States and other meat-eating countries had come out with the same advice. Expert opinion seemed unanimous.

Then the Food and Nutrition Board of the National Research Council was heard from. The NRC, a division of the National Academy of Sciences, is a private group of respected scientists who often advise the government on policy. The council's Food and Nutrition Board establishes the Recommended Daily Allowances (RDAs) that tell us how much of each nutrient we need in our diets. At one time, the board's RDA committee had noted the association between animal fats and heart disease. But now the board declared that "people should not be made afraid of the food they eat." It "found no reason" why all Americans should be told to cut down on cholesterol, although it recognized the wisdom of low-cholesterol diets for the "high risk" population.

Coming just when many people had decided to change their diets, the NRC announcement had two major effects. The first was general confusion among the newspaper-reading public. The second was a flood of protest from other experts. Some objected because there were no heart doctors or public-health scientists on the panel. Instead, there were biochemists, the sort of scientists who seek laboratory proof of cause and effect, and thus distrust statistical evidence. Dr. William Castelli, the heart specialist who directed the famous Framingham study, pointed out that the majority of American men have blood cholesterol levels that put them in the "high risk" category. Starting choles-terol-lowering diets early in life, he believes, can help avoid risk later. And as few people know their cholesterol levels, how many can assume that they are not "at risk"?

The NRC panel's recommendations were further questioned when the board's ties with the food industry were revealed by Jane Brody in the *New York Times*. It turned out that two of the report's panel members were food-company executives. Others, employed by universities, had received grants from or worked as paid consultants to the egg, meat, or dairy industries. The chairman of the panel had represented the egg industry at the Senate hearings on cholesterol. A former member who worked on the Dietary Goals had been dropped from the panel.

The whole controversy was a discouraging example of how hard it is for the public to evaluate official pronouncements. But once the issue was aired, it was clear that the NRC group did not have any new evidence that would contradict the other agencies' reports. What's more, a different subgroup of the National Academy of Sciences came out the next year in favor of changing our diets. This group, formed to review the link between diet and cancer, advised cutting down on all fat, in-cluding fatty meats, high-fat dairy products, and oils. The panel warned specifically against smoked and cured meats such as bacon, ham, and sausages. And, like the Senate committee, it recommended eating more whole grains, fruits, and vegetables.

Meanwhile, still more evidence was building up on the heart front. One argument of the conservative NRC group was that association does not prove cause and effect. Despite the evi-dence linking dietary fat with high blood cholesterol levels and heart attacks, there was no proof that changing our diets would change the other factors. But these connections were confirmed by two important studies released in 1981.

The first was a twenty-year study of 1,900 men employed in the Western Electric plant at Hawthorne, Illinois. The study found that the more cholesterol and saturated fat a man ate, the higher his blood cholesterol was likely to be. Also, the more likely he was to die of a heart attack over the twenty-year period. Eating more polyunsaturated fat was associated with lower cholesterol levels and fewer heart attacks. The study also found that blood cholesterol levels dropped in men who cut down on foods containing saturated fat and cholesterol.

The other study, conducted in Norway, followed 1,200 middle-aged men with high blood cholesterol levels and diets high in animal fat. Half the men were advised to replace whole milk, butter, and red meat with skimmed milk, polyunsaturated oil, and fish and chicken. They were also told to eat high-fiber bread and limit eggs to one a week. Five years later this group's blood cholesterol levels averaged 13 percent lower than those of the 600 men who continued on their old diets. Their heart attack rate was 47 percent lower. Though cancer rates were not part of the study, it was found that the men who changed their diets also had fewer deaths from cancer.

You will notice that none of the expert advisors suggest giving up meat altogether. People who eat red meat on occasion and chicken or fish the rest of the time will meet the dietary goal for fat at least as well as those who give up meat and fish but substitute eggs, cheese, or cream sauce. But adopting a sensible meatless diet can be one way to meet all the goals, and experts agree that those who choose this way can do so safely.

The Chemical Stew

Most people who give up meat for health reasons are worried about fat and cholesterol. But critics of today's factory-farm methods are also concerned about DES, DDT, PCB, and other humanmade substances that end up in our meat. Unlike bacteria from spoiled meat, these chemicals usually don't make people sick right away. For this reason it is difficult to pin down just what their effects really are. But some have caused cancer and birth defects in laboratory animals. Some have caused cancer and other health problems in workers who make or use them. Others have been blamed for the emergence of new disease germs which evolve in animals but go on to infect people.

Many scientists associated with consumer-interest groups believe that dozens of chemicals now used in farming and food processing should be outlawed. But there is no one government agency responsible for making these decisions. The Food and Drug Administration regulates additives in food. The Environmental Protection Agency is responsible for controlling chemicals that find their way into our lakes and rivers—and, consequently, into the fish people eat. The Department of Agriculture deals with farmers, ranchers, and the companies who supply them with drugs, chemicals, and animal feed. Each agency has its own procedures, regulations, and conflicting claims on its favor. And in many cases, the officials of these agencies feel more loyalty toward the makers and users of the chemicals than they do for the consumers.

DES (DIETHYLSTILBESTROL)

During the years between World War II and 1980, the great American beef habit was at its peak. Those were also the years when the beef we ate was brought to its peak with the help of DES. DES, short for diethylstilbestrol, is a synthetic chemical that imitates a natural female hormone. During the 1950s and 1960s, doctors prescribed DES for pregnant women thought to be in danger of miscarriage. It was also given to poultry and livestock, usually in the form of a tablet implanted in the animals' necks, after a university scientist found that it made the animals grow fatter and faster on less feed. But DES had some unfortunate side effects. In the late 1950s, a male restaurant worker who subsisted mostly on surplus chicken necks began to develop breasts, fatty hips, and a high voice. The changes were traced to the concentration of female hormones in the chicken necks. As a result, DES was banned from chickens, but still allowed in cattle and sheep. And other similar hormones are still used in chickens.

As early as the 1950s, DES was found to cause cancer and birth defects in mice and rats, but officials hoped that humans would not be affected. Then in 1970, several teen-age girls were found to have a rare form of vaginal cancer. It turned out that all of their mothers had taken DES during pregnancy. The drug's effect on humans was now clear, and consumer-interest groups pressed the government to ban DES in meat. The Food and Drug Administration and the Department of Agriculture replied that such a move would make meat more expensive. This did not appease the critics, and the FDA did make some moves to outlaw DES. But the law banning DES did not go through until 1979, after thirty other countries had banned the drug.

Then in 1980, FDA and USDA inspectors found DES implants in 200,000 cattle bound for slaughter. They estimated that at least 500,000 cattle had been treated with the drug since the ban. As neither the FDA nor the USDA is equipped to check more than a small proportion of the cattle that end up in butcher shops or supermarkets, consumer representatives wonder how effectively the ban will be enforced. If it is observed, cattlemen might simply switch to one of several similar hormones that have been synthesized since DES was developed.

ANTIBIOTICS

Another growth-drug farmers use is penicillin, the mold that made medical history with its power to combat bacterial infections. When penicillin and other antibiotics were new, farmers used them on animals as doctors did on people, to cure infectious diseases. But these diseases became so common among animals raised on crowded factory farms that farmers started feeding antibiotics routinely, just to prevent infection. For reasons still not understood, they found that antibiotics also made the animals grow faster. Today, almost all our poultry, pigs, and veal calves, and more than half of our cattle, get antibiotics added to their feed. Half of all the antibiotics produced in this country now go into feed for meat animals.

The trouble with widespread use of antibiotics is that the bacteria they are meant to kill eventually become resistant. At first, most of the bacteria are killed; but a few strong ones might survive. Their offspring inherit their ability to resist the drugs. In time, a whole new strain of resistant bacteria develops, and the antibiotics are useless against them. What's more, the resistant strains can transfer their resistance to other types of bacteria. Some of these have already infected people. One "new bug" epidemic in England killed forty-one babies. Public-health authorities traced the disease to animals doctored with antibiotics. As a result the drugs were banned in England, except when prescribed by veterinarians.

In this country, the use of antibiotics on healthy animals is still being debated. The livestock and chemical industries have fought FDA attempts at regulation and persuaded Congress to block a proposed ban. In 1979, an organization of scientists called CAST (Council for Agricultural Science and Technology) issued a report essentially clearing the practice. At the same time, however, seven microbiologists hired as expert consultants resigned from the CAST panel, charging that negative evidence had been deleted from the report. It turned out that CAST is an industry-funded group that usually supports controversial agribusiness practices. CAST's conclusions on antibiotics lost credibility, and medical doctors joined the seven specialists in expressing concern.

NITRATES, NITRITES, NITROSAMINES

The terms are confusing, and so is the issue. It involves additives that also exist in natural food and chemicals that are harmless in themselves but dangerous in combination.

As former FDA scientist Jacqueline Verrett explains it, the compounds sodium nitrate and potassium nitrite have been used in curing meat since ancient times. Nitrates are sometimes found in water, and they also occur naturally in certain vegetables. Nitrates themselves are not dangerous, but bacteria in the body can change nitrates into nitrites. In the stomach, nitrites can combine with chemicals called amines to form nitrosamines. And tests with animals have found nitrosamines to be "very potent" causes of cancer, genetic damage, and birth defects.

According to Verrett, meat packers since the 1930s have been adding nitrites to bacon, ham, sausages, bologna and other lunch meat, and smoked fish. As with the chemicals fed to meat animals, an FDA ban on nitrites has been debated for years. But again, meat companies protest. They warn that nitrites in packed meat are necessary to protect consumers from botulism, a deadly food poison that can develop in improperly canned or plastic-sealed fish and meats. For their part, consumer groups point to the sausages and packaged meats that do not contain nitrites or botulism germs. They also point to instances where unnecessary amounts of nitrites are added to bacon, sausages, and lunch meats simply for the fresh red color they give the meat.

In 1981, a committee of the National Academy of Sciences released a report on nitrites in food. The committee recommended reducing the amounts in cured meats, but noted that we are exposed to higher nitrite levels from other sources. These include cigarette smoke, cosmetics, some vegetables, and drinking water contaminated with fertilizer runoff. Other experts, however, pointed out that the vegetables containing nitrites also have high levels of vitamins A, C, and E, and the mineral selenium, which are thought to block nitrosamine formation. The amines needed *for* nitrosamine formation are found in meats and cheeses, as well as drugs and tobacco. Finally, in 1982, the National Academy of Sciences's panel on diet and cancer recommended that we severely limit our consumption of smoked fish, ham, bacon, frankfurters, and processed lunch meats. These meats, the panel noted, are high in fat, nitrites, and other cancer-causing substances. The panel also recommended eating fruits and vegetables high in vitamins A and C, as well as vegetables in the cabbage family, such as broccoli and cauliflower, which can also act against cancer-forming agents.

PESTICIDES

Like antibiotics, synthetic pesticides were originally hailed as a boon to human health. DDT, the first of the new miracle pest killers, killed mosquitoes that carried the deadly malaria germ. It was dramatically effective in killing other insect pests responsible for destroying food crops. In time, however, DDT was found to kill birds and fish as well as its intended victims. Gradually the pest species became resistant, and farmers began using more and more DDT with less and less success. As the new chemicals don't break down in the soil like natural organic substances, DDT began to build up in our lakes and rivers, in fish, and in the tissue of animals that ate DDT-sprayed plants. Environmentalists became concerned and pressed the Environmental Protection Agency to outlaw DDT.

After six years of delays and court battles, DDT was finally banned. But by then chemical companies had developed other, similar chemicals that were far more potent. In farm workers exposed to high doses, the new pesticides have been associated with skin problems, sterility, headaches, stomach cramps, emotional disorders, and cancer. According to a *Washington Post* article, an FDA official estimated in 1969 that pesticides caused 80,000 worker poisonings and 800 worker deaths every year. Worldwide, the World Health Organization estimated that pesticides were poisoning at least half a million people and killing 10,000 people a year. Since then, workers in a chemical plant making the pesticide kepone have suffered liver damage, brain damage, and sterility. In very low doses, these pesticides have caused liver cancer and birth defects in rats and mice.

Since the ban on DDT, three more synthetic pesticides (but not kepone) have been banned. But each separate chemical must be considered and tried separately. In each case, a public-interest group called the Environmental Defense Fund has gathered evidence and petitioned the Environmental Protection Agency to outlaw the pesticide. In their turn, the companies that make the chemicals in question have hired lawyers, demanded more tests, and so delayed the ban for years. Meanwhile, more and more insects become immune to the spray, and the planet becomes more and more contaminated with poisons. The only encouraging development is that as the synthetic compounds become less effective, farmers are beginning to turn to natural methods of controlling pests.

It might seem perverse to list the pesticides sprayed on fruits and vegetables as an argument against eating meat. But one problem with these chemicals is that they become more concentrated as they move up the food chain. For example, when a cow eats sprayed grasses, the pesticide compounds are stored in her fat cells. This builds up until there is far more in the cow's tissue than there was in any of the grasses she ate. People who eat beef or drink milk from the cow get more of the pesticide than do people who eat only the sprayed crops. The people in turn store the compounds in their own fat cells. Women who breast-feed their babies have it in their milk. Compared to the risk to workers, the amounts of pesticide we get from food may be insignificant. But scientists have expressed concern about the effects on babies from pesticides in cows' or human milk.

Today, pesticides contaminate virtually all our foods, including fruits and vegetables. However, government tests have found that whole milk contained pesticide levels five times higher than those found in vegetables and fruits. Meat, fish, and poultry showed twice the level found in whole milk.

In a study of the milk of breast-feeding women, the Environmental Defense Fund found that vegetarian mothers had far lower than average pesticide levels. Vegetarian mothers who also avoided whole milk had significantly less than other vegetarians. The EDF recommended that pregnant and breast-feeding women drink only skimmed milk. A later study, reported in *New England Journal of Medicine* in 1981, found that total-vegetarian mothers' milk contained only 1 to 2 percent of the average levels, or even less, of all contaminants except PCBs. PCBs, discussed below, are now so widespread that we all have significant amounts in our systems.

PCBs

The U.S. Dietary Goals suggest eating fish instead of meat because fish fat is unsaturated. But with pesticides and other synthetic chemicals spilling into our lakes and rivers, fish has become one of our most contaminated foods. PCBs, short for polychlorinated biphenyls, are further ingredients in the meat or fish eater's alphabet soup. These humanmade, fire-resistant chemicals have killed livestock and caused cancer and birth defects in laboratory animals. For this reason the manufacture of PCBs was banned in 1976. However, the compounds are still with us in materials made before the ban. In 1979, poultry and egg products were recalled in several western states because PCBs had spilled into the chickens' feed. In smaller amounts, they now turn up in most animal fat, including humans'.

So far, fish from the ocean is thought to be relatively free from chemical contamination. But if government agencies were to ban all fish containing traces of pesticides or PCBs, almost all our freshwater fish would have to be declared unfit to eat. As a compromise, allowable "tolerance levels" have been established. But many fish still contain several times the legal levels of PCBs. One tested catch was found to have several hundred times the legal levels. At the same time, cancer researchers, environmental scientists, and many government scientists maintain that these compounds are not safe at any level. The higher the level the greater the risk, but there is always a small risk of cancer or genetic damage at the lowest level. And as we eat more and more contaminated foods, the levels in our bodies build up.

LEAD

People who live near the ocean may still enjoy unpolluted fresh fish. But concerned scientists have warned that once the ocean fish is canned, it might be contaminated with lead. In 1980, researchers at the California Institute of Technology found that canned tuna contains ten thousand times more lead than fresh

46

tuna. The lead comes from the solder that is used to join the edges of the metal cans.

Comparisons of skeletons show that we have five hundred times as much lead in our bodies as did prehistoric humans, and the effects are alarming. Doctors in Boston and Philadelphia have found brain damage and poor school performance in children who had especially high levels of lead in their bodies. These problems were blamed on the leaded gasoline from car exhaust, not on canned foods; but lead can be deadly whatever the source. In their report to *Science* magazine, the California researchers recommended banning all lead-based cans in food packaging.

Lead contamination is not limited to fish. In fact, some tuna comes in aluminum cans that are not lead-soldered. You can identify these because the bottom and side of the can are made from the same piece of metal, without seams. The use of lead solder is also widespread in canning fruits and vegetables. With acidic foods such as orange juice and tomatoes, the lead content can climb to dangerous levels after the cans are opened. The Department of Agriculture has recently warned that such foods, once opened, should not be stored in their original cans.

MEAT INSPECTION

Even if current laws and tolerance levels are safe, how sure can we be that the food we are eating is within the legal limits? According to the General Accounting Office, a congressional group that checks up on other government agencies, the chances are about one in seven that your last hamburger contained illegal amounts of a regulated chemical. The GAO reported in 1979 that 14 percent of the meat and poultry sold between 1974 and 1976 had more than the legal limit of substances thought to cause cancer, birth defects, or other health problems. According to the GAO, there are 143 hazardous drugs and chemicals that can end up in meat, but Department of Agriculture inspectors test for only 43. And as it takes six to twenty-five days to get the results of the tests taken at the slaughterhouse, the meat will already have been sold by the time it is found to be illegal.

In the past, meat inspectors did not have to worry about

humanmade chemicals, and so the inspection system was set up to check for germs. Even so, consumer advocates have never been satisfied with the thoroughness of the checks. They note that an inspector has only three seconds per carcass to check for almost thirty diseases that can infect humans. The U.S. Center for Disease Control in Atlanta estimates that two million Americans a year get salmonella poisoning from bacteria in meat. Half the chickens sold in this country are infected, but inspectors overlook it because cooking the chicken will kill the bacteria. Sometimes, though, the chicken is insufficiently cooked, and sometimes the germs are transferred to other food from knives and countertops that came in contact with the raw chicken. Salmonella is rarely fatal, but it can subject its victims to days of nausea, stomach cramps, diarrhea, and fever.

Newspaper readers are sometimes shocked to read about the microscopic life that thrives inside those sterile-looking supermarket cases. Investigators for the magazine *Consumer Reports* have found high bacteria counts in supermarket hamburger and frankfurters. In frozen food cases, an inspector for the U.S. Department of the Interior found fish that had been packaged four years earlier. One supermarket butcher has testified that lunch meat too old to sell is ground up and made into store-brand sausages. Every now and then a newspaper reports a bribery scandal, where state inspectors have been paid to overlook putrid conditions in hams, sausages, and lunch meat. (These are the meats in which spoilage can most easily be disguised.) In 1971, Dr. Jean Mayer reported that more than forty of the seventy USDA meat inspectors in Massachusetts were under indictment for accepting bribes.

Vegetarians like to tell the allegedly true story of a man at a dinner party who ate everything else that was served but kept passing up the meat dishes. Finally, the woman sitting next to him asked if he was a vegetarian for religious or humanitarian reasons. "Neither," the man answered. "I'm a meat inspector."

No doubt most meat inspectors do eat meat, though they may be choosier than their neighbors about what it is and where it comes from. And probably most people, given the information available to a meat inspector, would favor more thorough inspection but still go on eating meat. Given the level of risk, few people give up meat just to avoid germs and chemicals.

Nevertheless, critics maintain that more careful handling and inspection would reduce the risk from bacteria. Consumer advocates are even more critical of growth hormones, antibiotics, and nitrites. These chemicals pose an unnecessary risk because they are deliberately added to our food. Pesticides, too, are deliberately introduced to the environment. The exact health effect of any one of these substances is hard to assess, and our environment is now so contaminated with chemicals that can cause cancer or genetic damage that it's hard to fix the blame for any particular case. The question is whether it makes sense to add to the chemical stew.

Should the government allow even a slight risk to the public just to fatten livestock? If outlawing growth hormones does make meat more expensive, will consumers be willing to pay higher prices for safer food? Should we support an industry that misuses antibiotics to the point where people might be defenseless against new diseases? Can we rely on the government to decide what health risks are worth taking, or should we make some decisions of our own?

Vegetarianism is just one answer to some of these questions. For most people, it is a drastic one. Many who are concerned about food safety feel that they shouldn't have to give up meat; they should be able to buy it undoctored. But those who choose vegetarianism, for whatever reason, will not be paying for questionable extras that consumers never asked for.

CHAPTER
6

The Cost of Meat

In 1980 Polish factory workers went on strike against their government-run industries. Their action was taken up by other Polish workers and farmers, and in a short time all of Poland seemed united in protest. Before the government clamped down, the workers had moved from demanding an independent union to calling for a total restructuring of the Polish political system. But the grievance that had triggered the first expressions of discontent was the rising cost of meat.

There is something about high meat prices that moves people to protest. To most of us, living the good life means, at the very least, affording meat. When people who have taken meat for granted find it no longer affordable, they feel cheated.

Americans, on the average, spend a smaller percentage of their income on food than do the Poles or most of the world's people. But Americans too grumble about the rising cost of meat. Their grumbles changed to a more contained sort of protest in 1973. The steep price rises of recent years were just beginning, and people were not yet conditioned to spending just a little more each time they passed through the checkout counter. Consumers blamed the stores, the middlemen, the cattlemen, and the government, and complained that something should be done.

One Connecticut woman decided to do something. She

called for everyone in her state to give up meat for a week as a protest against rising prices. With TV and newspaper coverage, the movement spread to other disgruntled consumers with similar ideas. The result was the National Meat Boycott in the first week of April 1973.

For seven days, millions of American families lived on omelets and peanut-butter sandwiches and tuna fish. Newspaper food pages featured meatless recipes for those who wanted to experiment with more interesting fare. Meat wholesalers reported sales drops of 50 to 75 percent, and retail sales in middle-class areas were running only 20 percent of normal. In poorer areas the drop was not as spectacular, partly no doubt because the poor did not have so far to drop. Then, too, the poor were probably more skeptical about what this kind of action would do for them.

Few of the people participating in the boycott had any clear idea of what it would accomplish. Most were simply fed up with high prices and wanted to make their feelings known. But according to its leaders, the goals of the boycott were to bring about a freeze on meat prices and a change in government trade policies. Existing policies, the boycotters charged, encouraged the export of American meat and feed grains but put limits on imports in order to keep domestic prices high.

Government trade policies did not change, but the boycott did slow the rise in meat prices. By 1976, Americans were eating more beef than ever before. But in 1978, with grocery prices generally up 10 to 20 percent, the cost of beef rose 45 percent. By early 1979 consumer agencies were remembering the 1973 boycott and calling for "beefless Wednesdays."

Beefless Wednesdays never caught on. By this time, consumers weren't in the mood for mass gestures. Many Americans were already having meatless days out of sheer economic necessity. Hamburger accounted for half the beef that was consumed. By this time, too, people had other reasons for buying less meat. Perhaps the meatless week of 1973 made Americans realize that there were alternatives. The Dietary Goals made them aware of the health hazards of high-meat diets. The consumer movement made the public more suspicious of the products meat producers and processors were offering. The health-food movement acquainted many with eating styles that don't depend on meat. And so, as prices rose, red meat no

51

longer seemed a commodity that must be had at any cost. Alternative protein sources looked more and more attractive. A pound of lentils or dried beans cost only $.69 in 1980, when ground chuck, the standard hamburger beef, was $1.69 a pound. Tofu, the Asian soybean curd now well known in America, was $.60 a pound. Ground sirloin, a more expensive hamburger beef, cost $2.09 a pound, three times as much as beans. In the same supermarket, porterhouse steak cost $3.00 and sirloin steak $4.00 a pound, bone and all.

By 1980 American meat sales had dropped 17 percent from their 1976 peak. Mainstream American food writers were coming out with meatless cookbooks designed to spare their readers' arteries and pocketbooks. Such menus were no longer just for kooks. True, you could still find hard-pressed shoppers who believed their families, especially the males, needed steak to keep up their energy. Reflecting that mentality, one market analyst predicted that the conflict between economy and nutrition would be the "battle of the eighties." But consumers aware of current thinking in nutrition have not been torn by such a battle. To them, cutting down on meat is good nutrition and good economy.

COST TO TAXPAYERS

Besides paying high prices for high-fat meat and milk, Americans also help support these industries through their taxes. Without government help, the dairy industry would have to lower milk prices or produce less milk. But as it is, the federal government sets a minimum price that all distributors and dairy processors have to pay to farmers. If producers cannot sell all their milk at this price, the USDA buys up the surplus. To discourage farmers from watering their milk to get more money, the government price supports are based on the fat content of the milk. The more fat in the milk, the more the farmer gets for it. But this practice has encouraged dairy interests to promote high-fat whole milk, even for teen-age dieters. It has also encouraged farmers to breed cows that give especially fatty milk, despite all the evidence that high-fat milk is less healthful.

What happens to the extra milk that the government is required to buy? Some goes to the army and other public institutions, and some goes to feed children under the school lunch program. Some of the surplus milk, with fat removed, goes back to farmers in dry form for animal feed. In 1982, with much publicity, some processed cheese was distributed to the poor, who had been hit by cuts in more substantial food-aid programs. But a good deal of the surplus goes unused. According to USDA figures, several hundred million pounds of surplus milk, cheese, and butter are put into storage each year.

It might seem strange that the government insists on paying for dairy products we have no use for. But Washington observers point out that the dairy lobby contributes large funds to top officials' political campaigns. In 1972, Richard Nixon secretly accepted a pledge of two million dollars in return for a 6 percent increase in the guaranteed price of milk. The news, when it came out, added one more count to the Watergate scandal that drove Nixon from the Presidency. In 1976, the dairy industry gave generous contributions to key senators and representatives. Two years later, Congress passed a law requiring twice-a-year increases in the price support. In 1980, candidates for federal office collected over a million dollars from the dairy industry. From that election, however, President Reagan came into office pledged to cut federal spending. Congress then voted to skip one increase and to make small adjustments in future increases. Still, the subsidies cost taxpayers almost two billion dollars in 1981 and slightly over two billion in 1982. In addition, consumers must pay more for milk each time the subsidized price goes up. And dairy farmers, to stay afloat, continue to increase their output and add to the surplus.

Other government subsidies come in the form of tax write-offs. By favorable tax treatment for the companies, the government effectively pays about half the cost of huge irrigation projects that benefit feed grain producers. Yet these projects are dangerously depleting our water resources and are often less productive than more modest and economical irrigation methods.

In addition to such direct supports, large producers also benefit from research conducted by scientists in government agencies and tax-supported universities. In the book *Hard Tomatoes, Hard Times,* Jim Hightower tells how the University of Georgia developed a conveyer belt to speed up the process of loading broiler chickens onto trucks. Hightower believes the companies who benefit should be paying for this research. Some of the research might actually harm consumers. The hormone DES was developed at public expense at the University of Iowa, then turned over to a private drug company to sell for profit. Still other projects are designed to deceive consumers. Hightower describes how tax-supported research came up with a chicken-feed additive that gave the chickens' skin a "pleasing yellow tinge." This doesn't improve the meat, but it does improve sales for the companies.

Hightower shows how large producers supply funds to university researchers and get back far more than they contribute. Through these financial arrangements, says Hightower, agribusiness interests exert strong influence on public universities. Nutrition textbooks, from the elementary to the college level, contain charts and other "teaching aids" furnished by the industry. Helen Guthrie's *Introductory Nutrition,* a leading college nutrition text, lists the Borden dairy company and several meat, egg, and food industry organizations as sources of "reliable nutrition information." And only after the Dietary Goals were published did textbooks stop lumping vegetarianism with dietary "fads." Until then, too, college texts emphasized only the nutrients in eggs, meat, and dairy products. Cholesterol concerns were dismissed as "controversial."

Of course, the meat and dairy industries are not the only branches of agribusiness that get government support. Hightower's classic example is the "red rock" tomato developed at Rutgers University. The tomato has very little juice and less flavor but it is easy to pick by machine, so it is now the standard tomato on sale everywhere. As a result farm workers have lost their jobs and consumers are deprived of a delicious food, but the companies save money.

EVERYBODY PAYS FOR AGRIGIANTS

During the 1970s it became clear to most observers that government policies since World War II have aided large agribusiness firms at the expense of small farmers, farm workers, and consumers. Year by year, the number of operating farms gets smaller and the size of the average farm gets bigger. Between 1940 and 1980 over four million farmers went out of business, often because they couldn't afford the land and equipment needed to compete with the giants. Those who remain often work long hours under contract to large food or drug companies. The companies sell the farmers their equipment and the farmers must work harder to keep up the installment payments.

Farmers are not the only victims of food-industry giants. Studies of agribusiness impact have found small-town stores forced out of business because the large corporations do not buy their supplies and machinery locally or spend their income in the community. With fewer farms, rural workers lose their jobs or earn less than before. Some are forced to go on welfare or food stamps, adding to taxpayers' expense. Consumers are so remote from the people who make the decisions that they have no control over the quality and type of food that is offered for sale. The concentration extends throughout the food industry, allowing large companies to charge high prices without fear of competition. Such practices are said to cost American consumers about sixteen billion dollars each year.

Officials used to maintain that large farms were to everyone's advantage, because they could produce more food at less cost. Former Secretary of Agriculture Earl Butz made no bones about his sympathy for the giants. "Get big or get out" was his now-famous advice to small farmers caught in the squeeze. But Butz's successor, Bob Bergland, said in 1980, "It is a myth that the biggest farms are the most efficient." A USDA study released by Bergland found that moderate-sized, family-owned farms were most efficient. Yet 95 percent of our vegetables come from farms owned or controlled by large corporations. The average corporate farm in California is eight times the size the USDA judged most efficient in terms of best return on energy expended.

Just before leaving office, Bergland warned that unless government policies change, 1 percent of the nation's farms will control 50 percent of farm production by the year 2000. Today, the top 3 percent controls almost half of all farm sales. However, the policies of President Reagan's Secretary of Agriculture, John Block, continue to favor large producers.

How does the meat industry fit the trend toward fewer and bigger producers? Chicken production is a highly concentrated industry. According to a 1975 government publication, 97 percent of our broiler chickens are produced by agribusiness giants or by farmers under contract to them. The largest supplier, with the cozy name of Holly Farm, has a million and a half breeder hens in one operation. The hens lay five and a half million eggs a week. The eggs are hatched and sent off to "independent" farmers, who raise them and send them back to Holly Farm processing plants for slaughter and packing. Three months after hatching, the chickens lie wrapped in plastic in supermarket cases.

Pig farming is not yet as concentrated as poultry farming, but it is heading rapidly in the same direction. Cattle are raised and fed by large meat-packing companies, and the companies in turn may be owned by huge multinational conglomerates. ITT, a communications conglomerate that buys and sells companies the way kids trade baseball cards, produces ham, sausages, and bacon. ITT also owns the companies that bring us Hostess Twinkies and Wonder Bread. Cargill, the world's largest grain-trading company, is also the number-one cattle feeder and the fourth largest in poultry operations. Cargill also owns our second largest meat packing company. (The largest meat packer is owned by a petroleum company.) It is not surprising to see Cargill involved in meat operations, as more than three quarters of our grain crop goes to feed livestock.

TAKING ACTION

It is tempting to envision the vegetarian movement as one extended boycott that would cut into the fat of these interlocking operations. However, the dynamics are not that simple. Beef production has dropped since Americans cut back on meat in the late 1970s, but prices have climbed. And the small farmers are the least able to survive the cuts. The large grain sellers continue to manipulate feed prices and markets. With the domestic meat market "softening," they can turn to a growing foreign market in formerly meatless countries. Then, too, as the dairy subsidies illustrate, government policy can encourage production even when the market for it does not exist.

Considering these realities, critics of agribusiness see political change, not changes in personal diets, as the most likely way to break up the growing concentration of power among food producers. Nevertheless, changing our own diets is one step individuals can take to establish our personal independence from the giants. For food activists and others involved in alternative food programs, vegetarianism is only one part of a larger movement. For many, looking into meat issues is the first step in thinking about food in political terms. "It all began when I gave up meat," said one young woman who works full time on a project involving small farmers and rural workers. "People questioned that and I found myself looking further and further into the food economy in order to explain my decision." Others concerned about food issues use their power as consumers by participating in projects that help them and their neighbors eat better for less.

Buying vegetables directly in urban farmers' markets is one way in which consumers can support small local farmers while getting the best deal for themselves. In the 1970s, hundreds of American cities established or revived markets where farmers and city dwellers could trade to their mutual benefit. Several small farmers in the New York City area were on the verge of going out of business when the city established Greenmarket. Now the farms are thriving. Greenmarket farmers set up their trucks in different neighborhoods on different days of the week, and they are welcomed by devoted crowds in all of them. The customers get better food than they would in supermarkets for comparable or lower prices. The farmers get more money for their food than they would from wholesale distributers, and they thrive on the appreciation they get from city people just finding out how good fresh vegetables can be. Farmers realize that the city folk are not drug-crazed muggers, shoppers realize that farmers are not grass-chewing hicks, and both realize that they have a common interest outside the agribusiness system.

More and more people committed to food reform are joining co-ops, in which groups of people get together to buy food at wholesale prices. Some co-ops seek out small independent farmers, or farmers who sell pesticide-free food. Co-ops can also pool their buying power to persuade their suppliers not to handle foods that are being boycotted by farm workers and other groups. The important thing is that the members make the choice. The point of the co-op movement, according to a Catholic priest I talked to in Hoboken, New Jersey, is not just to get cheap food. It also shows people that together they can do for themselves what the commercial establishments are not doing for them.

From cooperative buying, some groups go on to cooperative

farming in community gardens. School systems also sponsor gardening projects, where students can grow food for their families. Under the Youth Garden Program of the Cleveland, Ohio, public schools, students from third graders to high school seniors have been growing vegetables since 1904. In 1974, 21,000 young gardeners in Cleveland grew more than $622,000 worth of vegetables.

More recently, action for food reform has moved inside the schools. One nutritionist in Fulton County, Georgia, has converted the public-school lunch program to a natural-food plan that attracts more students to the cafeteria than ever ate at school before. Fulton County students have also become involved in nutrition projects and organic gardening. In Oakham County in rural Massachusetts, students cook with natural whole foods and help plan ethnic menus for the school lunch program. Other schools across the country have introduced pita sandwiches and tofu for lunch and outlawed junk-food vending machines in cafeterias. The tofu, it must be said, has not always been a hit. These measures were initiated by teachers, parents, or nutritionists, but in other systems students have taken the initiative. In colleges, students have already transformed their dining programs by demanding natural foods and vegetarian choices. Junior- and senior-high-school students might not win vegetarian lunch programs as such, if there are few vegetarians at the school. But programs that emphasize natural whole foods and adopt the Dietary Goals will end up offering a lot more meatless selections.

Students can also be on the watch for industry salesmanship in health and nutrition classes. The Dairy Council is the biggest supplier of school nutrition information, and much of its material is designed to sell high-fat products because they bring the biggest profits. Large meat companies also provide schools and colleges with free material extolling the nutritional value of meat. In 1980, when government agencies were telling people to limit their meat eating, the National Live Stock and Meat Board decided to fight back through the schools. "There is no doubt that vegetarianism is growing," said a Meat Board report. But as government money for textbooks becomes harder to get, the board reasoned, teachers will welcome their free "teaching aids." Alongside this material students might suggest a reading of *Eating in America,* the U.S. Senate report that presents the Dietary Goals.

Groups or individuals interested in turning around their school food services can get some practical ideas from the 32-page booklet "Eating Better at School: An Organizer's Guide," put out by the Center for Science in the Public Interest. It is available for $2.00 from the CSPI, at 1755 S Street, NW, Washington, DC 20009. For those interested in delving further into food issues, the same organization has compiled a resource book for high-school and college study. Titled *Food: Where Nutrition, Politics and Culture Meet,* it is available from CSPI for $5.50.

CHAPTER
7

Think of the Starving

When I was growing up around 1940, my parents used to urge me to finish my dinner by reminding me of all the starving children in China. I couldn't see how my overeating would help the Chinese children, but my parents' point was that I should feel grateful for the food I had. In their view, the proper way to express my appreciation would be to eat everything on my plate.

Most American children have heard the same admonishment, although the location of the starving children might vary from Biafra to India to Kampuchea, according to which food emergency has most recently been publicized. Some children have a perfectly rational answer: "If you're thinking about the starving children, why don't you send them my extra food?" Today, many young people have decided to do just that, in an indirect way. By passing up their meat, they hope to make more food available to those who need it.

The idea took root in 1971 when a young woman named Frances Moore Lappé stirred up the American conscience with a paperback book, *Diet for a Small Planet.* Lappé wrote the book to make people aware of the wastefulness of the American meat-centered diet. Lappé discovered that over 78 percent of all our grain and 95 percent of our unexported soybeans go to feed livestock, not people. But for every seven pounds of grain and soybeans fed to the animals, we get only one pound of edible meat. As a result the average American consumes almost a ton of grain in a year. Most of these 2,000 pounds we consume indirectly, by eating meat from grain-fed animals. The average Indian consumes only four hundred pounds of grain a year, almost all of it directly.

Most Americans believed in 1971 that humans need meat for protein. Lappé showed that animals give us less protein in the form of meat than we give them in feed. According to her figures quoted in *Animal Factories,* beef cattle give us back less than 5 percent of the protein they take in. Pigs give back less than 12 percent and chickens less than 18 percent. For this reason Lappé called the meat animal a "protein factory in reverse."

For Americans who had forgotten how to eat without meat, Lappé went on to explain that we don't need meat for protein. Combining grains with soybeans, lentils, chick peas, or any other kind of bean gives us protein that is just as valuable as meat. Lappé urged people to eat "low on the food chain," eating the plant protein directly or mixing it with small amounts of milk, cheese, or fish. If the livestock feed we would save this way were given to people instead, it could feed all the starving and severely malnourished people in the world.

Defenders of beef eating argue that cattle do not use up that much humanly edible food. Many beef animals, they point out, graze on grassland. In recent years, some livestock raisers have gone back to range-feeding their cattle, and the amount of grain fed to livestock has declined by a small margin. However, figures from the 1970s show that 70 percent of our beef cattle are still "finished" on grain, and over three quarters of our grain crop still goes to livestock.

What's more, it would not be possible to return all cattle raised today to grazing land. There just isn't enough land. As it is, it takes twenty times as much crop and grazing land to feed a person on a meat-based diet as it does to feed someone who lives on beans and rice. World resource experts warn us now that overgrazing is wearing out existing rangeland. A National Academy of Science committee reports that the world's tropical rain forests are being destroyed at the rate of fifty to a hundred acres a minute to make grazing land for cattle. Experts use such phrases as "biological catastrophe" in forecasting the results. The World Watch Institute, an independent research group that assesses global resource prospects, warned that the loss of the rain forests will "change the nature of life on the planet for all time." The solution, then, is not switching back to range-fed cattle, but cutting back on cattle-raising altogether.

Grain and land are not the only resources being wasted by meat animals. While the world approaches serious shortages of energy and water, meat eaters use more than their share of both. Where it takes three hundred gallons of water a day to grow food for one vegetarian, a typical omnivore requires twenty-five hundred gallons. Much of this water is drawn from underground reserves that are being used up faster than rain can replenish them. Machinery and fertilizer involved in feeding and raising farm animals use extravagant amounts of fossil-fuel energy. Measured in the same energy units, the fuel energy that goes into a hamburger is three times what the hamburger gives back in food energy. In contrast, corn and soybeans give back six to seven times the energy put into growing them.

Whatever input and return you choose to measure, current methods of raising livestock come off as an inefficient way to get food. According to the more conservative estimates of World Watch President Lester Brown, the average Russian or American omnivore uses roughly four times as much grain, land, energy, and fertilizer as a vegetarian consumes directly.

As Brown's mention of the Russians reminds us, North Americans are not the only overconsumers. The people of cattle-raising Australia, New Zealand, Uruguay, and Argentina eat more beef per capita than we do. Western Europeans eat less than we do, but more than their share. The Russians and Japanese seem to be rushing to catch up with us in meat consumption, and other less-developed countries are making efforts in the same direction. But far from justifying our consumption, that only compounds the problem.

According to Brown, the world's resources cannot support a growing population of meat eaters. He predicts that shortages will soon force changes for all of us. As Brown puts it, our "days of unrestrained materialism are numbered. The change will be either mandatory or voluntary."

The changes that Brown urges are important for our food security, and some Americans have changed their diets out of concern for our limited resources. Once again, though, voluntary diet changes have to be supported by changes in government policy aimed at conserving these resources. As long as companies are given tax advantages for depleting the water supply and public lands are managed for the benefit of ranchers, the current disregard for environmental impact is likely to continue.

So far, we have been talking about our own food resources. The problem of getting food to the world's hungry is even more complicated. It is not a simple matter of allocating grain to cattle or to people. If large numbers of Americans gave up meat, the grain we saved would not automatically be available to the hungry. Brown acknowledges that feeding less corn and beans to cattle here will not get that corn and beans to the people who need it.

A U.S. Presidential Commission on World Hunger reached a similar conclusion. The Commission reported in 1980 that more than one-eighth of the world's population suffers from some form of malnutrition, and the proportion is growing. (United Nations officials take a dimmer view; they classify a full one-fourth of the world's people as severely underfed.) But, said the Commission, the chief cause of hunger is poverty, not overpopulation. In other words, people are hungry because they cannot buy the food that is available.

Frances Moore Lappé now agrees that food scarcity is not the cause of hunger, but she does not agree that poverty explains the problem. To her, poverty and hunger are both symptoms. The cause of food inequality is a lack of power. In the book *Food First,* written with co-author Joseph Collins, Lappé argues that the land and resources now exist to feed all the hungry people in the world. However, the hungry people do not control the land and resources in their own countries. Instead, food production is controlled by large landowners and foreign (mostly American) food companies that grow luxury crops for export. Instead of growing corn and beans to feed its own people, Mexico sends tomatoes and lettuce to the United States. Mexico imports corn and wheat, which is sold to those Mexicans who can afford to buy it. Ninety percent of Mexico's peasants remain undernourished. Brazil sends us vitamin C-rich oranges, while Brazilians suffer from vitamin C deficiency. Half of Brazil's basic grains go to livestock that most Brazilians cannot afford to eat. Peanuts are a basic protein food in Africa, yet half the peanuts grown in Africa go to feed cattle and poultry in Europe. Colombia grows carnations on land that could be growing food for hungry Colombians. Expensive sugar, pineapples, and bananas are exported from the Philippines, where the people are landless and underfed. The money for all these export crops goes not to the people who work the land but to the large corporations that control the operations.

If poverty were the cause of hunger, says Lappé, then simply sending food to the hungry would be a solution. But instead of sending food, Lappé urges Americans to work for food self-reliance here and elsewhere. We should oppose government aid to countries with unpopular governments, where the poor will not benefit from the aid. Instead we should support aid to countries such as Nicaragua that are attempting to give the rural population more control over food production.

This policy, Lappé notes, is "exactly the opposite" of the one our government has followed. At present, our food aid does not go to feed or aid the hungry. Instead it goes to people who can pay for it, mostly in developed countries, and to governments we see as our military and political allies. Two-thirds of our grain exports now go to feed cattle. Another motive behind our food aid programs, Lappé has concluded, is to create export markets for American corporations. Instead we should encourage agricultural development for basic foods, so the people in the poorer countries can feed themselves.

Lappé now maintains that people misunderstood *Diet for a Small Planet.* At the time that *Diet* came out, people had to learn that they could make changes in their own diets. They had to realize that the land could feed more people if it was not feeding livestock. But, says Lappé, "I didn't mean that if each of us only ate one less hamburger a week the hungry could be fed." In 1982 Lappé brought out a new edition of *Diet for a Small Planet.* In the new version she emphasized that changing our diets is not an answer to world hunger. Changing our diets is simply a way of saying "I have a choice." In taking this step, Lappé tells us, we can stop feeling guilty and start acting responsibly. Giving up meat and processed foods is one way that we can take control over our own diets. But the way to get food to the hungry is to work for political change that gives people control over the land and resources in their own countries.

Other analysts agree that the problem of hunger is political in nature. Patricia Kutzner, director of the World Hunger Education Service, believes that some vegetarians give too much attention to changing their own life-styles. In her view, this can make them unduly smug. To make her point, Kutzner quotes a Third World representative to the 1978 World Food Conference. "If you Americans really want to help my hungry people," this frustrated delegate burst out, "eat all the meat you want but get your government to change its trade policies. Then, we will all be able to eat." Kutzner, however, doesn't say to "eat all the meat you want." She believes that changing your diet can be the first step in beginning to live "the examined life." This requires bringing your life-style into harmony with your values and beliefs. Like Lappé and Collins, she also believes that taking charge of your own diet can be the first step in working for food self-sufficiency worldwide.

If giving up meat is not a solution to world hunger, it can be a way of recognizing the problem and refusing to be part of it. Those who wish to take a more active part in the solution can get in touch with organizations that are working to empower the hungry and educate people about food inequality. Young people who aren't in a position to donate money or work in the field can study the issues these groups raise and participate in some of their projects. For example, Oxfam America, a group committed to food self-sufficiency, sponsors a one-day fast every year on the Thursday before Thanksgiving. People send the money they would otherwise spend on food to Oxfam's self-help programs in poor countries. Individuals can participate in the fast privately or organize group fasts among family members, neighbors, classmates, and co-workers. For information on the fast, write to Oxfam America, 302 Columbus Avenue, Boston, MA 02116.

The American Friends Service Committee, associated with the religious Society of Friends, also sponsors a number of food-related social programs. With other church groups, it supports the Nestlé boycott, a response to the company's marketing of infant formula in Third World countries. Members refuse to buy Nestlé Company products because its salespeople, sometimes dressed as nurses, persuade breast-feeding mothers to switch to formula feeding. Many mothers can't afford to keep up their purchase of the formula, but once they have made the change, their own milk dries up and they can't go back to breast-feeding. Others have to mix the formula with badly polluted water. The result, according to the United Nations World Health Organization, is widespread malnutrition and about a million infant deaths a year. When the WHO met on the issue in 1981, the United States was the only country to vote against restrictions on formula promotion. For information on the Nestlé boycott, write to INFACT, 1701 University Ave SE, Minneapolis, MN 55414.

Lappé's organization, the Institute for Food and Development Policy, publishes a variety of inexpensive books and pamphlets on the economic aspects of food issues. Among them is a $2.45 paperback titled *What Can We Do,* which profiles actual grass-roots activists in the areas of agriculture and nutrition. For a list of its publications, write to the Institute for Food and Development Policy, 1885 Mission Street, San Francisco, CA 94103.

C H A P T E R
8

Summing Up

Balancing the evidence on all fronts, the case against meat seems a strong one. But if we look back at the arguments one by one, we might find the case for moderate meat eating to be just as strong.

☐ The callous practices of today's factory farms pay off because the huge demand for meat makes overcrowding and mechanization profitable. But if people would eat less meat altogether and then choose from a wider variety of animals and a wider variety of organs from the animals, fewer cows and pigs would be raised. Those that were could then live more naturally.

☐ The earliest humans lived mostly on fruits and seeds, but meat had a place in their diets from the beginning.

☐ The amounts of meat consumed today give people more saturated fat and cholesterol than their bodies can handle; but occasional or small amounts of meat can be tolerated.

☐ The chemicals that end up in today's meat might not be safe, but the risk is no doubt very small for people who eat very little meat.

☐ As food prices rise, Americans are learning that they can eat more economically without red meat. Still, a little chopped sausage or ham hock to flavor a vegetable stew or bean dish will probably be affordable.

☐ Meat eaters in the United States, Canada, and other developed countries use more than their share of world resources. But the planet can support some meat animals, especially those that don't compete with humans for food. And though the grain now fed to livestock could feed all the hungry people of the world, those people would not get the grain if we stopped raising livestock. What the people in poor countries need is a chance to raise their own food on land now controlled by the wealthy.

In the last few years, Americans have already cut back significantly on red meat, mostly from concern about cholesterol and rising prices. But the proportion of true vegetarians will probably always be small. Still, even those who don't go all the way can benefit from learning how to cook and eat meatless meals.

In any case, there are always people who are dissatisfied with half-way measures. To radicals and saints, and to the idealistic young, total commitment is a more attractive virtue than moderation. Many young people, once they start thinking about animals' rights, begin to question their own right to kill and eat other creatures. Some, comparing hunger on other continents with overindulgence on ours, just can't enjoy a hamburger or steak even once in a while. Even people who are interested only in saving their own money or health often find switching to vegetarian meals more satisfying than just eating less meat. Some find that after they break the meat habit they lose the taste for flesh. Some believe it is more consistent to avoid all animal products, including milk. But that brings up the question of whether humans can live on plants alone.

Whether the decision is to give up just meat, meat and eggs, or all animal products, new vegetarians are bound to run into people who think they are endangering their health. Even those who sympathize with the idea will want to know more about vegetarian nutrition before taking it up. Can you get enough protein on a vegetarian diet? Can you grow as tall if you don't eat meat or drink milk? Will all those starchy carbohydrates make you fat? How about all those vitamins and minerals the meat ads tell us beef is best for? Are vegetarians exposing themselves to deficiency diseases that meat eaters don't have to worry about?

The next section of this book is designed to answer these

questions, plus others that you might not think to ask. It won't tell you whether to become a vegetarian, or what kind of vegetarian you should be. But it will give you the information you need to make the decision, and to eat well if you decide for some form of vegetarianism.

PART

2

Vegetarian Nutrition: What You Need

9

Becoming a Vegetarian

By now you have probably concluded that vegetarian diets are more likely to improve than endanger your health. But you can't simply give up meat and end up with a healthful diet. For one thing, people who get most of their nonmeat foods from cans, freezers, snack packs, and commercial bakeries have to learn to cook with real whole foods. The rewards in flavor alone can be a revelation. But along with the fun of learning to cook and the pleasure of learning new tastes comes responsibility. For teen-agers especially, going vegetarian usually involves taking over the planning and preparation of their own meals. This requires a little knowledge of nutrition, a little self-discipline, and some consideration for the other people who share your kitchen.

Many people hesitate to give up meat because they think vegetarian cooking takes more time. Most vegetarians claim that it doesn't. With so-called natural-food stores now selling frozen fake meats and instant lentil burgers, it can take as much or as little time as you want it to take. But for those of you who have never had to prepare your own meals, then yes, vegetarian cooking will take more time. That's why you shouldn't try to make too many changes at once. If your family has never made a big deal of meals and cooking, then you probably shouldn't plan to make pasta from scratch or throw a Mexican dinner for six until you get used to cooking your own meals with dried beans or packaged spaghetti. As fixing your own meals becomes part of your daily routine, you will gradually become interested in trying new foods and doing more elaborate cooking.

FAMILY HASSLES

One of the biggest problems faced by vegetarian teen-agers is not how to eat or how to cook, but how to cope with family hassles. Most parents today are more tolerant of meatless diets than they were ten or even five years ago, because more and more adults are now learning that their own high-meat diets can cause health problems. What's more, so many people are becoming vegetarian these days that it's no longer looked on as a far-out thing to do. Still, many parents will be uneasy if their sons or daughters drop meat altogether, unless they can be convinced that their offspring know what they're doing.

One way to convince them that you know what you're doing is to have the nutritional answers at hand. This book should help you answer your parents' questions. If they want more technical detail, refer them to some of the books listed as sources in the further reading section at the end of the book. If you think personal contact would work better than a book, suggest that they talk the matter over with some vegetarian adults (if you know any) or with your family doctor. When parents get emotional about their children's food habits, referring them to a rational outsider might calm them down where trying to outshout them yourself will have the opposite effect.

Once your parents understand that you *can* be well fed without meat, they will want to make sure that you *will* be. Simply sharing the peas and potatoes and dessert, while passing up the pork chop, won't impress them. If they see you planning alternative meals and shopping for the groceries you need, they'll be more inclined to trust your judgment. When they see you consistently preparing your own balanced meals, they should gradually stop urging you to taste just a few bites of meat.

Whatever you do, don't try to force your family into your way of eating. They have a right to their choice just as you have a right to yours, and they also have a right to eat in peace.

74

Besides, it won't work. There is nothing like a self-righteous new vegetarian to drive the mildest of parents to an orgy of conspicuous flesh consumption. Instead of trying to persuade them, try enticing them by cooking the family a special meatless meal once a week. (Make a big deal of it. Get out the candles.) That, and your own example night after night, is more likely to make your point. I know many families, including my own, that have gone vegetarian after a teen-age family member took the initiative. But if your family doesn't, just be thankful they accept your decision, and let it go at that.

And if they don't accept your decision? In some families, food has been an emotional issue since infancy, when parents set out to stuff food down their kids and the kids learned that they could upset their parents by refusing it. In other cases, the parents are so unsure of themselves for one reason or another that they take any departure on the kids' part as a challenge to their own way of life. All too often, the kids respond by rushing straight into the rebellious behavior that seems to be expected of them. In these families, the safety of vegetarian diets is not the real issue. If the generations weren't fighting over meat, they'd be fighting over something else.

Let's suppose that you have really turned off meat, you are not doing it to spite your parents, but they refuse to see it that way. At worst, where reason and example and experts' assurance fail, you might have to choose between eating with your family and eating your way, alone. Fortunately, very few parents are so irrational. Most are simply concerned and need to be reassured that their teen-age children are sensible enough to take care of their own needs.

TAKING CARE OF NUTRITION

Just what those needs are is the subject of the next few chapters. You will find that food from plants can meet almost all of them, and that eggs and dairy products can take care of the rest. You can use the material in these chapters to answer your own nutrition questions, or to answer parents or other people who suspect that you are being faddish or irresponsible by not eating meat. If you are not that interested in nutrition but just want to make sure your diet is adequate, then you should at least study the chart of key nutrients on pages 130-3, the food-group chart on page 140, and the sample meal plan on page 141. If you have any questions about these condensed summaries, you can then turn back to the fuller explanations. You might want to keep a record of what you eat each day, and check it out against what the charts say you should be eating. You might discover that you are not eating as wisely as you think you are.

If your daily record passes the comparison test, if you read the next seven chapters diligently and guard against every risk they mention, there is yet another pitfall to be avoided. That is the danger of becoming too concerned about nutrition. People have eaten well for thousands of years with very little meat and no knowledge of the amino acids, vitamins, or minerals that we will be talking about in the next few chapters. Given a variety of real food to choose from, all they needed was a sense of hunger and a sense of taste. Today, some nutrition-minded vegetarians might do well to add a sense of proportion.

Eating properly is important, but there is more to eating well than eating properly. You might be getting all the nutrients your body needs, but if your dinner is not a high point of your day, you can be missing out on one of life's basic pleasures. Whatever they say about not living on bread alone, good food enjoyed in good company can feed the soul. And the conversation generated at a good meal can refresh the mind along with the body.

While looking into the science of eating, we shouldn't disregard the art. Every culture that gets past the subsistence stage develops skills and customs that make eating more than a refueling operation. In her cookbook, *Classic Italian Cooking,* Marcella Hazan gives us an eloquent description of the art of eating in Italy. "An Italian meal," says Hazan, "is a story told from nature, taking its rhythms, its humors, its bounty, and turning them into episodes for the senses." When we get too deeply into vitamins and minerals, Hazan's words can bring us back to all our senses.

CHAPTER
10

The Nutrients

When my daughter Deirdre decided to become a vegetarian, I worried that she might not get enough of the right kind of protein. Most meat-eating parents seem to share that fear. Another common worry is that vegetarians might get fat from eating too much starchy carbohydrate. The fact is that most meat eaters get far more protein than they can use, and the extra amounts don't do them any good. As for starchy carbohydrates, doctors are now telling meat eaters to eat more of these essential foodstuffs. And we know that doctors are also advising meat eaters to cut down on animal fat.

All this makes vegetarian diets seem superior, and they can be. But in addition to protein, fat, and carbohydrate, the three foodstuffs that build our bodies and give them energy, we need other substances from food. Our bodies can't make use of the foodstuffs without vitamins and minerals, and a few of these nutrients are not as easy to get from plants. Your meat-eating friends might never have heard of vitamin B_{12} or zinc, but what you read about them in the chapters to come might affect your decision to stick it out as a vegetarian. It should affect how you eat as a vegetarian.

The next few chapters will go into just what carbohydrates, proteins, vitamins, and the other nutrients are, why we need them, how much we need of each one, and how well vegetarian

77

foods supply them. You will learn that all whole foods supply a combination of nutrients. No food is pure protein, and only a highly refined food such as white sugar is pure carbohydrate. Meat is a high-protein food, but most meat is also high in fat. Dried beans are high in both protein and carbohydrate. Bread, rice, and spaghetti are high in carbohydrate, but they also contain protein that is important for vegetarians.

As you read about which foods supply which nutrients, you will understand why no one should give up meat, fish, eggs, and milk all at once. Such a move would be especially unwise for anyone under about age twenty-one. Like it or not, teen-age bodies are growing and changing so fast that they need more of most nutrients than do either adults or children. Among these nutrients are protein, vitamin D, iron, and zinc, all plentiful in foods from animals. Humans of all ages need vitamin B_{12}, which is found almost exclusively in foods from animals. If you are willing to take supplements and spend more time studying food and cooking, you can manage to get all the nutrients you need without eating animal products. But teen-agers who are not used to planning and preparing their meals will have enough to do adjusting to a meatless diet. Those who continue to eat eggs and dairy products will be covered while they learn to cook with different vegetarian foods.

When considering how much of each nutrient we need, we will often refer to the Recommended Daily Allowances, or RDAs. These standards have been established for each nutrient by a group of experts we will call the RDA committee. Its full title is the Committee on Dietary Allowances of the Food and Nutrition Board, a division of the National Research Council of the National Academy of Sciences. The RDAs are established by estimating the amount of iron, vitamin D, or other nutrient needed by the average person of a certain age and sex. These figures are then increased to protect people who need more than average amounts. Most people don't need the full amount, but you might be one who does.

The RDAs are used as guidelines by nutritionists and dietitians planning meals and diets for large groups of people. They are recognized as authoritative standards by vegetarian and nonvegetarian nutritionists, and any who disagree with particular recommendations feel called upon to justify their departures. In cases where qualified nutritionists question specific RDAs, the arguments on each side will be presented.

The RDAs are only mentioned here to give you an idea of how well a vegetarian diet can meet each requirement. Individuals planning their daily meals should not make a fetish of RDAs. The committee makes clear that no one diet has to meet every requirement every day. Let's face it; we all know people who live on processed junk food, with long stretches between one green vegetable and the next. But in the long run, people who eat properly are likely to feel more energetic, look more alive, resist colds and illness better, and enjoy their food more than people who live on junk food, with or without meat.

If this review of three foodstuffs, a dozen vitamins, and twenty essential minerals makes vegetarian eating seem too complicated, remember that meat eaters also need all these nutrients. A few minerals may be harder to get without meat or fish, but vegetarians who eat sensibly can come out ahead.

CHAPTER
11

Carbohydrates

We usually think of fuel as the oil and gas we burn to drive our cars, heat our homes, and keep our refrigerators and other appliances going. But our bodies also need energy in order to move around, to keep warm, and to keep our hearts, brains, and other organs working. Carbohydrates are the major fuel we burn to get that energy. Inside our cells, carbohydrate combines with oxygen, not in a burst of flame as wood or oil does in a furnace, but much more slowly so that the energy is released over a period of time.

Vegetarian diets tend to be high in carbohydrates for the simple reason that carbohydrates are made by plants, not animals. Only green plants are able to make food from the carbon dioxide (CO_2) in the air and the water (H_2O) in the soil. In the process of photosynthesis, plants use the sun's energy to change these compounds into the carbon-oxygen-hydrogen compounds we call carbohydrates. Animals have to get the energy they need by eating the carbohydrate stored in plants. Animals, including humans, can store some carbohydrate in their livers for a short-term supply of energy. But beyond that, when animals eat plants, the carbohydrate they don't use right away is changed into fat and stored in that form. When people eat animals, they are getting their energy indirectly from plants, but not in the form of carbohydrates. Milk is the only animal food that gives us any noticeable amount of carbohydrate. About 5 percent of cows' milk is made up of a carbohydrate called lactose.

When we don't get enough carbohydrate, our bodies can change fat and protein into energy. But these processes can burden the kidneys with extra waste products to get rid of, leaving us feeling more tired than before. Besides, as we'll see, the body has other uses for proteins. Only protein contains the building material we need to grow and to replace worn-out tissue. When protein is burned for energy, it can't be used for the other work that only protein can do.

As for fat, people who rely on fat for energy end up eating more fat than is good for them. We have already talked about the serious diseases that have been linked with Americans' high-fat diet. Because of these connections, doctors are advising us to eat more carbohydrate and less fat.

Most people in the world have always relied on carbohydrates for most of their energy. Until recently, this was true of Americans, too. But now, only about 45 percent of our calories come from carbohydrates. The number-one U.S. Dietary Goal

is to increase that proportion to 58 percent. To accomplish this, the Senate committee suggests that we eat more fruit, more potatoes and other vegetables, and more grain foods such as bread and rice. In countries with a low incidence of heart disease, the people get up to 85 percent of their calories from carbohydrates. Most comes from grain foods or potatoes. In America, vegetarians are already in line with the experts' recommendations. Most vegetarians get about 60 percent of their calories from carbohydrates. Among vegetarians who don't eat eggs and milk, the percentage is higher.

SUGAR AND STARCH

If carbohydrates are nutritious foods, then what about so-called "junk food"? Popular diet books often link the two together, yet it's hard to believe that we should drink more Cokes and eat more potato chips and candy bars. In fact, no one (except maybe the Coke and potato-chip and candy-bar companies) would suggest that. But some carbohydrate snacks are nutritious. Pizza, for example, is a well-balanced combination of carbohydrate, fat, and protein, with carbohydrate predominating, as it should in a meal. And the main problems with potato chips are not the carbohydrates but the fat the chips are cooked in and the salt that is added. What nutritionists deplore is not carbohydrate itself, but the kind of carbohydrate foods that Americans have been eating. In Coke and candy bars, we find a completely nonnutritious carbohydrate—namely, sugar.

Seventy years ago, our grandparents got more than two-thirds of their carbohydrates from starchy foods such as bread, cereal, corn, and potatoes. Today, more than half of our carbohydrates come from sugar. The Dietary Goals call for doubling our consumption of starchy carbohydrates and cutting back on sugar.

One reason for switching back to more starch and less sugar is that foods high in starchy carbohydrates also contain other nutrients. Most of the people in the world have always obtained most of their protein from starchy foods. These foods also contain vitamins and minerals, some of which our bodies need in order to make use of the carbohydrates. The sugars that we get in foods like soft drinks, candy bars, and desserts are called "empty calories" because they furnish nothing but energy. People who eat sweets instead of other foods are missing out on other nutrients that their bodies need for growth and health.

Besides inflicting us with empty calories, sugar is a leading cause of tooth decay, which afflicts 98 percent of all American high-school students. In countries where sugar is not an every-day food, only 1 to 5 percent of the population have acquired cavities by their early twenties.

A third problem with sugar is its lack of staying power. Sugar is called a quick-energy food because it is made up of just one or two basic carbohydrate units. (White table sugar is a double sugar, called sucrose, which breaks down into molecules of two single sugars, glucose and fructose.) Sugar is so easily digested and passed into the bloodstream that you feel a lift right away. But the benefit doesn't last. Ordinarily the body tries to keep the amount of sugar in the blood at a fairly even level; but the chemicals that control this balance tend to overreact to a sudden flood of glucose. The result is a drop in blood sugar about two hours after the snack. You are left then with a letdown feeling and the urge to eat again.

Unlike sugar, starches give a longer-lasting benefit. Starches are complex carbohydrates, made up of very long chains of sugar molecules. Starches have to be broken down into simple sugars before being absorbed through the walls of the intestine. This slows down the whole process, and after starches are absorbed, they are distributed through the body at a more controlled rate.

It might turn out that sugar is to blame for even more serious problems. Some studies suggest that people who eat large amounts of sugar are more likely than others to suffer from heart attacks, high blood pressure, and diabetes. The makers of the Dietary Goals found "no clear links" between sugar and heart disease but cited "some evidence" connecting it with diabetes. In any case, the empty calories, dental cavities, and aftereffects of a sugar rush seem reason enough to cut down on sugar.

There is nothing wrong with eating a little sweet food now and then. Many scientists believe that we are born with a taste for sweets. This had survival value in the days before humans grew their own food, when people roamed about gathering whatever grew wild. Many poisonous plants have a bitter taste, and so a dislike for bitter flavors could be lifesaving. Many nutritious foods, especially fruits, are sweet, and so an inborn sweet tooth was an advantage. The harmful effects of sugar have only showed up recently, since people started eating large amounts of pure sucrose. In 1976, the average American ate about a cup of refined sugar a day. This was more than twice as much as our ancestors ate a hundred years earlier.

Soft drinks are a good (or a bad) example of the rising use of sugar. Today 25 percent of the sugar we eat comes in soda pop. In 1930, the average American drank about 50 eight-ounce servings of soft drinks a year. In 1960, sales were up to 200 servings per person. By 1981, it was 618. That's about a can and a half a day. But that's just an average. In reality, some people drink none at all, and the average teen-ager drinks far more. Teen-agers are also the best customers for sweets in general. Some get more than half their calories from sugar.

Manufacturers take advantage of the preference for sweets by adding sugar to foods that are not naturally sweet. Yogurt, an ancient staple in the Middle East, did not become popular here until yogurt makers started adding syrupy fruit preserves to the packages. Sales of dry breakfast cereals picked up about a generation ago, when someone in the cereal business thought of spraying the flakes with sugar. Now some commercial cereals have more sugar than any other ingredient. A few are more than half sugar.

When you start reading the labels on food packages, you will notice that large amounts of sugar are added to commercial spaghetti sauce, ketchup, fruit drinks, and even bread. "Health food" breads simply substitute brown sugar, honey, or molasses for the white sugar. These sweeteners may taste better, but they are still essentially sugar. Like commercial white sugar, molasses is a product of the cane-sugar plant. Blackstrap molasses has the most white sugar separated out and usually contains iron and other nutritious minerals along with the sucrose. Brown sugar is simply white sugar with a little molasses or caramel coloring mixed in, and honey is just another double sugar made up of glucose and fructose. The best thing to be said about honey is that you might use less, because it tastes sweeter than sugar. Molasses, too, has a stronger taste, so you would tend to use less.

Some food labels list corn syrup or dextrose instead of sugar. These terms only deceive consumers who don't realize that

84

these ingredients are also simple sugars, without any nutritional value. Dextrose is just a commercial name for the glucose that is extracted from cornstarch.

People who fear that sugar might make them fat often switch to "diet" soft drinks, which contain saccharin or other artificial sweeteners. However, medical authorities have warned that these substitutes do not help people lose weight. In laboratory studies with fat rats, the animals fed saccharin ended up fatter than those who did not get saccharin. Like sugar, saccharin lowers blood sugar and makes the animals more hungry later on, so they eat more than ever. Other laboratory tests here and in Canada found that rats fed large amounts of saccharin develop bladder cancer. Because of these findings, the U.S. Food and Drug Administration proposed a ban on saccharin in 1977. But the diet-food industry launched a huge advertising and lobbying campaign to discredit the FDA's evidence, and Congress decided to settle for a warning label. One congressman contributed some laughs, if not much light, by suggesting that the label read, "Warning: the Canadians have determined that saccharin is dangerous to your rat's health."

Since 1977, other agencies have come out in support of the FDA proposal. A National Cancer Institute study found that heavy users of artificial sweeteners have a 60-percent higher risk of bladder cancer than do nonusers. In 1980, a National Academy of Sciences report agreed that saccharin slightly increases the risk of bladder cancer, partly by increasing the risk from other cancer-causing substances in our diets. As cancer usually develops over a period of many years, cancer specialists fear a rise in bladder cancer if the teen-agers who use diet drinks today continue to do so through life.

If sugar substitutes are just as bad as sugar, how do you feed that inborn sweet tooth? Maybe a better question would be, how do you retrain it? The fact that people seem to be born with a taste for sweet foods does not mean that it is "natural" to want everything to taste like sugar. If we have come to that state, it is because we are getting sugar in most of our foods without even being aware of it.

John and Karen Hess, who wrote about the corruption of our food tastes in *The Taste of America,* believe that Americans eat so much sugar because they are starved for flavor. With so much of our food coming out of laboratories and packages, we forget what real fresh food tastes like. The Hesses say their own children grew up with good-tasting, old-fashioned foods and never craved sweets. This is true in other families, including my own, where soft drinks and junk foods are not forbidden but simply aren't kept around. By the time my son Eric was in junior high school, he was making his own granola because the granola sold in stores (including health-food stores) was too sweet. My daughter Deirdre will drink grapefruit juice for breakfast, but she says orange juice is too sweet. (This is a personal taste the rest of us don't share.) Deirdre orders cheesecake now and then in her favorite vegetarian restaurant, but ordinarily when we go out to dinner, no one wants dessert. I know a few other people who grew up drinking fruit juice and milk instead of soft drinks. None of them can imagine why anyone would voluntarily drink a Coke or Pepsi. One teen-age apple-juice freak complained that Coke tastes like something you would put in your car, not your stomach.

If you are already addicted to sugar, it is harder to kick the habit; but not as hard as you might think. The first rule is not to have sweets around. Stock up on fruit, nuts, seeds, peanut butter, and other nutritious snack food that you like. Drink fruit juice instead of soft drinks. If you like yogurt, buy it plain and try it with fresh fruit instead of fruit preserves. Or add your own honey, but cut down gradually on the amount. (There is no need to cut it out completely.)

Because sugar does give you a temporary pickup, be sure you get the good food you need so you don't need the sugar fix. Sugar is no worse for vegetarians than it is for meat eaters, but it can fill you up so you don't eat enough of the starchy foods you need. When you learn to do without sugar, you can better appreciate good vegetarian food. If all this virtuous eating sounds unbearably dull, you can always go fry up a batch of hot chiles.

FIBER

In addition to sugar and starch, a third type of carbohydrate plays a role in our diets. This is the indigestible fiber (sometimes called roughage) found in whole grains, fruits, and some vegetables. Because humans can't digest this material, it was once thought to be unimportant. Americans came to eat less and less of it as they cut down on starchy carbohydrates. Now, when Americans do eat wheat and rice and other grains, it is usually in the white, refined form. These grains have had the fiber stripped off, along with most of the vitamins and minerals. But as fiber consumption went down, diet-related diseases went up. Now many medical authorities believe that fiber helps protect against bowel cancer. According to the theory advanced by Dr. Denis Burkitt, fiber adds bulk to the diet, which keeps the waste material moving through the intestines and gives cancer-causing agents less of a foothold. In countries where people eat more fiber, bowel cancer is rare.

Some doctors question whether fiber itself is the important factor. They point out that diets high in fiber tend also to be low in fat. It well may be the fat that makes the difference. Either way, vegetarians are better off than meat eaters, because their diets tend to be higher in fiber and lower in fat. One study found that lacto-ovo-vegetarians eat twice as much fiber as meat eaters, and vegans eat almost twice as much as lacto-ovo-vegetarians.

CHAPTER
12

Fat

Whatever the ill effects of too much fat, we do need a certain amount. Fat foods contain needed vitamins, and the fat helps to carry these vitamins through our bodies. Fats are made up mostly of chemical compounds called fatty acids, and at least one of these, linoleic acid, is an essential nutrient in itself. But we can get the linoleic acid we need when only 2 percent of our calories come from fat. In 1974, most Americans got over 40 percent of their calories from fat, and the Dietary Goals call for reducing this to 30 percent. In nonmeat-eating countries of Asia, people get about 10 percent of their calories from fat.

When the Senate's Dietary Goals told people to cut down on "saturated" fat and eat proportionately more "polyunsaturated" fat, they were effectively advising us to eat less animal fat and get more of our fat from vegetable oil. Though the meat and dairy industries protested, margarine makers responded with commercials of shoppers and diners announcing gleefully, "It's polyunsaturated!" Not everyone knew what the word actually meant, but people got the message that polyunsaturated spread was the kind to buy.

You don't have to know what "saturated" means chemically to decide what kind to buy, but the word makes more sense if you do. Whether a fat is called "saturated" or "unsaturated" depends on whether it is filled up, or "saturated," with hydrogen. Like carbohydrates, fats are made up of carbon, hydrogen, and oxygen, but in different proportions. Most fatty acids contain even-numbered chains of carbon atoms, attached to a unit called an acid. (The oxygen is in the acid part, which isn't pictured here.) When in the chain, each carbon atom has room for two more attachments. When all of the attachments are filled with hydrogen atoms, the chain is "saturated" with hydrogen. This is called a saturated fatty acid.

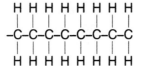 Saturated fatty acid

In unsaturated fats, two or more hydrogen atoms are missing. Without them, the unattached carbon atoms attach to each other in what is called a double bond. If only one pair of hydrogen atoms is missing, the fat is called monounsaturated.

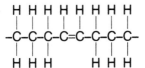 Monounsaturated fatty acid

If there is more than one double bond, the fat is polyunsaturated.

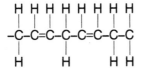 Polyunsaturated fatty acid

In Chapter 4 we talked about the problem of cholesterol building up inside the blood vessels. We saw that eating saturated fats, as well as cholesterol itself, can result in higher cholesterol buildup. On the other hand, eating polyunsaturated fats helps to lower the cholesterol levels. Monounsaturated fats have no effect on cholesterol levels.

Actually, no food fat is entirely saturated or unsaturated. All are made up of different fatty acids, some saturated and some unsaturated. But in general, animal products have more saturated fats, and vegetable oils have more unsaturated fats. The exceptions are coconut and palm oils, which are very high in saturated fats. Chicken and fish have a healthier balance of all three kinds of fats, which is why the Dietary Goals recommend eating less red meat and more poultry and fish. Beef is high in saturated fat and very low in polyunsaturated fat. The fat portion of cows' milk is also high in saturated fat. Lacto-vegetarians can control this by drinking skimmed or low-fat milk.

Only vegetable oils are very high in unsaturated fats. Olive oil and peanut oil are high in monounsaturated fat. Most other vegetable oils are higher in polyunsaturated fat. These include corn oil, a good all-purpose cooking oil. Safflower oil, a health-food favorite, is even higher in polyunsaturated fats and lower in saturated. As for that polyunsaturated margarine, it is and it isn't. If you read the label, you will probably find that the margarine has been "partially hydrogenated." This means that hydrogen atoms have been added to turn some of the unsaturated fat into saturated fat. Saturated fat is solid at room temperature, but unsaturated fat is liquid. Adding hydrogen to vegetable oil makes it spreadable like butter, which is highly saturated. As a rule, the softer margarines are less saturated than the firmer ones. If the label lists liquid fat as the first ingredient, then you know that most of the fat is still unsaturated.

Just how low our saturated-fat intake should be is still being debated. While most authorities consider moderate amounts acceptable, some vegetarians maintain that less is better and none is best. But it is agreed that saturated fat is not an essential nutrient. A small amount of fat is essential, but we can get all we need from vegetable oil, or from the fat content of whole grains, seeds, and nuts. There is no Recommended Daily Allowance for fat, because Americans are in no danger of getting too little. The only people known to suffer from fat deficiency have been hospitalized patients who can't eat at all and must be fed intravenously.

Currently, fat accounts for about 40 percent of the average meat eater's calories, but only about 33 percent of the average lacto-ovo-vegetarian's calories. Vegetarians who change from whole to skimmed or low-fat milk products can bring their fat intake well below the 30 percent recommended in the Dietary Goals. Total vegetarians get even less fat, and virtually no saturated fat.

CHAPTER
13

Protein

From the recommendations we've seen so far, vegetarians seem to be doing better than meat eaters. Medical authorities are advising us to eat more carbohydrate, which we can only get from plants. They are also saying we should cut down on fat, especially animal fat. Now nutritionists are telling us that Americans eat more than twice as much protein as we need. Many Americans seem to plan their diets on the assumption that if protein is good, then more protein is better. Nutritionists know, however, that the extra protein we eat is just wasted. This is how it works:

All protein contains nitrogen, in addition to the carbon, oxygen, and hydrogen present in carbohydrates and fats. (Much protein also contains sulphur, but that's not involved here.) Plants make protein using nitrogen compounds they absorb from the soil, and animals get the nitrogen they need by eating plant protein. But when we eat more protein than we need, whether we get it from plants or from animals, the nitrogen is separated off and washed out of the body in urine. If our diets are short in carbohydrate, the remaining elements will be changed to glucose and burned for energy. If the body already has enough fuel, the glucose will be changed to body fat. In other words, the extra protein will wind up like any other extra calories.

Instead of "the more the better," then, today's nutritionists are telling us that "enough is enough."

One problem with the large amount of protein that Americans eat is that it usually comes in the form of meat. Meat usually contains a good deal of fat, so that along with the protein meat eaters usually get more fat than is good for them. And, of course, meat is an expensive way of getting either calories or protein.

HOW MUCH IS ENOUGH?

This doesn't mean that protein is not important. Protein is an important part of every living cell. Except for their water content, our bodies are half protein. Half of that is in our muscles, one-fifth in our bones, and one-tenth in our skin. The hemoglobin in our red blood cells is protein. The enzymes that digest and help us make use of food are proteins. The antibodies we need to fight infections are proteins.

Growing bodies need protein to build up new tissue in the muscles, bones, blood cells, and throughout the body. Even after we stop growing, we need protein to repair and replace the old tissue that is constantly being used up and worn out. And the body cannot make protein from fat or carbohydrate. We have to eat protein-containing food.

To give us enough of this necessary building material, the RDA committee recommends 56 grams of protein a day for males fifteen and over. A larger man might need more, a smaller man less. For boys between eleven and fourteen, the RDA is 45 grams, and for females between eleven and eighteen it is 46 grams. Grown women need only 44 grams.

Now let's see how well a vegetarian diet can supply those 44 to 56 grams. To make it difficult, we will start with what most people would consider a low-protein meal, the spaghetti recipe given on page 228. Here is the list of ingredients, along with the protein content of each:

1 lb. spaghetti .... 56 grams protein
2 eggs ....12 grams
½ cup grated Parmesan cheese ....20 grams
½ cup olive oil.. —

2 cloves garlic.. —
black pepper .... —
$$\overline{\text{88 grams protein}}$$

With the spaghetti, the recipe suggests having a tossed salad with a cup of chick peas added. The chick peas add another 24 grams of protein, and even the salad greens will have about 4 grams of protein. This brings the total to 116 grams. If the recipe is divided among six people, each one will get 19 grams of protein. Give each person a glass of milk (9 grams protein) and he or she has now consumed 28 grams of protein in one meal. That is more than 60 percent of the 44 to 46 grams recommended for the whole day. A larger person who needs 56 grams of protein a day will probably eat at least a quarter pound of spaghetti, so we should allow one-fourth of the entire recipe for him. (Actually, our family splits this meal four ways, and two of us are in the 120-pound category.) Instead of 19 grams, then, this person will get 29; and a glass of milk brings that up to 38 grams.

For breakfast, let's say the same people each have a ³/₄-cup serving of oatmeal (4.5 grams of protein), with ¹/₄ cup of milk (2.25 grams) poured over. Add two slices of whole-wheat toast (4.8 grams), and the breakfast protein comes to a little more than 11.5 grams. With a glass of milk (9 grams) and an 8-ounce glass of orange juice (1.7 grams), it's a little more than 22 grams. (The breakfast might also contain some sugar or honey on the oatmeal and some butter on the toast, but there is no protein in sugar and no protein worth counting in butter.) For lunch, a peanut-butter sandwich (12 grams) and a glass of milk (9) give you 21 grams of protein.

This makes a day's total of 71 grams of protein for the person who needs 44 to 46, and 81 for the larger person who needs 56. Most likely, both of them will snack during the day, maybe on a cup of yogurt (8 to 12 grams) or 3¹/₂ ounces of seeds and nuts (about 20 grams), or both. You can see that getting enough protein is not hard, as long as you eat real food instead of filling up on sweets.

Without milk or eggs you can still get enough protein by eating dried beans. Instead of the spaghetti recipe, a total vegetarian might have the Cuban beans and rice recipe on page 216. A cup of the cooked black beans from that meal would give the vegan 22 grams of protein, and a cup of the brown rice would add 4 grams. Without milk, the vegan would still be getting 49 grams of protein for breakfast, lunch, and dinner. The snack would add 20 more. That brings the day's total to 69 grams.

COMPLETE AND INCOMPLETE

If it's that easy, why are vegetarians so often warned about protein? As you might know, it is not just the amount, or quantity, of protein that matters, but also the quality. Meat is often described as a "high quality" or "complete" protein, and plant protein as "incomplete" or "low quality." These terms refer to the fact that meat and plant protein contain different combinations of amino acids.

All protein is made up of amino acids, which are the real building blocks of life. When we digest proteins, we break them down into separate amino acids. Later our bodies take up these amino acids, and recombine them to make new proteins. About twenty amino acids are involved in this body-building job, but our bodies can make most of these out of whatever protein is available. They do this by breaking down other amino acids and recombining their parts. But nine of the twenty amino acids are essential in our diets, because we cannot make them ourselves. And if any of them are missing, we are not able to make use of the ones that are available. In this sense, an incomplete protein is just as bad as no protein at all.

Meat is called a "complete" protein because animals' bodies contain the amino acids in patterns that are very close to the combinations humans need. In almost all plants, there is a shortage of one or more essential amino acid. To say that animal protein is "complete" and plant protein "incomplete" is an exaggeration. Still, the protein food we get from animals gives us all the amino acids we need in proportions that allow us to use them efficiently. This is true whether we are getting the protein from meat or fish or eggs or milk. In fact, the protein in eggs and milk is more "complete" than the protein in meat and fish.

In plants, some foods are better sources of protein than others. Grains are quite high in protein, but not as high as meat. And the protein in grains is of a lower quality. All grains contain all nine essential amino acids, but they contain less of the amino acid lysine than animals do. Lysine is called the "limiting" amino acid for grain, because the shortage of lysine limits how much use we can make of the other amino acids. Rice has more lysine than most other grains do, so that an adult who ate nothing but brown rice could get enough protein if he or she ate lots of rice. But the same person would need far less meat (or eggs or milk) to get the same protein value. And growing children or teen-agers need more protein per calorie than adults do, so they could not get enough from rice alone. Nuts and seeds have a higher concentration of protein than grains do, but they too are low in lysine. Also, nuts are high in fat; and it would be hard to get enough protein from nuts and seeds without getting too many calories.

We have mentioned that dried beans are good protein foods. These members of the pea family are often called legumes, because of the family's botanical name, Leguminosae. In England, they are sometimes called pulses. In India, they are dals. Some of the legumes sold in American supermarkets are kidney beans, navy beans, lima beans, chick peas, and lentils. (The fresh or fresh-frozen green beans we eat as vegetables belong to the same family, but they are not as high in protein.)

Legumes are especially high in protein because of a particular group of bacteria, the *Rhizobia*, that live in small nodules on the roots of the legume plants. These "nitrogen-fixing" bacteria can combine nitrogen with hydrogen to form ammonia, which the legumes then use to make amino acids. (As you can guess from the name, the ammonia makes up the "amino" part of the amino acid. The acid part is made from the carbon-hydrogen-oxygen compounds originally produced by photosynthesis.)

Because of the help they get from the *Rhizobia,* dry beans contain far more protein per ounce than grains do. In fact, some beans have a higher protein content than you will find in some meat. But bean protein is of lower quality than meat protein, because beans are low in the amino acid methionine. Now at last comes the interesting point for vegetarians: It turns out that beans have more than the needed amount of lysine, the limiting amino acid in grains. And grains are low in lysine but high in methionine. Like Jack Sprat and his wife, the amino acid patterns in beans and grains complement each other. Eating them together gives you more usable protein than eating both of them separately. Put together, the amino acid pattern of beans and grains is of just as high a quality as the pattern in meat.

This happy chemical match has inspired some of the world's most satisfying meals. In India, spicy dals made of chick peas or lentils or mung beans are traditionally eaten with rice or bread. The Mexicans mix kidney or pinto beans with corn tortillas or rice. Italians combine white beans and macaroni in their classic dish called *pasta e fagioli.* The people who developed these combinations hundreds and thousands of years ago had never heard of amino acids. But they knew that grains and beans tasted better together, and they knew that people who ate both were better fed than those who had to live on one or the other.

In 1971, Frances Moore Lappé's book, *Diet for a Small Planet,* brought this common knowledge to Americans who

96

had forgotten how to eat without meat. From Lappé, young people concerned about the use of world resources learned that they could safely eat "low on the food chain" by combining complementary protein. From Lappé, America's new vegetarians learned the first rule of complementarity: *Combine grains with legumes.*

Not all legumes have exactly the same amino acid patterns, nor do all grains. Soybeans are often classified as a complete-protein food because their amino acid patterns are very close to those found in meat. Soybean protein is of a lower quality than the protein in milk and eggs, but higher than that of any other plant.

Peanuts, usually classified as legumes, are slightly short in methionine and tryptophan, and lower still in lysine. Because of the shortage of lysine a peanut-butter sandwich is not as high quality a meal as other grain-legume combinations. But milk is very high in lysine, so a glass of milk with the peanut-butter sandwich gives you a high-quality meal.

This brings us to Lappé's second point: *A small amount of complete protein food can raise the quality of any protein.* According to Lappé, mixing a little meat or fish in with your beans or rice makes all the protein as usable as the meat protein. Milk, cheese, and eggs will do the same. Because all animal proteins are especially high in lysine, this principle works especially well with grains.

In a world where meat has been a luxury for most people, this is the way animal foods have traditionally been used. Italians have made an art of cheese and pasta combinations. Mexicans often add a little cheese to their bean-tortilla combinations. The Japanese eat large amounts of rice, sometimes with soybean curd and sometimes with small amounts of fish. Both boost the protein quality of the rice. Europeans cook small amounts of meat in vegetable stews, and fill up on wheat or rye bread.

Now, if you go back and look at that sample day's menu, you'll find that all the meals contain complete protein. The milk for breakfast balances the oatmeal and toast. The milk, bread, and peanut butter for lunch make a complementary triangle. At dinner, the chick peas complement the spaghetti; and the milk, cheese, and eggs add substantially to the complete protein count. The beans and rice in the vegan meal complete each other. But it will take a soy product or other legume to balance the vegan's breakfast oatmeal and boost the value of the sandwich at lunch.

Like most new ideas, Lappé's explanation of protein complementarity seemed very complicated to a lot of people. Her book contained about fifty charts and tables, most of them comparing the protein value of various foods and showing how the different amino-acid patterns fit together. But vegetarians don't have to worry about whether chick peas or lentils go better with rice. Perhaps not every individual grain-bean combination will have a protein quality equal to milk and eggs; but neither does meat. As long as people have had enough to eat and were not limited to just one food, the human race has got along for thousands of years without adding up the amino acids in their meals.

According to Lappé, the complementary proteins had to be eaten together at the same meal. Shortly after *Diet for a Small Planet* was published, one researcher reported that amino acids remain in the intestines for several hours after they are eaten. This would mean that protein eaten earlier in the day could combine with other protein eaten later. However, other protein authorities warned that the complementary protein still had to be eaten within a period of three or four hours.

Some nutritionists now feel that Lappé made too much of matching protein in any case. They point out that only a small proportion of protein intake has to be in the form of complete protein. According to Dr. Mark Hegsted, the Harvard nutritionist who helped formulate the U.S. Dietary Goals, "the quality of diet protein is of little or no significance unless the diet protein is of very poor quality comparable to that of white flour." Dr. Hegsted said, though, that protein quality should still be considered important during the growing years.

In the 1982 edition of *Diet for a Small Planet,* Lappé agrees that she was probably unduly concerned about complementing protein. She now recognizes that "even without meat, the average person who eats a varied diet of whole foods and only modest amounts of sugar and fat is getting his or her recommended protein allowance."

It is interesting that the current debate is not whether we need animal protein but whether we need complete protein at all. Today, all nutrition and medical authorities acknowledge that beans and grains or cheese and grains can make a complete-protein meal. Whether we can get by on lower protein values is of interest to nutritionists involved in establishing requirements and feeding the hungry. But few Americans are so poor that they can't afford a cup of beans with their rice or a sprinkling of cheese on their spaghetti. As long as essential amino acids are considered important for growth and health, it is sensible to eat foods or combinations of foods that contain enough of all of them. And as long as we eat for pleasure as well as for health, we will surely want to mix different protein foods in ways that centuries of good cooks have found to be most satisfying.

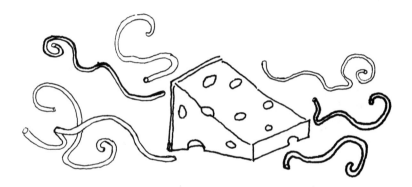

CHAPTER

14

Vitamins

If you think of food as the fuel that keeps your body going and the building material it uses for growth, then vitamins are not food at all. But they are essential nutrients, because without their help you would not be able to make use of the food you do take in. Like proteins, fats, and carbohydrates, vitamins are organic compounds, which are usually defined as containing carbon atoms in their molecules and occurring in living organisms. And like proteins, fats, and carbohydrates, but in far smaller amounts, vitamins are present in different combinations in the various foods we eat.

Once ingested, most vitamins link up with particular enzymes, which are protein substances produced within the body itself. From then on the vitamins and enzymes work together to make sure that the digested proteins, fats, and carbohydrates get absorbed through the intestinal walls, transported to the cells, and later broken down into "burnable" fuel or recombined to build new tissue.

All these processes involve a highly complicated series of chemical reactions, and yet the vitamins that are called for at innumerable stages along the way are needed in only very small amounts. For example, to maintain your particular weight and activity level you might require an ounce and a half of pure protein a day and over half a pound of carbohydrate, but no more than two milligrams of vitamin B_6. (Two milligrams (mg) means two thousandths of a gram, or just seventy millionths of an ounce.) Of vitamin B_{12}, you need only three micrograms (mcg). This is only three-millionths of a gram, or one ten-millionth of an ounce. Just the same, doctors warn that a diet lacking in these small amounts can lead to serious deficiency diseases or even death.

Fortunately for vegetarians, most of these necessary substances are present in the plants we eat, and what we don't get from plants can be found in milk and eggs. But without any animal products, total vegetarians could be missing one crucial vitamin, B_{12}, and they might have trouble getting enough riboflavin (B_2) and vitamin D. This chapter will look at all the vitamins and consider how well vegetarian diets supply them.

COBALAMIN—VITAMIN B_{12}

B_{12} always heads the list of vitamins that total vegetarians are warned about. The reason is that cobalamin is not naturally present in plants and we cannot get along indefinitely without it. A lack of B_{12} will eventually cause serious problems in the digestive and nervous systems, and in the bone marrow where red blood cells are formed. Without B_{12} these blood cells do not divide normally but simply grow bigger. The result is a disease called pernicious anemia, which used to be fatal until doctors discovered that a substance found in animal liver could clear up the symptoms—if it is given in time.

Not all pernicious anemia comes from a lack of B_{12} in the diet. In fact, vegans often point out that most people who get the disease are meat eaters. It seems that these patients, mostly older people, are unable to absorb cobalamin through their intestinal walls. However, the substance must be there in the first place in order to be absorbed, and it must come from outside the body—whether in food, pills, or (for those whose digestive systems can't absorb it) by injection.

Another old vegan argument has it that B_{12} is manufactured by microorganisms in our own intestines and so is not needed in the diet. Nutritionists answer that this is only partly true. Cobalamin is made by bacteria in the soil, and in animals' intestines. However, with humans the catch is that the bacteria do their work in the large intestine but absorption takes place in the small intestine. Nutritionists believe that whatever amount is made this way occurs too far along the intestinal tract to do us much good. About all we wind up with is a lot of B_{12}-rich material to flush down the toilet.

What about strict vegetarians in India who go all their lives without meat or milk? First of all, most Indian vegetarians do drink milk or eat yogurt. Those who don't, according to B_{12} authority Dr. Victor Herbert, are probably saved by farming methods that are more organic and food-storing practices that are less hygienic than ours. Their grains and vegetables are likely to be contaminated with insects and with small residues of the manure they use as fertilizer. The manure is so rich in vitamin B_{12} that unnoticeable traces of it supply enough.

You might know some total vegetarians here who appear to be perfectly healthy after two or three years without any B_{12} whatever. As cobalamin can be stored in the liver, deficiency usually takes a few years to show up. Sometimes it takes much longer. For reasons that are not understood, some vegans seem to get by indefinitely. One young woman in California went for eight years without any animal products or supplements and seemed to be healthy. Then she had a baby and decided to breast-feed. Within a few months the baby was in critical condition in the hospital. The diagnosis was B_{12} deficiency, due to a lack of the vitamin in the mother's breast milk. For all we know, the mother might have continued to be healthy. Perhaps some vegetarians can make better use of intestinal B_{12} than our nutritionists believe. But B_{12} deficiency is so serious that it's not worth the risk to find out.

Total vegetarians who don't take B_{12} in any form might not suffer from the early symptoms of deficiency, but this is not an advantage in the long run. What happens is that folacin, another B vitamin, "masks" the B_{12} deficiency by easing the anemic symptoms. Folacin is especially plentiful in the usual vegetarian diet high in dried beans and leafy vegetables. The disease then progresses unnoticed, until the nervous system has been severely damaged. At first the victim might notice nothing more upsetting than tingling or numbness in the hands and feet. Then he or she might become depressed, or have trouble remembering or concentrating. Sooner or later the person starts hallucinating and generally freaking out. By then it might be too late to save his or her life.

Why, if B_{12} is that essential to health, have some vegans been so reluctant to take it? One reason might be that at one time all cobalamin obtainable in shot or pill form was extracted from animal liver. To many strict vegetarians, taking liver extract would violate their principles. The British playwright George Bernard Shaw, mentioned earlier as a prominent vegetarian, was faced with this dilemma when he developed pernicious anemia at the age of eighty-four. The word got out that Shaw was taking liver extract. Soon the founder of the short-lived American Vegetarian party, a man named Symon Gould, wrote Shaw an angry seventeen-page letter calling him a "phony vegetarian." But Shaw was not one to be cowed by criticism, and he simply wrote back a straightforward note to the effect that "you would take it, too, if your life depended on it."

Whether Mr. Gould would or would not have given in to save his life we will never know. The important thing is that today no one has to make the choice. In 1973, after a twenty-five-year effort, a way was found to synthesize cobalamin from inorganic chemicals. So now you can buy B_{12} tablets that are not made from liver or from any other animal material. (Finding the right dose will be harder, though. B_{12} is often marketed in megadoses more than one hundred times the required amount.)

More recently, in 1977, researchers at Cornell University found that cobalamin is produced by the bacteria involved in the fermentation of the soy products miso and tempeh, described in Chapter 17. According to Dr. Kieth Steinkraus, who directed the studies, a typical three-and-a-half-ounce serving of tempeh gives you about five micrograms of B_{12}, which is more than you need for a day's supply. Some natural-food stores now carry tempeh with B_{12} listed on the nutrient label.

It is also possible, for vegans who just don't like the idea of taking pills, to get the required amount from brewer's yeast that has been enriched with synthetic vitamin B_{12} or specially grown in a vitamin B_{12}-rich medium. Sometimes called nutritional yeast, this dietary supplement is not to everyone's taste. However, a favorite snack among college vegetarians is nutritional yeast sprinkled over popcorn—no butter, no salt, just nutritional yeast, and maybe a shake of garlic powder. It grows on you. Be aware, though, that not all brewer's yeast is enriched with B_{12}, even when it is sold in health-food stores. If it is, B_{12} will be listed on the label.

In health-food stores and some drugstores, you can also buy commercial "soy milk," the liquid squeezed from soybeans. Soy milk is often fortified with vitamin B_{12}, usually for babies who are allergic to cows' milk. However, as the label will show, the amounts of the vitamin per serving in the milk made for babies are small compared to adolescent and adult requirements. Some total vegetarians make and fortify their own soy milk, though like brewers' yeast soy milk doesn't taste especially good and does not in itself contain B_{12}.

If fish, eggs, milk, or cheese are part of your regular diet, there is no need to eat liver or take supplements in order to avoid pernicious anemia. As mentioned earlier, only tiny amounts of cobalamin are needed. The American RDA for adults and adolescents is only three micrograms a day, and the United Nations expert group that sets world standards recommends only two micrograms. Most Americans actually take in much more—an average of ten micrograms daily. Most of that comes from meat, poultry, and fish, but almost a third of the total comes from eggs and dairy foods. That amounts to just about the recommended three micrograms.

Lacto-ovo-vegetarians can get three micrograms from two glasses of milk and an egg, or simply three glasses of milk. That much milk is recommended in any case for teen-agers, meat-eating or not. The chart on pages 130-1 lists the amounts of B_{12} in different nonmeat foods.

RIBOFLAVIN—VITAMIN B_2

Another B vitamin that total vegetarians might be short of is riboflavin, which we need to make food available for growth and energy. No life-threatening disease has been traced to riboflavin deficiency. However, diets low in riboflavin can lead to cracked skin at the corners of the mouth, sore, swollen lips and tongue, and eyes that are painfully sensitive to light. The best sources of this nutrient are milk, organ meats (such as liver), and other animal products. Without them, vegans have to eat lots of leafy green vegetables and whole or enriched grains, which also contain some riboflavin. The chart on pages 130-1 shows how much it takes. Lacto-vegetarians have no trouble getting enough riboflavin from milk, supplemented by normal portions of greens and grains.

THIAMIN—VITAMIN B$_1$

Getting enough thiamin is no particular problem for a vegetarian. The average American gets about a quarter of his thiamin from meat; but that is only because the average American eats a lot of meat. Most of the world's people have always obtained their thiamin from carbohydrate foods such as rice and wheat. Because our bodies use thiamin to change carbohydrates into energy, this arrangement worked well—until the middle of the nineteenth century, when it became a common practice to "refine" or "polish" rice and other grains by stripping off the germs and outer layers. As we now know, it was the nutritious parts of the grains that were being thrown away. The result of the practice was that people who had been getting by on a mostly rice diet began to literally waste away from beriberi. This was the first of several diseases found to be caused by vitamin deficiency.

Now thiamin and a few of the other nutrients removed during refining are put back into rice, bread, flour, and breakfast cereal in a process known as enrichment. The only Americans who have to worry about thiamin deficiency today are those who rely too much on empty carbohydrates in the form of alcohol or sugar. (However, we'll see as we go along that many of the other nutrients taken out of whole grains are not included in the enrichment formula.)

NIACIN

Like beriberi, pellagra is a deficiency disease we now know only by its name. But a few generations ago it was common among poor people in our southern and southwestern states. Many of them had to live on almost nothing but cornmeal, which lacks the B vitamin niacin. Without it, they developed symptoms that doctors referred to as the three D's: diarrhea, dermatitis (rough, blotchy skin), and dementia (insanity). A fourth D, death, often followed, and those who didn't die filled up several mental institutions. Some asylums had to be specially built just to house pellagra victims, and house them is about all they did. The patients never recovered.

Today, refined corn and wheat products are enriched with niacin. Most Americans get about a quarter of their niacin supply from bread and cereal and almost half from meat. However, vegetarians can substitute dried beans to make up for the absence of meat. Peanuts and soybeans are especially high in niacin, and a four-ounce square of the soy cake, tofu, gives you fifteen milligrams. This just about takes care of the adolescent RDA of fourteen to fifteen milligrams for girls and eighteen milligrams for boys.

PYRIDOXINE—VITAMIN B$_6$

Meat also accounts for almost half of the average American's supply of pyridoxine, which we need in order to make use of protein. But again, you can do as well on a steady diet of dried beans, whole grains, fruit, and leafy vegetables. Enriched grains won't help, as pyridoxine is not one of the nutrients added to refined grains during the enrichment process.

OTHER B VITAMINS

Folacin, sometimes called folic acid, has already been mentioned as the substance that acts with B$_{12}$ to control the formation of red blood cells in the bone marrow. Folacin gets its name from the Latin word *folium,* meaning "leaf," because there is so much of it in spinach and other leafy vegetables. It is also found in whole grains, dried beans, and several other vegetables—all part of a reasonable vegetarian diet.

Pantothenic acid was named from the Greek word meaning "all," because it is present in all living cells. We could not get energy from foods without pantothenic acid, but because the substance is present in all food groups this is not a problem. Organ meats, eggs, and fish are excellent sources; but fortunately for vegetarians so are whole grains and dried beans. The only people who might possibly wind up with a pantothenic-acid deficiency are those who live almost totally on processed foods. This is because the vitamin is removed in the process of refining grains and is easily destroyed by canning and freezing.

Biotin also helps the body to convert all types of foods into energy sources. It, too, is present in almost all foods, and especially high in organ meats, egg yolks, and dried beans. Unless

106

you happen to eat an enormous amount of raw egg whites, which interfere with biotin absorption, deficiency is not a realistic worry.

Choline and inositol are sometimes classed among the B vitamins. However, no RDA has been set for them, no deficiency has ever been observed in humans, and as both can be synthesized by the body, it is not certain that they are needed in the diet at all. We do know that choline and inositol help the body to handle fats. In addition, choline is being studied as a possible weapon against mental illness and memory loss, especially in old people. (If your memory and mental functions are already normal, though, choline does not make them any sharper.) In any case, both choline and inositol are found in most foods.

THE Bs AS A GROUP

You might wonder why there are so many B vitamins when there is only one vitamin A, one vitamin C, and so on. The answer is simply that many of the Bs are found in the same foods and so it took a while for early investigators to realize that they were actually different substances. When the separate chemicals began to be isolated, each one was given a different number. Later still, chemical names were assigned to both newly discovered vitamins and those already known by numbers. They continued to be listed together as a "B complex," because they often tend to work together and to depend on each other's presence for proper functioning—but then this is true of other vitamins and minerals as well.

One property that the B vitamins do have in common is that they all dissolve in water. Because of this, they tend to leak out from vegetables into cooking water. One way to avoid this is to use a vegetable steamer. This will allow the food to cook without being immersed in water. Their water solubility also means that ordinarily, if you take in more B vitamins than you can use at the time, the excess will be washed out in your urine. You can't save it up, and for that reason you need constant new supplies. On the other hand, vitamins A, D, E, and K dissolve in fat and not in water. As a result, extra amounts can be stored in the body's fat cells and used later on when the diet doesn't supply them.

VITAMIN A

Of the four fat-soluble vitamins, vitamin A is found only in animal-origin food, especially liver, whole milk, butter, and egg yolk. But we can get along without preformed vitamin A, because our bodies can make it out of carotene. As the name suggests, carotene is the deep orange material found in carrots and in other orange vegetables such as squash and sweet potatoes. Orange fruits, such as peaches, apricots, and cantaloupe melons, are also good sources. So are dark-green leafy vegetables, the darker the better. Spinach and broccoli are high in carotene, and the darker outer leaves of lettuce have more than the lighter inner leaves. You don't see the carotene in green vegetables because the orange is covered up by the deeper chlorophyl color.

Vitamin A is important for growth and reproduction, and for healthy mucous membranes, especially in the eyes. In undeveloped countries, thousands of children go blind each year for lack of vitamin A. An early sign of the problem is poor night vision, a phrase which really refers to the ability of our eyes to adjust to darkness. We all have some trouble getting used to a dark movie theater, for example, but drivers who just can't see the road after passing another car's headlights might be suffering from a mild vitamin A deficiency.

Total vegetarians who eat green salad most days and orange vegetables often don't need to take vitamin-A pills. Nor will vitamin-A pills clear up pimples, as some skin doctors once hoped. In fact, as the body can store up vitamin A, large doses in pill form can build up and cause headaches, dry skin, kidney damage, and other health problems. You can't overdose on carotene, though. The only harm known to come from eating too many carrots is that huge amounts over a period of time can cause a person's skin to turn orange too.

CALCIFEROL—VITAMIN D

Vitamin D is the only substance classed as a vitamin that doesn't have to come from food. As long as we get enough sunlight, we can make our own. Vitamin D is especially important during the growing years because it helps the body make use of the minerals calcium and phosphorus to form strong, straight bones and healthy teeth.

Vitamin D deficiency was not a problem in preindustrial times when people spent more time out-of-doors and the skin color of different populations had evolved to suit the amount of sunlight they were exposed to. But then came factories, and with them indoor jobs, air pollution, the movement of dark-skinned people to smoggy northern cities—and the crippling bone disease known as rickets. A way had to be found to get vitamin D to growing children, and so most commercial milk is now fortified by exposing it to artificial ultraviolet light. As milk contains the calcium and phosphorus that call for this vitamin, it is the reasonable food to fortify. In fact, milk and butter already contain small amounts of vitamin D that the cows get from sunlight in summer, but these amounts are usually not enough. Without fortification, fish-liver oil is the only good food source, a fact once deplored by helpless children whose parents confronted them with spoonfuls of cod-liver oil. Thanks to the milk treatment, rickets is again rare and cod-liver oil has vanished from our medicine chests.

Only small children are crippled by rickets. Without the ability to assimilate calcium and phosphorus, their fast-growing bones become too soft to hold up their bodies. The leg bones actually bend under the weight. Even if the children get enough vitamin D and calcium later, their bones never straighten out. But even though you are too old for rickets, you need vitamin D throughout your teens in order to reach your full growth. A good supply of vitamin D and calcium now might also help prevent softening of the bones in later life. It is thought that our bones continue to add mass well into adulthood. At about age thirty-five they begin to deteriorate. If they haven't built up enough mineral density by then, the loss can result in aching, fragile bones years later.

Teen-age total vegetarians, who do not include milk in their diets, might ask their doctors about other kinds of fortification, especially during the winter. But it's not good to take vitamin-D pills on your own. Like A, D can be dangerous in excess. The possible effects include vomiting, diarrhea, and kidney damage.

VITAMIN E

Vitamin E has been called the reproduction vitamin because of findings that without it both male and female rats were unable to produce offspring. But the same results might occur if other nutrients were taken away, and in any case no one has ever found that extra amounts of vitamin E help people with fertility problems. In fact, vitamin E has also been called the vitamin in search of a disease, because deficiency in humans is practically nonexistent. We know that vitamin E helps us to make use of polyunsaturated fats, and that the more polyunsaturated fats you take in, the more vitamin E you need. But as polyunsaturated fats in the form of vegetable oils are also the chief sources of vitamin E, it is likely to be there when you need it. And as animal-derived foods are not good sources, vegetarians are not missing out on vitamin E.

VITAMIN K

Vitamin K gets its name from a Danish word for coagulation, or clotting, because it helps to form the blood-clotting protein that keeps us from hemorrhaging when we bleed. Vitamin K is synthesized by microorganisms in our small intestines. Supplies might be low in certain newborn infants and in some people who have been taking high doses of antibiotics. Otherwise deficiency is almost unheard-of. The very little you might need in your diet is easily supplied by leafy green vegetables.

ASCORBIC ACID—VITAMIN C

Vitamin C is the one water-soluble vitamin that is not included among the B vitamins. It is not of special concern to vegetarians, but it is interesting because of the controversies and uncertainties connected with it, from Columbus's time to the present.

Every history of nutrition tells about the large number of sailors who suffered and often died from a disease called scurvy, which occurred only when they were off at sea for months without fresh food. Without understanding why, the British navy discovered during the 1700s that they could prevent scurvy by including lemons in the sailors' rations. Today the "antiscurvy factor," as it was first called, is known by the

110

more scientific-sounding name "ascorbic acid." Most people just call it vitamin C. We know that it works by helping to form collagen, a component of healthy connective tissue. We have learned that vitamin C helps the body to absorb calcium and iron and to make use of several of the B vitamins. It is involved in healing wounds and fighting infections. But not everyone agrees on how much ascorbic acid we should get. Even the RDA committee has changed its mind. In 1974 the recommended amount was reduced from sixty to forty-five milligrams a day; in 1980 it went back up to sixty.

It takes only about ten milligrams of vitamin C a day to prevent scurvy, and that amount is sure to be present in anything like a normal diet. But our bodies use up more than that each day, and they can store up amounts greater than what they normally use. According to the committee, the sixty milligrams now recommended gives us a reserve supply of a month or more. Amounts greater than that are not as efficiently absorbed, so the committee concluded that they are not needed.

Still, there are people who believe that we need more. They point out that other higher animals take in many times as much vitamin C as we do. Adjusting for body weight, we would have to consume at least two grams a day, or about thirty-three times the RDA, to match what gorillas get from their plant diets. Exactly that amount was recommended by the Nobel Prize-winning chemist Linus Pauling in his book, *Vitamin C and the Common Cold.* Dr. Pauling's past achievements and the prestige of the Nobel Prize won his book a lot of serious attention. Since its publication in 1970, many people have been taking large doses of vitamin C in pill form in the hopes that it will help them ward off colds. However, studies done since Pauling's book was published don't seem to back up his claim for ascorbic acid as a cold preventive. Some researchers are afraid that long-term overdoses might have harmful consequences, such as an increased need for the substance once the pills are discontinued. Nevertheless, as the body during infection can use up more than normal amounts of ascorbic acid, the old home remedy of drinking lots of orange juice and hot lemonade when down with a cold still seems to make sense.

We usually associate vitamin C with orange juice, and citrus fruits are the most common source of ascorbic acid. But several other fruits, including strawberries, will do almost as well.

111

Tomatoes and potatoes are good sources of vitamin C. So are green peppers and cabbage if eaten raw, but ascorbic acid is a fragile vitamin and much is lost to heat when these vegetables are cooked. Mere exposure to air will destroy it in cabbage shredded for salad too far ahead of mealtime, or in orange juice that is allowed to stand in a uncovered container. And though fresh broccoli and spinach are good sources even when cooked, once they begin to wilt you can be sure that much of the vitamin C they started out with has already escaped. Nevertheless, it is easy to get your recommended sixty milligrams of vitamin C. One six-ounce glass of orange juice is all it takes. And vegetarians are at no disadvantage because ascorbic acid is practically nonexistent in meat and animal products.

ON RDAs, SUPPLEMENTS, AND OTHER NUMBERS GAMES

The confusion over vitamin C is a good illustration of the complications you run into when you try to be too exact about computing vitamin needs and intake. In the first place, the need for any one nutrient varies from person to person and from time to time. Smokers, for example, might use up more vitamin C than do nonsmokers. Women on the birth-control pill seem to need extra amounts of several B vitamins. Pregnant women need more of everything. B_6 needs go up with the amount of protein eaten. And people who are physically active use up more than average amounts of most nutrients. The official Recommended Daily Allowances are based simply on the amounts that the average person is thought to need to reach full growth and perform at his or her best. A safety margin is added to these figures to allow for people who need more than average amounts. The RDAs' purpose is to serve as guidelines for dietitians and others responsible for feeding large numbers of people. It was never intended that individuals go around counting and measuring the vitamin content of their meals.

Even if you wanted to, you could never be sure how much of any given nutrient is present in a particular food simply by consulting a table. For example, vegetables begin to lose their C and B vitamins as soon as they are picked. More is lost in freezing and canning and in cooking water when the vegetables are boiled. Fruits grown in the sun have more vitamin content

112

than those grown in the shade. Some varieties of apples and potatoes have more than others. And as we'll see, the amount of iodine, zinc, and other minerals present in any food depends on the amount in the soil where it grew.

The reaction to all this should not be anxiety, but confidence that, overall, a sensible and varied diet of fresh, whole foods will average out in your favor. After reading this chapter you will realize that there are many good reasons for eating leafy green vegetables. There is no need to remember that a half cup of raw spinach gives you about 50 percent of your daily vitamin A requirement. You should also realize that going for several days without *any* greens won't be disastrous; the body can easily make up for a short-term lack. Still, it's a good idea to get in the habit of eating sensibly every day so that you don't end up always intending to do it right tomorrow. It's surprising how many people do deceive themselves this way. In one government survey, women questioned about their families' eating habits almost all claimed to serve well-balanced meals. Yet when asked to recall the previous night's dinner, most reported meals or snacks that didn't come close to meeting the standards they thought they were following.

To some people, vitamin pills seem to be the answer to poor eating habits and uncertain food values. Yet almost all nutritionists agree that most people who buy vitamin supplements don't need them. They believe that anyone who makes a habit of a varied, balanced diet is wasting money on vitamin pills. This certainly holds for lacto-ovo-vegetarians as well as for meat eaters. In this sense, though, a vegan diet can't be considered balanced. It does require some supplementary form of vitamin B_{12} and possibly vitamin D and some minerals as well.

Of course, many nonvegan diets are poorly balanced. Survey after survey has found that many people in this country rely too much on sugar and processed foods and substitute junky snacks for balanced meals. Teen-agers' diets tend to be most unbalanced of all, and teen-age girls are worse off than boys. (Boys might not eat any more wisely, but as they are usually bigger and often more physically active, they simply eat more, period. This automatically gives them more nutrients along with the calories.) Nevertheless, the best way to remedy the situation is to eat properly, not to try to supplement a bad diet with pills.

From time to time one vitamin or another is promoted as a cure or preventive against cancer. In 1982 the National Academy of Sciences panel on diet and cancer seemed to give respectability to this position. In addition to advising against high-fat, low-fiber diets and nitrate-cured meat and fish, the panel advised eating foods high in beta-carotene and vitamin C. Beta-carotene is the vitamin-A precursor found in dark green and orange vegetables. However, the panel specified that these vitamins should be obtained through food, not pills. Taking large doses of a vitamin in pill form is usually wasted effort and sometimes dangerous. As Dr. Jean Mayer has remarked, "At five, ten, a hundred, or a thousand times the normal level, vitamins are drugs and should be treated accordingly." Such megadoses might be useful in treating diseases, but this is a job for specialists who can judge when they are needed and in what amounts.

It might seem more reasonable to take the vitamins that are sold together in multivitamin combinations. But even they might well be lacking in some necessary nutrient that is yet to be discovered. The missing ingredient might be so abundant in real food that no deficiency disease has turned up. Most multivitamins also leave out some elements we do know are needed in very small amounts. Some pills include minerals that we might already be getting in excess. They often throw in ridiculous amounts of certain B vitamins that are already abundant in food. This probably won't hurt you, but it just means that you will be pouring a lot of expensive stuff through your body and flushing it down the toilet.

If you still prefer to take vitamin pills just for insurance, at least choose a multivitamin that does not exceed the RDAs for the nutrients it does provide, and be aware of what is missing. Remember that junk food and pills cannot take the place of good meals—either nutritionally or as one of life's major pleasures. Remember, too, that the most common diet-related diseases in this country are dental cavities (from too much sugar), heart disease (associated with too much animal fat), obesity (too many calories), and iron-deficiency anemia. Anemia is the only one of the four that is caused by a lack in the diet.

As it happens, iron is one nutrient that might be short in an otherwise wholesome vegetarian diet. You might not be much worse off in this respect than meat eaters who don't eat liver, but nevertheless getting your share of iron from a meatless diet might take special attention. Zinc is another essential mineral that is harder to get without meat; and without milk, vegan teen-agers have to make a special effort to get the recommended amounts of calcium. It is not only that these three minerals are easier to find in meat or milk than in vegetables; they are also easier to absorb from meat and animal products than from the plants in which they do occur. As all three are of special importance during the years between eleven and eighteen, they will get special attention in the following chapter on minerals.

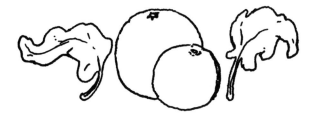

Minerals

ost people don't think of chromium, cobalt, or copper as being edible; but in fact these are only a few of more than twenty minerals that we need in our diet. So far, all the nutrients we've talked about have been organic substances, made up essentially of different combinations of just four elements: carbon, hydrogen, oxygen, and—in the case of proteins and some vitamins —nitrogen. When you include the nonorganic hydrogen-oxygen compound, water, 96 percent of our body weight consists of these same four elements. That remaining 4 percent is where the mineral elements come in.

Luckily, getting enough of most essential minerals is not a problem. Many specialists worry more about people taking too much. You don't need a prescription to buy iron, zinc, selenium, or copper in pill form; but most doctors and nutritionists disapprove of such self-medication. They warn that taking just a little too much of any one mineral, even when it is not toxic in itself, can interfere with the body's use of other essential nutrients.

Still, some minerals might be short in an average diet, vegetarian or otherwise. Surveys have found that large numbers of Americans don't get the recommended amounts of iron. Recently, evidence has turned up that zinc might also be scarce, especially in meatless diets. And total vegetarians who are still growing might have trouble getting enough calcium. The purpose of this chapter is to inform you about mineral needs, especially those you might not be meeting. It will not equip you to decide whether you, in particular, need supplements. That requires professional judgment and sometimes special lab tests. If, after reading this, you feel that you might not be getting enough zinc, for example, the safe thing would be to check with a doctor. (*Don't* take the word of the salesperson who stocks mineral pills, however knowledgeable he or she might seem.)

Almost *every* responsible diet book gives the same advice about mineral supplements: Don't take them without asking a doctor. What they usually don't mention is that not all doctors are up on nutrition, and not all are sympathetic toward vegetarian kids. If your family doctor dismisses your questions, you might have to look further for advice. One good bet would be an organization of doctors in group practice with a nutritionist on the staff.

If your community has a free youth clinic, you can probably find someone there who is open-minded and experienced with teen-age nutrition problems. Otherwise, explaining your situation on the phone before making an appointment might save you from spending money on a doctor who isn't equipped or inclined to advise you. Fortunately, doctors in general, and younger doctors especially, are becoming more aware of the virtues of vegetarian eating. And a growing patients'-rights movement is making them more aware of the need to answer questions instead of just giving orders.

IRON

During the 1960s and early 1970s, different government agencies conducted a number of nutrition surveys in the United States and Canada. People were asked about their eating habits and what they had eaten the previous day, and in some cases blood tests and other lab tests were taken to measure the level of different nutrients in their bodies. In every case, whether the group studied was college students in Iowa, poor people across the country, a cross section of Americans, or a representative sample of Canada's population, one finding stood out: People were not getting enough iron. Teen-agers' diets were found to be especially low in iron, and teen-age girls were worse off than boys. Yet teen-agers also need more iron than anyone except for pregnant women, who are usually advised by their doctors to take iron pills.

Teen-age boys are growing especially fast and need iron to build up more and more red blood cells. Iron is an essential part of the hemoglobin in these cells, the red material that carries oxygen through the body. When the hemoglobin level falls too low, anemia can develop, leaving the victim unusually tired and weak. (Untreated anemia can eventually lead to death, but people are likely to go to a doctor long before this stage.) Girls don't need quite as much iron for growing, but they need extra amounts to make up for the iron lost in the blood each month during menstruation.

Actual anemia is not a common disease in this country, and some specialists question whether we have a real deficiency problem. However, most believe that many Americans are at risk in regard to iron. That is, they are probably less prepared than they could be to fight off infection and more likely to develop anemia as a result of blood loss, pregnancy, or other stress situations.

Low iron intake is not limited to vegetarians; but as liver is the only food that is really loaded with iron, this nutrient is harder to obtain from a meatless diet. Also, iron exists in two different forms, and the form found in meat and fish is easier for the intestines to absorb.

Part of the problem with vegetarian iron sources has been blamed on a compound called phytic acid, which is present in the outer layers of whole grains, especially oats. It is also found to a lesser extent in nuts and dried beans. It seems that phytic acid binds up iron and other minerals in those foods and makes them harder for the body to absorb. Phytase, an enzyme in our intestines, breaks down some of the phytic acid, so that not all of the minerals in the food are wasted; but people who don't eat meat still need to take in more of the minerals in order to get the same benefits. Whole-grain bread is a better source of minerals than other whole grains, because the same enzyme occurs in yeast. While the yeast is working to make the dough rise, the phytase works to destroy much of the phytic acid in the flour. Enriched breads and cereals have iron added, but some studies have found this iron to be less well absorbed.

How, then, do vegetarians get enough iron? Some eat rai-

118

sins and other dried fruits for their high iron content; but you have to eat a lot of dried fruit, and consequently a lot of calories, in order to get much iron. (Of course, a dried fruit does not contain any more iron than the whole fruit did originally. But without the water there is simply more iron per unit of weight, and you are likely to eat more of the fruit that way.) Spinach contains iron, but again, you are not likely to eat that much spinach. And spinach also contains oxalic acid, another substance thought to bind up minerals. Tofu and other soy products are better sources of iron, and the iron from soybeans is well absorbed—almost as well as from meat. Eggs and certain vegetables, such as potatoes, brussels sprouts, and acorn squash, also contain some iron.

If you don't eat meat, you can make the iron you do get more absorbable by including a vitamin C-rich food such as broccoli, potatoes, tomatoes, or grapefruit with your meal. Like meat, ascorbic acid helps to change the iron in vegetables to a more usable form. Be aware, though, that this iron-absorption job tends to use up the ascorbic acid, so it can't be counted as your vitamin C for the day.

Another way to boost the amount of iron in your meals is to cook in an old-fashioned iron skillet. This is especially effective with acidic foods, such as tomatoes or lemon juice, which are cooked for a long time. A serving of tomato-based spaghetti sauce cooked in iron for two or three hours will give you about five times your daily requirement of eighteen milligrams of iron. Even with other foods cooked for a shorter time, a few milligrams of iron will be picked up. Oddly enough, this form of iron is easily absorbed. It is interesting that the only populations known to suffer from an excess of iron are Bantu groups in Africa who live mostly on cereal products and beer that have been cooked or fermented in iron pots for long periods of time. Americans, though, with our different cooking and eating habits, are more likely to benefit than to suffer from iron-pot cooking.

ZINC

Vitamin C and iron pots make it fairly easy for vegetarians to avoid iron deficiency. But nutritionists have only recently become concerned about zinc deficiency, and nobody has yet

119

come up with a vegetarian shortcut to getting enough zinc. There is no doubt that eating small amounts of meat or seafood makes it easier to get the required fifteen milligrams of zinc. As you will see from the chart on pages 132-3, vegetarians have to add up small amounts from a number of foods, such as eggs, cheese, milk, and whole-wheat bread. White bread has very little zinc, because about 80 percent is lost in refinement and not put back into enriched bread. Zinc is abundant in wheat germ and is also present in brown rice and other whole grains, and in many dried beans and nuts. But the amounts vary, according to the zinc in the soil where the plants were grown. Also, because of phytic acid, not all the zinc in whole grains gets absorbed. According to the RDA committee, people who don't eat meat should probably take in far more than fifteen milligrams of zinc in order to absorb the needed amount.

Zinc is especially important for young people, because it is needed for physical growth and sexual development. Teenagers have lower zinc reserves in their bodies than those in other age groups, and they tend to use up large amounts during periods of physical and emotional stress. In Egypt and Iran, severe zinc deficiency was found in a number of undernourished young men in their late teens who lived mainly on unleavened bread. They were all small for their age, had small sex organs, and generally looked younger than they were.

Nothing so extreme has turned up in this country, but nutritionists were concerned by a 1972 study of 150 middle-class school children in Denver, Colorado. More than a third of the children examined had low zinc levels in their bodies. Some were suffering from actual zinc deficiency and were not growing as rapidly as they should have been. A later study of low-income children in Denver turned up more widespread zinc deficiency with low zinc stores in more than two-thirds of the children. Why the difference between the two groups? According to the researchers, the poorer kids probably got less zinc because they ate less meat. Probably, though, they also got less milk and eggs and didn't eat whole-grain bread. Well-fed vegetarians such as the Seventh-day Adventists are not known to suffer from zinc deficiency. Nevertheless, growing vegetarians should be aware that meatless diets can be short in zinc.

A common symptom of zinc deficiency is a loss of appetite

or a change in the sense of taste. Food might seem to lose its flavor, or everything might develop an obnoxious taste or smell. Healing is also slow when there is not enough zinc, and the healing process normally uses up so much of it that some people temporarily lose their sense of taste while recovering from surgery, burns, or broken bones. Of course, a common cold can also temporarily destroy your sense of taste, and so can worry or unhappiness, so don't assume that you have a zinc deficiency just because your food seems tasteless.

CALCIUM, PHOSPHORUS, AND MAGNESIUM

About 2 percent of your body weight is calcium and another 1 percent is phosphorus, which means that those two elements make up three quarters of the body's mineral content. (The other one quarter is shared by at least fifty other minerals, not all of them known to be useful.) More than 98 percent of the calcium is in our bones, another 1 percent goes to the teeth, and much of the rest is used by the nerves and muscles, including the heart. Nutritionists are currently at odds about how much calcium we actually need and how much we can get without drinking milk; but it is agreed that growing bodies between the ages of ten and eighteen need more calcium than at any other time in life.

Milk, cheese, and other dairy products are the best sources of calcium, and without them total vegetarians will have a hard time getting the 1,200 milligrams recommended by the RDA committee. (An eight-ounce glass of milk contains about 300 milligrams.) What's more, the lactose in milk makes the calcium easier to absorb. Whole grains and beans contain calcium, but in smaller concentrations. Also, much of the calcium in beans and grains is bound up by phytic acid. Leafy green vegetables contain calcium, but some of them contain oxalic acid. (Broccoli and kale do not have oxalic acid.) Some of the tofu made in this country is coagulated with calcium sulphate during processing, so that a four-ounce square ends up with about 150 milligrams. However, if you buy fresh (unpackaged) tofu, you can't always find out how it was made.

So much for the bad news. On the other hand, vegetarians can take comfort from the fact that both high-fat and high-protein diets also interfere with calcium absorption. For that reason the committee has set the RDAs quite high to suit the average American meat eater who is oversupplied with both fat and protein. Too much phosphorus, another element that is high in meat, also increases the need for calcium. The Canadian RDAs for calcium are lower than ours, and the British and World Health Organization recommendations are about half of ours. The American RDA committee acknowledges that people who don't eat meat can get by on "considerably less" than the RDA.

As for phytic acid, it is now agreed that people who are used to getting their calcium in this form are able to handle phytic acid. The United Nations committee of food and health experts has established that milk drinkers can adjust to a diet of whole grains and soybeans. After a few weeks or months without milk, their bodies learn to break down the phytic acid and absorb the calcium from the beans and grains.

Some American nutritionists question our experts' promotion of milk and our high-calcium RDAs. They point to populations elsewhere in the world that stop drinking milk in early childhood when they are weaned from their mother's milk. These people do not grow as tall as Americans do, but that does not make them less healthy. Unless they are generally undernourished, they do not seem to suffer from calcium deficiency. But they also tend to get more vitamin D from sunlight than we do, and that helps them to make better use of the calcium they do get from plants.

No one denies that milk-drinking populations are taller than others. In China, researchers have found that babies' growth rate slows abruptly when they are taken off their mother's milk and put on rice. In Japan as in China, the people have always been small compared to Americans; but now Japanese teenagers and young adults are very close to their American counterparts in height. Why the change? Nutritionists note that milk is not a traditional food in Japan, but today the Japanese are drinking fifteen times as much milk as they did before the end of World War II. The Japanese are also eating considerably more meat than they used to. But except for the possible social advantage of being tall, the Japanese don't seem to be better off for their change in diet. Instead, they are beginning to suffer from the same diseases that plague fat-fed Americans.

There are other complications in the calcium picture. In

1982 a special calcium committee established by the American Society for Clinical Nutrition recommended increasing the adult RDA, especially for those under age thirty-five. Not until then do the bones stop adding mass. The committee believes that higher calcium intake in young adulthood might reduce the rate of osteoporosis, the "brittle-bone" condition that is common among older Americans. Osteoporosis is rare, however, in countries where calcium intake is lower than ours. People in those countries also consume less fat and protein, and the committee chairman has noted that Americans' high meat consumption has much to do with our elderly population's bone weakness.

Whatever our adult RDA should be, then, experts agree on two points: Vegetarians in general need less calcium than meat eaters do; but because of their rapid bone growth, teen-agers need more than either younger children or adults whose bones are fully formed. To reach their full growth, then, teen-agers will still benefit from some milk or dairy products. Besides being convenient sources of calcium and vitamin D, dairy foods give growing vegetarians the riboflavin, complete protein, and vitamin B_{12} that omnivores get from meat. It is possible but harder to get enough calcium from plants. As a substitute for milk, vegan societies in this country recommend drinking soy milk with calcium, vitamin D, and other vitamins added.

About 80 percent of the phosphorus we take in combines with calcium to build and strengthen bones and teeth. Phosphorus is found in most foods; and a diet that contains enough calcium and protein is not likely to be short in phosphorus. On the other hand, too much phosphorus from meat, additives, or soft drinks containing phosphates might interfere with calcium absorption.

Magnesium is another mineral that works closely with calcium, phosphorus, and vitamin D. Over half of the magnesium we take in ends up in our bones, though like the other two minerals it is found throughout the body. The best sources are all vegetarian—whole grains, nuts, beans, and leafy vegetables.

SODIUM, CHLORIDE, AND POTASSIUM

Our language is full of reminders of the value that has been placed on salt since ancient times. Our word "salary" comes from the Latin word for salt, because part of the pay of ancient Roman soldiers was a guaranteed salt ration. Consequently, a man who wasn't much of a worker was considered "not worth his salt." In medieval times, salt was assigned a special place at the dinner table and so were all the guests, so that those of high rank sat "above the salt" and those of lesser station were placed "below the salt." My own grandmother used to maintain that "a kiss without a mustache is like an egg without salt." I found out later that she was improving on a quotation from Rudyard Kipling, who had a character compare an egg without salt to "kissing a man who doesn't wax his mustache."

It's true, we could not get along without salt. Our lives depend on maintaining a very delicate balance in body fluid within and between the cells. And that balance depends on the workings of three elements: Two of them are sodium and chloride, the elements that make up ordinary table salt, and the third is potassium.

Important as it is, most Americans take in far more salt than they need. Sodium occurs naturally in food, and much more is added in processing. Consumers usually add more from the salt shaker, in cooking and at table. But all this sodium can be harmful to people who are susceptible to high blood pressure. That condition usually doesn't show up until middle age, but to avoid trouble later on it is best to break the salt habit early in life.

People like salt because it brings out the taste of foods, but the amount of salt that most of us use tends instead to make everything just taste salty. For more variety and better flavor, use less salt in cooking and experiment with herbs and spices instead. At the table, sampling the food as it is served instead of automatically reaching for the salt can help sensitize your taste buds to other flavors. Cutting down on salt might be hard to get used to, but before long you will find that you have developed a distaste for food that is heavily salted. When you do, you will be a step ahead of meat eaters, because plant-origin foods generally have far less salt to start with.

As for potassium, the only people who have to worry about it are those who already have high blood pressure and are taking medication to help their kidneys get rid of salt. The potassium is flushed out along with the sodium, and occasionally supplements are needed to correct this.

TRACE ELEMENTS

Besides calcium and phosphorus, we need only four other minerals in amounts over 100 milligrams a day. They are magnesium, sodium, potassium, and chloride. The others, including iron and zinc, are often called trace elements because they are present in the body in such small amounts that at first only traces were detected. Most trace elements are so common in whole food that no one who eats sensibly has to worry about getting enough.

Selenium offers a good example of the claims and controversies surrounding particular vitamins and minerals. Selenium supplements are sold in health-food stores in the belief that they can protect against cancer. Selenium in foods varies according to the amount in soil where the foods are grown, and some studies show higher cancer and heart disease rates in low-selenium areas. But selenium can be toxic at high levels, and the RDA committee is confident that a balanced diet provides all we need, without supplements. Seafood, and then meat, are the best sources, but whole grains are also good. As the foods we buy in any one area are likely to come from many different parts of the country, eating a variety of grains and brands is good insurance against a low-selenium diet.

Fluorine, another controversial mineral, is well known for its role in preventing tooth decay, which is why it is added to the drinking water in many communities. Some groups oppose this practice because high doses of fluorine can be poisonous, and putting it into the water supply robs individual citizens of their choice in the matter. But the American Dental Association, which supports fluoridation, maintains that fluorine is toxic only in amounts about 2,500 times greater than anyone is likely to get from water. The dentists point out that many other essential minerals and some vitamins are also poisonous at very high levels.

Iodine is used by the thyroid gland in the neck, which plays an important role in regulating physical and mental growth. Without iodine, the thyroid can enlarge and cause an ugly swelling called a goiter. Women with iodine deficiency sometimes give birth to dwarfed and mentally retarded children, called cretins. As with zinc and selenium, the amount of iodine in food depends on the amount in the soil where the food was grown; and in certain parts of this country the soil and water are very low in iodine. This is especially true in the Great Lakes area, which used to be called the "goiter belt" because that condition was so common there.

Then, about fifty years ago, manufacturers began adding iodine to table salt. This gives us all the iodine we need, and goiters have just about disappeared. We need only very small amounts of iodine, so no one has to take too much salt in order to get enough. Most supermarkets today stock both iodized and noniodized salt.

But now, iodized salt is becoming controversial. Critics argue that heavy salt users might be getting too much iodine because iodine is now used in a number of commercial food processes and additives. They say that iodine deficiencies in local soil are no longer important, because most foods are now shipped from one part of the country to another. Nevertheless, the RDA committee still recommends iodized salt for people living in noncoastal regions.

Cobalt is not known to be useful in itself, but it is of interest as the only mineral that is actually part of a vitamin molecule. (That explains why vitamin B_{12} is sometimes called cobalomin.)

Just for the record, **manganese, molybdenum, copper,** and **sulphur** are also known to be essential to humans. **Nickel, tin, vanadium,** and **silicon** have been found to be essential to animals and so are probably needed by humans as well.

Some trace-element specialists are afraid that synthetic fertilizers and food processing might be paving the way for widespread, low-grade mineral deficiencies. The fertilizers boost plant growth by enriching the soil with certain elements such as nitrogen and phosphorus, but they don't put back other elements that might be used up in the process. Defenders of the practice say that the plants themselves could not grow if essential minerals were missing—but we already know that soils low in zinc, selenium, and iodine produce plants that are also low in the same minerals.

126

There is no question that refining grains and substituting highly processed concoctions for real whole foods rob people of many nutrients they used to be able to take for granted. **Chromium** is one essential mineral that is now less abundant in the standard American diet than in that of more traditional cultures. Among the best sources are corn oil, cheese (but not milk), and whole grains (but not white rice or bread, as 80 percent is lost in milling and not put back).

With trace minerals as with vitamins, the best policy is not pills but a sensible variety of whole foods. Eating a variety increases your chances of hitting all the nutrients, and eating whole foods ensures that you will get all the vitamins and minerals they had to start with. Trace minerals in pill form might give you more than you need of some minerals but crowd out others that are not in the pill. The body absorbs the minerals from the pills, but as a consequence other minerals in your food might be less well absorbed.

CHAPTER
16

Summing Up:
What You Need

fter reading the last five chapters, you've seen which of the foodstuffs, vitamins, and essential minerals are easy to get from plants and which ones are usually provided by meat. You've seen that most nutrients are just as easily available to vegetarians as to omnivores, but a few are not. The chart on pages 130-3 shows those that are not.

As the chart will remind you, iron and zinc are the only nutrients that lacto-ovo-vegetarians have to be concerned about. You can get enough of both from a meatless diet, but it has to be a wholesome diet. Vegetarians who have to get trace elements from plants can't afford to live on refined foods and junky snacks.

You probably realize by now that it is harder to get all the essential nutrients from a vegan diet. We've seen that, practically speaking, vitamin B_{12} is not naturally present in plants. Milk is still the best source of calcium and the only food source of vitamin D. Riboflavin is present in many vegetables and grains, but it takes a lot of vegetables and grains to make up for the amounts usually obtained from meat and milk. Without milk and eggs, zinc is scarcer for vegans than for other vegetarians. And because of the complicated interaction among nutrients, careless vegans might not be benefitting from some of the ones they do get. You need calcium and iron, for example, in order to absorb vitamin B_{12} and to convert carotene into vitamin A. And neither vitamin D nor calcium can do its job without the other.

Vegans willing to make the effort can be just as healthy as omnivores, if not more so. But you can't simply give up all meat and animal products without some serious planning. Especially during the growing years, you will probably have to resort to supplements that people on more balanced diets can do without. Whether you take the supplements in pill form or in fortified yeast or soy milk, it is best to consult a doctor or nutritionist on the right formula for you.

Another caution: Switching from a standard American diet to a healthful vegan life-style involves such drastic changes that it should not be done cold turkey. I recently read a book by a doctor advising his adult readers to cut down on sugar, salt, and animal fats—not give them up entirely. He suggested making this moderate change in three stages and staying at each stage for a year before moving on to the next. Most people are probably too impatient to wait three years, but those who have strong feelings against eating anything that comes from animals should at least make the break gradually. It's one thing to read about the nonanimal sources of the nutrients you need, but it takes time to learn to live with them. Give up meat first, and use eggs and milk as a bridge while you get used to an everyday diet based on such foods as brown rice and tofu.

KEY NUTRIENTS FOR VEGETARIANS

The nutrients listed in this chart are the ones that careless vegetarians or vegans might be missing. Those who give up meat and fish should check to make sure they are taking in enough zinc and iron. Only those who also give up eggs and dairy products have to worry about calcium, riboflavin, and vitamins B_{12} and D.

All values given are approximate, as there is often considerable variation from sample to sample.

The cheeses given as sources for vitamin B_{12} and other nutrients are only examples. Other cheeses also contain these substances, but in general the ones listed here are the best sources among the more popular cheeses.

You might be surprised to see meat and fish samples listed in a vegetarian nutrition chart, but I believe you should have this information in order to compare for yourself and make your own choices.

All nutrient values listed for vegetables, legumes, rice, and pasta are for cooked portions.

Nutrient	RDA	Sample Meat and Fish Sources	Egg and Dairy Sources	Vegan Sources	Results of Deficiency
* VITAMIN B_{12}	3 mcg	3½ oz beef liver 80 mcg 3½ oz canned tuna 2.2mcg 3½ oz beef 1.8 mcg 1 frankfurter .5 mcg 3½ oz chicken .4 mcg	1 cup creamed cottage cheese 1.2 mcg 1 egg 1 mcg 1 cup plain yogurt with added nonfat milk solids 1 mcg 1 cup whole or skimmed milk 1 mcg ¼ cup nonfat milk solids (dry skimmed milk) 1 mcg 1 cup buttermilk .5 mcg 1 oz Swiss cheese .5 mcg 1 oz cheddar cheese .25 mcg 1 oz mozzarella cheese .25 mcg 1 cup plain yogurt without added milk solids .25 mcg	3½ oz tempeh 5 mcg nutritional yeast fortified soy milk vitamin supplements (pills) } check labels for exact amounts of these nutrients	intestinal pain, diarrhea, constipation pernicious anemia menstrual irregularity eventual deterioration of central nervous system

Nutrient	RDA			Deficiency Symptoms
*RIBOFLAVIN	males 11–14 1.6 mg males 15–18 1.7 mg females 11–18 1.3 mg	3½ oz ground beef .2 mg 3½ oz chicken .2 mg	1 cup creamed cottage cheese .56 mg 1 cup plain low-fat yogurt with added milk solids .5 mg 1 cup whole milk .4 mg 1 cup skimmed milk .34 mg 1 cup plain whole-milk yogurt .3 mg 1 oz cheddar cheese .13 mg 1 egg .13 mg	*Vegetables* 1 cup okra .3 mg 1 cup asparagus .27 mg 1 cup cooked spinach .26 mg 1 cup butternut squash .25 mg 1 cup cooked kale .24 mg 1 stalk broccoli .23 mg 1 cup brussel sprouts .21 mg	cracks and soreness at corners of mouth itching, watering and stinging eyes face rash and scaling skin
*VITAMIN D	10 mcg		1 cup whole or skimmed milk 2.5 mcg	exposure to sunlight	rickets in small children limited bone growth in children and adolescents soft, fragile bones in later life
*CALCIUM	1200 mg	½ cup canned tuna 15 mg 3½ oz chicken 12 mg 3½ oz ground beef 11 mg	1 cup plain yogurt with added nonfat milk solids 400 mg 1 cup skimmed milk 300 mg 1 cup whole milk 290 mg 1 cup plain yogurt without added milk solids 270 mg ½ cup ricotta cheese 260 mg 1 oz Swiss cheese 260 mg 1 oz edam cheese 225 mg 1 cup creamed cottage cheese 210 mg 1 oz cheddar cheese 210 mg 1 oz gouda cheese 196 mg 1 oz mozzarella cheese 145 mg	*Legumes* 4 oz tofu 150 mg 1 cup soybeans 145 mg 1 cup white beans 100 mg 1 cup chick peas 100 mg *Vegetables* 1 cup cooked bok choy 250 mg 1 cup cooked kale 200 mg 1 cup okra 150 mg 1 stalk broccoli 135 mg	rickets in small children limited bone growth in children and adolescents soft, fragile bones in later life

continued

Nutrient	RDA	Sample Meat and Fish Sources	Egg and Dairy Sources	Vegan Sources	Results of Deficiency

**IRON	18 mg	3½ oz calf liver 14 mg
		3½ oz canned oysters 5.6 mg
		3½ oz ground beef 3 mg
		¾ cup canned tuna 2 mg
		3½ oz chicken 1.5 mg
			1 egg 1 mg	*Legumes and Nuts*
				1 cup chick peas 7 mg
				1 cup black or
				  white beans 5.5 mg
				1 cup lentils 3 mg
				4 oz tofu 2.3 mg
				1 oz almonds,
				  cashews, or peanuts 1–1.3 mg
				1 cup mung
				  beansprouts 1 mg
				Grain Foods
				1 cup oatmeal 1.7 mg
				1 cup enriched rice 1.4 mg
				1 tbs toasted wheat germ .9 mg
				1 cup brown rice .8 mg
				1 slice bread, whole
				  grain or enriched .5–.8 mg
				Vegetables
				1 cup tomato juice 2 mg
				½ cup acorn squash 1.7 mg
				1 cup cooked kale 1.6 mg
				1 stalk broccoli 1 mg
				⅔ cup brussel sprouts 1 mg
				1 baked potato or
				  sweet potato 1 mg
				Fruit
				½ cup dried apricots,
				  prunes, or raisins 2.5 mg
				1 banana 1 mg
				Other
				1 tbs blackstrap molasses 3 mg
				cooking in an iron pot
				  (see pp. 197–8)
					anemia, characterized by weakness and fatigue

| **ZINC** | 15 mg | 3½ oz canned Atlantic oysters 75 mg
3½ oz canned Pacific oysters 9 mg
3 oz ground beef 3.8 mg
2 oz calf liver 3.5 mg
3½ oz typical fish 1 mg
3½ oz canned tuna 1 mg
½ chicken breast .7 mg | 1 oz parmesan cheese 1.5 mg
1 cup plain yogurt 1.1 mg
1 cup whole milk 1 mg
1 cup creamed cottage cheese 1 mg
1 oz cheddar cheese 1 mg
1 oz mozzarella cheese 1 mg
¼ cup nonfat milk solids (dry skimmed milk) .75 mg
1 egg .5 mg | *Legumes and Nuts*
1 cup black-eyed peas 6.7 mg
1 cup chick peas 2 mg
1 cup lentils 2 mg
1 cup split peas 2 mg
1 cup dry beans 1.8 mg
1 cup green peas 1.3 mg
1 oz cashews 1.2 mg
1 oz almonds .7 mg
1 tbs peanut butter .5 mg

Grain Foods
3 oz granola 1.8 mg
1 cup brown rice 1.2 mg
1 cup oatmeal 1.2 mg
1 tbs wheat germ 1 mg
1 cup pasta (amounts for whole-grain pasta not available) .7 mg
1 slice whole-wheat bread .5 mg

Vegetables
1 cup corn .7 mg
1 cup cabbage .6 mg
1 cup onions .6 mg
1 cup carrots .5 mg
1 cup tomatoes .5 mg | retarded growth and sexual development
slow healing of wounds
loss or distortion in sense of smell and taste |

KEY

Portion: 3½ oz = 100 grams

Abbreviations:

mg = milligram, or one thousandth ($\frac{1}{1000}$) of a gram

mcg = microgram, or one millionth ($\frac{1}{1,000,000}$) of a gram

*Vegans take note

**All vegetarians take note

Principal source:
Jean A.T. Pennington and Helen Nichols Church, *Food Values of Portions Commonly Used.* 13th ed. (New York: Harper & Row, 1980).
Other Sources:
Dr. Carl V. Moore, "Iron," in Robert S. Goodhart and Maurice E. Shils, eds., *Modern Nutrition in Health and Disease.* 5th ed. (Philadelphia: Lea & Febiger, 1973), for information on iron pot cooking.
M.L. Orr, *"Pantothenic Acid, Vitamin B$_6$ and Vitamin B$_{12}$ in Foods."* Home Economics Research Report No. 36, Agricultural Research Service, USDA, for vitamin B$_{12}$.
Dr. Keith Stemkraus, New York State Agricultural Experimental Station, Cornell University, for vitamin B$_{12}$ content of tempeh.
Yogurt labels for vitamin B$_{12}$ content.

PART 3

Putting It Together

Food Groups

So now you know what nutrients you need, why you need them, and which ones you might be short of if you don't eat meat. But how can you be expected to remember all that whenever you sit down to a meal? That's where the four food groups come in. Just as the National Academy of Sciences has established RDAs to guide professional nutritionists, the U.S. Department of Agriculture devised food groups to help consumers plan their daily meals. Food-group charts were reproduced in textbooks from grade school to college, and handed out wherever the government dispensed nutrition information. The food-group plan, it was thought, would benefit producers by promoting their products and consumers by advising them on nutrition. The idea was that if people would eat foods from each recommended group, they would automatically get the nutrients they need.

There is nothing sacred about four food groups. When the USDA first came out with the plan, there were twelve. That proved cumbersome, and so the recommended foods were regrouped and called the Basic Seven. Essentially, the seven categories were green vegetables, citrus fruits, potatoes and other vegetables, bread and cereal, milk, meat, and butter. Still later, the three fruit and vegetable groups were clumped together, and the butter group was dropped on the reasonable assumption that people would get enough fat anyway. From then on, people were taught to choose from four food groups: meat, milk, bread and cereal, and fruit and vegetables.

During the 1970s, consumer-minded nutritionists began to question the four-group plan. The "new nutrition" had made clear that food groups give only one side of the picture: They point out the beneficial elements in particular foods but ignore the possible hazards. The "milk-group" lists made no nutritional distinctions among skimmed milk, whole milk, and high-fat cheeses. And the very name "meat group" for the protein category gave red meat a misleading status. In almost all textbooks, poultry, fish, and eggs were listed as possible substitutes for red meat. But other protein foods such as beans were usually mentioned later, in smaller print. In some elementary school texts beans were not listed at all.

Not until 1980, after several government food and health agencies had adopted new nutrition guidelines, were the food

groups changed again. By then Bob Bergland was Secretary of Agriculture and Carol Tucker Foreman, a former consumer representative, was Assistant Secretary for Food and Consumer Services. Foreman's staff did not make any major changes in the four-food-group concept but did change the "meat group" heading to "meat, poultry, fish, beans, and eggs." It is not as easy to remember, but it does put a nonanimal protein on the same line as meat. Now, more and more nutrition charts contain a more inclusive "protein group" instead of a "meat group."

As any food-group plan is simply a convenient way to remember what to eat, there is no one right way to arrange a chart. Various organizations, vegetarian or otherwise, have their own versions. The chart on page 140 is similar, but not identical, to the Foreman plan. The major difference, besides eliminating meat, is that this chart puts more emphasis on whole grains whereas the USDA guide treats whole and enriched grains as equals. Whole grains are especially important to vegetarians because they contain trace minerals that other people get from grain-fed or grass-fed animals.

At first glance, a food-group chart might seem hard to remember, or hard to follow. Isn't it a lot of trouble to work all those different servings into one day's eating? It's not, if you remember that the servings don't have to be big ones, and they don't have to be separate dishes. For example, a cheese and tomato sandwich gives you food from every major group. (Cheese can qualify for both the milk and the protein groups.) The sample meal plan following the chart shows how easy it is to squeeze in all the recommended servings from the food groups.

When you are planning your diet around four food groups, it is more interesting if you have a variety of foods to choose from within each group. Switching off among different grains, beans, and vegetables also ensures that you won't miss any of the vitamins and trace minerals that might be more prevalent in some foods than in others that seem similar.

139

FOOD GROUPS FOR VEGETARIANS

Bread and Cereal

4 or more servings daily*,
  mostly whole grains
Include:
2 to 4 slices whole-grain bread
2 servings chosen from: rice, pasta,
  rolled oats, other grain products,
  and seeds

Whole grains provide protein, B
  vitamins, vitamin E, iron, and
  other trace minerals
Enriched grains provide some B
  vitamins, protein, and iron

Beans and Other Protein Foods

2 servings daily* (can be
  skipped when dairy products
  are substituted)
Choose from:
soybeans, tofu, tempeh, and other
  soy products
pinto, kidney, black, navy, pea, and
  other dry beans
split peas, lentils, chick peas
nuts
eggs

Beans, peas, nuts, and eggs
  are good sources of protein, B
  vitamins, and trace minerals
Eggs alone provide vitamin B_{12}

Dairy Products

4 servings daily* (vegans need
  fortified soy milk or other
  substitutes)
Choose from:
milk, buttermilk, yogurt, cheese,
  and cottage cheese

Dairy products are good sources of
  protein, calcium, riboflavin, and
  vitamin B_{12}
Commercial milk is also fortified
  with vitamins A and D

Vegetables and Fruit

4 servings daily*
Include:
1 serving citrus fruit, melons,
  berries, tomatoes, or raw
  cabbage
1 serving dark green or deep yellow
  vegetables
1 serving dark green leafy
  vegetables

Foods listed with citrus fruits are
  good sources of vitamin C
Dark green and deep yellow
  vegetables are good sources of
  carotene for vitamin A
Dark green leafy vegetables provide riboflavin, iron, and calcium
All vegetables provide a variety of
  vitamins and minerals

*¾–1 cup = 1 serving

SAMPLE VEGETARIAN MEAL PLAN

This sample meal plan is only an example, set down to show how you can fit all the recommended food-group servings into a day's eating. It is based on the examples used in Chapter 13, "Protein," which deliberately were chosen to be typical, not supernutritious, high-protein meals. No doubt you will think of other combinations that fill the requirements just as well. Portions are not specified, because in most cases your own appetite will be the best guide to how much you should eat. Desserts and other foods can be added, depending on your calorie needs.

	Meatless	Vegan

Breakfast	orange or orange juice
	oatmeal with milk and
	  honey
	whole-wheat toast with
	  butter or nut butter
	milk
		orange or orange juice
		oatmeal with honey and
		  soy milk
		whole-wheat toast with nut
		  butter
		fortified soy milk

Lunch	peanut butter sandwich
	  on whole-wheat bread
	raw carrot sticks
	banana
	milk
		peanut butter sandwich on
		  whole-wheat bread
		raw carrot sticks
		banana
		fortified soy milk

Snack	yogurt with tahini apple juice	nuts, seeds, and raisins fortified soy milk

Dinner	spaghetti with parmesan
	  cheese and egg (p. 228)
	tossed salad with chick
	  peas
	steamed Italian green beans
		Cuban black beans and rice
		  (p. 216)
		tossed salad with tofu
		  dressing
		steamed squash

Snack	popcorn (nutritional yeast
	  optional)
		popcorn with nutritional
		  yeast

VEGETARIAN FOODS

The most exciting part of going vegetarian is the abundance of new foods you discover after you switch from meat-based meals to those that combine different foods from the earth. This chapter is only an introduction to the vegetarian foods most commonly available. As you become familiar with them, you will probably discover others on your own. Get in the habit of visiting ethnic markets and natural-food stores and asking about the exotic roots and grains and spices you find there. Browse, taste, experiment, and you'll learn why tracking down new foods has become a national enthusiasm.

BREAD AND CEREAL

Carbohydrate, protein, unsaturated fat, B vitamins, minerals, and fiber: The grain foods that come from the grassy plants called cereals have them all. Throughout history, most of the world's people have made wheat, rice, corn, or other grains the basis of their diets. Now American health officials are recommending that we go back to a heavier use of grains. For vegetarians, foods made from grains are especially important. Combined with milk or beans, they give us the high-quality protein and trace minerals that omnivores get from meat.

However, most of the rice, bread, and other cereal products sold in grocery stores are not from whole grains. For the past hundred years or so, the food industry has been "refining" grains (or "polishing" them, as the process is sometimes called). During refining, the nutritious parts of the grains are stripped off and only the white, starchy endosperm is left. Gone are the layers of bran around the endosperm. Gone, too, is the compact germ, the embryo that would grow into a new plant. Gone with them are a quarter of the whole grain's protein; at least half of the pantothenic acid, calcium, molybdenum, and chromium; and over two-thirds of the thiamin, niacin, riboflavin, vitamin B_6, folacin, vitamin E, iron, potassium, phosphorus, magnesium, zinc, and copper. Gone, too, is the indigestible fiber that helps to move food through the intestines.

We have already seen how people who lived mostly on white rice began to weaken and die from beriberi, and how doctors finally tracked down thiamin, the vitamin in whole grains that is needed to prevent the disease. We've seen, too, how a lack

142

of niacin caused pellagra in people who lived mostly on corn-meal. When these deficiency diseases were discovered, nutritionists began campaigning to have the vitamins added back to refined foods. Now, most refined cereal products are "en-riched" with thiamin, riboflavin, niacin, iron, and sometimes calcium. But this enrichment formula was established in 1941 and has never been changed, even though it is now known that more than twenty other essential nutrients are also lost in refinement. Enrichment has done away with the dramatic deficiency diseases. But compared to what they started with, enriched grains are still impoverished.

Whole grains in general are important for vegetarians, but **whole-grain bread** is especially so. Because the yeast in risen bread works to release minerals from phytic acid, bread is a good source of the zinc and iron that teen-agers need. Another reason for eating whole-grain bread is that it tastes good and gives you a sense of satisfaction you don't get from sponge-rubbery commercial white bread.

Back in the days before mass refinement, Europeans considered white bread a delicacy of the rich. The rich didn't suffer from mass deficiency diseases because they got enough other foods, including meat and other grains foods, to make up for what was lost in refinement. But even white bread in those days was more substantial, nutritious, and tasty than the air-blown factory product sold as bread today. You can't imagine anyone calling this Styrofoam stand-in the "staff of life." But you will realize why that term was once applied to bread when you try a homemade whole-wheat loaf like the basic recipe given on page 205. This bread doesn't even need butter, though it goes well with soft cheese, peanut butter, or tahini.

During the 1960s and 1970s, more and more people became convinced of the superiority of whole-grain bread. Many were taken aback, though, by the bread ratings in *Consumer Reports,* a magazine that advises shoppers on all sorts of products from cars to toothpaste. In 1976 and again in 1982, the *Consumer* company tested several commercial breads on laboratory rats. The rats were kept on diets consisting entirely of bread and water. Surprisingly, the rats on some enriched white breads did as well as or better than rats on whole-grain breads. In the 1982 test, the two top-performing breads were white and

143

some whole-wheat breads were among the poorest. The testers found, though, that the white breads with the best records contained added eggs, milk, and soy flour. These ingredients are not usually added to whole-wheat breads. Thus the experiment did not show that white flour alone is as nutritious as whole wheat. Dr. Mark Hegstead pronounced the findings "meaningless" in terms of human nutrition, and the testers acknowleged that rats fed nothing but bread cannot be compared to people on varied diets.

Adding eggs, milk, and soy products boosts the food value of white bread, but vegetarians who eat these foods anyway should still eat whole-grain bread for the trace minerals they might not get otherwise. If you buy commercial bread, be sure to read the label so you will know just what ingredients it contains. Some breads that look whole and dark may simply be colored with molasses or caramel. Beware, too, of names such as "grain," "wheat," and "health" bread that mean little but sound nutritious.

Not all the nonwhite breads are new and phony. Cracked wheat, for example, is not made from whole-wheat flour, but it is a traditional bread with more taste, texture, and food value than plain white bread. And, according to law, any bread labeled "100% whole wheat" must be just that. The "100% whole wheat" bread sold in supermarkets doesn't have the hearty texture and taste of old-fashioned bread, but it is made from flour that contains almost the entire wheat grain. If you read the labels on most other breads, you will find that enriched white flour is the first listed ingredient. As ingredients on all food labels must be listed in order of their proportion in the food, that means that the bread has more white flour than anything else.

Not all bread is made with wheat flour. The whole-rye bread and dark pumpernickel rye that are traditional in parts of Europe are deliciously hearty. But if you read the labels on supermarket rye or pumpernickel, you'll find that white wheat flour comes first again, and the darker look comes from molasses or caramel coloring. And don't let "egg" bread fool you. In most cases the egg content is next to nil, and the rich-looking yellow color is artificial.

One bread that has become popular in this country is pita bread, the Middle Eastern "pocket bread" used to make falafels

144

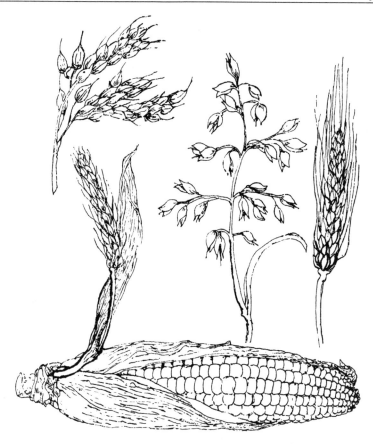

and other vegetarian sandwiches. (See page 252 for some ideas for pita-bread sandwiches.) In many ethnic stores, super-markets, and natural-food stores, you can buy both white-flour and whole-wheat pita bread. The great appeal of pita bread is probably not its taste but its shape. It's the perfect form for a portable sandwich. The pocket is achieved by rolling the dough out very thin so that during baking the air inside makes one large bubble.

Baking your own bread is immensely satisfying, but not ev-eryone wants to spend Saturdays that way. Another way to get fresh-baked bread is to look for a local bakery that bakes bread on the premises (so you can ask them what's in it), or a natural-food store that deals in fresh-baked bread.

Contrary to what most people still believe, bread is not fat-tening. A one-ounce slice of bread has no more calories than a one-ounce slice of lean roast beef.

145

If you make a habit of eating whole-grain bread, you can afford to skip whole grains at dinner now and then. Vegetarians should get used to eating whole-grain foods as a rule, and once they do, they often find refined flour products bland and mushy. But that doesn't mean they have to pass up all white-bread pizza and all dishes made with white rice or white pasta, just because they contain fewer nutrients than they might have.

Whole-grain *rice* is also called brown rice, because the bran layer makes it a little darker than refined, white rice. Brown rice is higher than white in protein, most vitamins, and minerals. It also has a fuller flavor, which most vegetarians come to prefer. But unless you live mostly on rice, the difference in protein is not important. Where white rice works better in a dish, or when you haven't time to cook brown rice, it won't hurt to use white rice once in a while. A possible compromise is converted rice, a white rice that ranks between ordinary white and brown rice in food value. It is prepared by steaming the grains before refining, a process that drives some of the outer vitamins and minerals into the kernel. However, it also changes the texture, and real rice fanciers reject converted rice on grounds of taste. By any standard, precooked instant rice is the worst buy of all, for it has lost taste, texture, and nutrients in processing.

Pasta, another familiar grain food, comes in a variety of forms. Pasta is the Italian name for spaghetti, macaroni, and other noodles made from semolina flour. This is refined flour made from a hard wheat called durum. You can get whole-wheat spaghetti and macaroni in some supermarkets, and natural-food stores now carry whole-wheat shells, elbows, lasagna noodles, linguine, and more. These products are chewier than white pasta and go well in hearty dishes such as the broccoli spaghetti on page 230 of this book. However, if you find whole-wheat spaghetti too heavy for some cheese and pasta dishes, why not use an enriched spaghetti, such as Buitoni, which has some wheat germ added back to the white flour? For a treat, go to an Italian specialty grocery for fresh-made pasta. This will cost more than the dried packaged kind, but it will have more body and flavor, whether it is made with whole-wheat or white flour or some other combination. It might inspire you to make your own, which is easy if your family has a pasta machine.

Corn, also called maize, was the basic grain of the American Indians and is still a staple food in Central and South America.

Other Americans know corn from the sweet corn on the cob that we eat as a vegetable; but people who live mostly on corn use dried field corn, another variety, and grind the kernels up into a flour, called cornmeal. In most supermarkets, cornmeal is sold only in refined form, sometimes labeled "degerminated." That just means that the nutritious germ has been taken out. It is worth going to a natural-food store for stone-ground whole cornmeal, for the texture as well as the vitamins and minerals.

Hominy and hominy grits, familiar to most people in the South, are made from corn kernels that have been soaked in lye to remove the bran and germ. Tortillas, the flat Mexican pancakes now sold in supermarkets across the country, are often made from refined, enriched corn flour. (You can also buy enriched wheat tortillas, but if you eat a lot of wheat in other forms, corn makes a change.) For more food value and more corn flavor, look for whole-grain corn tortillas in health-food stores.

Bulgur wheat, a staple in the Near East, is a parboiled wheat product. Like converted rice, it keeps about 75 percent of the whole grain's mineral and vitamin content. It is faster to cook than brown rice and makes an interesting change with lentils or chick peas.

Millet, a common food in parts of Asia and Africa, is most common here as bird or animal feed. But it can also be found in natural-food stores and can be cooked like bulgur wheat. Don't buy millet in a pet-food store; it might be contaminated with chemicals that aren't allowed in human food.

Another grain available in natural-food stores is *barley.* The "pearled" barley found in supermarkets is a refined product.

Oats, a staple in Scotland, are also fed to animals here. But Americans do eat oats as a breakfast food, most often in the form of Quaker rolled oats. (Running a roller over the hulled, whole grains smashes them down so that they will cook faster.) Rolled oats are not refined, but as oats are high in phytic acid, they are not a good source of trace minerals.

Another way to eat grains is in dry breakfast foods. However, you should read the labels to find out just what form of carbohydrate you are getting. Some breakfast cereals are so high in sugar that their nutritional value per calorie is very low. This is true no matter now much thiamin, niacin, and iron is sprayed onto the flakes. Government tests in 1980 found Kellogg's Sugar Smacks to be 56 percent sugar. Granolas, which are advertised as "natural" "health" cereals, ranged from 22 to 32 percent sugar. It's better to make your own granola, or to buy unsweetened breakfast cereal made from whole grains. Or skip the cereal and have yogurt and wheat germ with whole-wheat toast for breakfast.

Nuts and seeds are high-protein snacks that are good for breakfast and easy to eat on the run. Like grains, nuts and seeds can be combined with beans (or soy "nuts") for complete-protein meals. However, most nuts are higher in fat, which might be a disadvantage for weight watchers.

BEANS

Say the word "bean" and what comes to mind? In Mexico, it might be a hearty platter of black *refritos,* stuck with corn tortillas and topped with shreds of cheese and lettuce. In Japan, it might be the delicate soybean curd, tofu, deep-fried in sizzling oil and sprinkled with natural, aged soy sauce. In France, it might be a steaming bowl of white-bean soup, thickened with cream and fragrant with fresh herbs; in India, a bowl of lentil dal, with hot and aromatic spices mixed and fried for the occasion.

In this country, "beans" usually means a green vegetable, to be served on the "side" while the serious attention goes to meat. But green peas and beans, valuable as they are as vegetables, are not the foods that have supplied most of the world's people with their protein. This credit goes to the various dried beans, which belong to the same botanical family, Leguminosae, but are completely ripe and hard when picked from the plants. But dried beans suffer from a serious image problem in this country.

To an older generation of Americans, the word "bean" conjures up images of the 1930s depression. In those days, before food stamps and unemployment payments, jobless millions lined up for free bean soup; and penny-pinched working people ate beans at home, often in the form of a flavorless mush. Members of a younger generation raised on beef have inherited their parents' disdain for beans, whether they've tasted them or not. Worse yet, for many Americans beans

148

bring thoughts of an embarrassing condition that is technically known as flatulence and more commonly known as gas. Chances are you first heard about beans from the old children's rhyme, "Beans, beans, the musical fruit,/the more you eat the more you toot."

Nevertheless, beans can be used in so many satisfying meals, and they can provide so many essential nutrients, that anyone who gives up meat should make a point of trying beans. Beans are very low in fat, and the fats they do contain are mostly unsaturated. They are high in starchy carbohydrates, and so help meet the U.S. Dietary Goals that call for more carbohydrates in the American diet. Beans are high in protein, and combined with bread, rice, or other grain foods, bean protein is just as usable as what we get from meat. Beans are good sources of several B vitamins and some minerals, including iron.

As for beans' well-known "musical" properties, it's true that beans do sometimes cause intestinal gas. But this condition varies widely, according to the bean itself, the way it's prepared, and the experience of the eater. People who grew up in bean-eating cultures don't seem to be affected. Those who aren't used to beans can try to get used to them gradually, eating only small amounts at first, and starting with legumes that have a lower flatulence potential. Most people can tolerate lentils, split peas, lima beans, and chick peas. Most have no trouble at all with peanuts or tofu. Kidney beans and white beans are more likely to cause gas, and so are plain cooked soybeans. However, this can be reduced by soaking dry beans overnight and then changing the water before cooking them. But most people, once accustomed to beans, can skip this step without any noticeable discomfort.

Even though **dry beans** have lost status during America's prosperous decades, you can still find a wide variety in any supermarket. Most of us are familiar with *kidney beans* as an ingredient in chile con carne. (The Spanish name really means hot peppers with meat.) Other varieties of the kidney bean include pinto beans, pink beans, and the white beans called navy, pea, or Michigan beans. Split peas (green or yellow) are also common in supermarkets. So are lentils, a staple in Mediterranean cultures since Old Testament times. In one of the best-remembered stories in the Bible, Isaac's son Esau sells his

149

birthright for a "mess of pottage," which scholars tell us was lentils. You can also find dried garbanzos (otherwise known as chick peas or ceci beans) and, often, the delicious black (or turtle) beans used in Latin American cooking.

Americans have yet another objection to dried beans, and that is that they take an hour or more to cook, sometimes two or three hours. But once dumped into a pot of water they need no special attention. Teen-agers who prepare their own meals can easily cook up a pound of beans on a weekend or evening and reheat them as needed. But even if your idea of an everyday dinner doesn't go beyond opening a can, you can still find a variety of beans at the supermarket. Canned chick peas, kidney beans, and Italian white beans are common. Stores with Spanish-food sections also sell canned black beans (in Spanish, *frijoles negros*). All of these come plain, to be seasoned as you wish. They are better buys than canned New England–style "baked" beans, which are loaded with sugar. Canned soups are usually dismal, but the best of them, meatless or not, are those made from beans. They include Cuban-style black-bean soup and Italian minestrone. Progresso lentil soup is probably the closest any canned soup has come to the homemade version.

Another legume we're all familiar with is the **peanut,** which

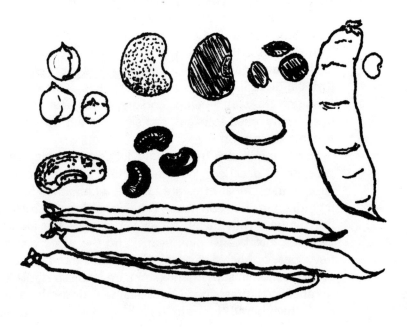

is not really a nut despite its name. We usually eat peanuts as a snack or a spread, but in some parts of Africa peanuts and sorghum, a grain, are the basic foods. Most commercial peanut butter has been adulterated with sugar and salt, and the oil has been partially hydrogenated to keep it from separating off. This means that some of the polyunsaturated fat is turned into saturated fat, the kind that doctors are telling us to avoid. In untreated peanut butter that sits around, you will find that a layer of oil will form at the top. However, you can easily mix it back in, with no loss of taste or food value. If you like, you can keep natural peanut butter in the refrigerator to keep it from separating. Plain peanut butter is available in natural-food stores, where you can often select the peanuts and put them through the grinder yourself.

Bean sprouts are a favorite food among health-food enthusiasts, who have learned that the vitamin content shoots up in sprouted beans. In addition, sprouting makes the minerals in beans more available because it destroys some of the phytic acid. Few of us are so starved for vitamins that our well-being hinges on the difference between sprouted and unsprouted beans. But bean sprouts are also fun to make, fun to throw into salads and stir-fries, and fun to eat. It takes about three days to sprout your own mung beans, the kind most often used for Chinese bean sprouts. You can buy whole mung beans in a natural-food store or an Oriental grocery. Alfalfa seeds also sprout well. They take four or five days to sprout and make fine, delicate, tiny sprouts that give a festive touch to sandwiches and salads. All other beans, including lentils, can be sprouted in the same way, but not all turn out as reliably as mung and alfalfa.

To sprout beans:

1. Put ⅓ cup of beans in a one-quart jar and fill the jar with cool water. Cover the open jar top with cheesecloth and attach the cloth to the jar with a rubber band. Let stand overnight.
2. In the morning, drain the water out through the cheesecloth. Fill with fresh water and drain well. Do not refill with water. Now lay the jar of beans on its side in a dark cupboard.

151

3. Rinse and drain the beans again that night. Continue to do this twice a day and return them to the cupboard each time. In about three days the mung sprouts will be about one and one-half inches long and will be ready to eat. Alfalfa sprouts will take four or five days and will be much smaller.

4. Put the sprouts in a large bowl or pan and rinse in cold water. Throw away any of the loose cases that float to the top. (This is just for appearances. It's not important to get them all.) Store in the refrigerator and eat within a few days, while you are sprouting more beans.

Soybeans are not usually found in supermarkets, but they are a staple in natural-food stores and Oriental markets. Soybeans in one form or other have been a basic food in Asia for thousands of years, and during that time the Eastern world has developed as many interesting uses for soybeans as the Western world has for cows and dairy products. Soybeans are an important food for vegetarians, as they are close to meat in protein value. Soybeans don't have to be combined with grains to give you all the amino acids in usable combinations.

By far the leading soy food in this country is *tofu,* made from pressed soybeans. Also called bean curd, it is often sold

152

fresh in the form of four-ounce white squares which are kept floating in water. You can also buy packaged tofu, in four- or eight-ounce squares. Japanese and most Americans pronounce the word TOE-fu; the Chinese say DOW-fu. Unlike cooked soybeans, tofu is very mild and delicate in flavor, even bland to our taste. It can be eaten cold or cooked, and is usually served with soy sauce and spices.

Before 1975, the only tofu made in this country was produced by Japanese- and Chinese-Americans for use in Oriental grocery stores and restaurants. Then William Shurtleff and Akiko Aoyagi published *The Book of Tofu,* which told Americans how the Japanese make and cook tofu. Since then, hundreds of tofu factories have sprung up across the country. (Still, we have a long way to go to match the 38,000 tofu producers in Japan.) Tofu is now served in American college dining halls and sold in natural-food stores, supermarkets, and produce markets. Business is so good that big food companies are now looking into tofu making. In 1979, the makers of Dannon yogurt and Kraft cheese products sent scouts to a "soycrafters" conference held at Hampshire College in Amherst, Massachusetts.

In 1979, Shurtleff and Aoyagi came out with *The Book of Tempeh,* and Americans learned about still another soy food. **Tempeh** (pronounced TEM-pay) is a staple in Indonesia just as tofu is in the Far East. But tempeh is a fermented food. This means that it is made by the action of bacteria and mold on cooked soybeans, just as different bacteria and molds act on milk to create cheese and yogurt. The end product is a compact, mold-covered block, with a more interesting flavor than tofu. Some say it tastes like chicken or cheese, but it really just tastes like tempeh. It is usually sliced and fried, and eaten with soy sauce.

Tempeh is not yet as popular here as tofu, but several American tempeh factories have opened, and fresh tempeh is beginning to show up in natural-food stores. Those who don't carry it fresh often sell tempeh kits; but making your own tempeh is a weekend project. Tempeh is of special interest to total vegetarians because it contains vitamin B_{12}, which is usually found only in food from animals. In this case, the B_{12} is made by bacteria during the fermentation of tempeh.

Miso (pronounced MEE-so), another fermented soy product, also contains vitamin B_{12}. However, miso is used more as a flavoring than a basic food. It comes in the form of a thick paste, usually heavily salted, and the salt alone makes it hard to eat much at a time. The Japanese often add miso to soups. It is also delicious mixed with tahini and spread on whole-wheat bread.

Soy sauce is another very salty soy product used to flavor foods. Most American soy sauce is a synthetic product; but the Japanese shoyu sold here and the tamari found in natural-food stores are made from aged, fermented soybeans. You can taste the difference.

Soy "milk" is a liquid made from ground soybeans cooked in water. Like cooked soybeans, soy milk has a strong flavor that most Americans find unpleasant. New methods have been developed to eliminate the offensive taste, but even when it does not taste terrible, soy milk has no positive flavor to recommend it. To compensate for this, sugar or honey is usually added to commercial and homemade soy milk.

Most soy milk sold in this country is made for babies who are allergic to cows' milk, but total vegetarians also use it as a substitute for cows' milk. Some vegans make their own soy milk, either from dry soy powder or from scratch—but the latter is a tedious and time-consuming process, especially considering the reward. However it is made, soy milk alone does not give you all the benefits of milk. It is high in protein but contains no vitamin B_{12} or vitamin D and only a fraction of the calcium in cows' milk; so these nutrients have to be added in the process. When they are, soy milk can be nutritious. Whether you'd call it a natural food or a supplement is another question, perhaps an irrelevant one. But drinking soy milk is a choice born of commitment, not taste.

Soy flour is ground soybeans, often added to bread and other baked goods to improve their protein quality. But soy flour does not rise like grain flour and it can give the bread a beany taste, so only small amounts are used.

Soybeans can be sprouted like mung beans, and the sprouts look very much the same. But **soy sprouts** have to be cooked before eating because raw soybeans are thought to inhibit growth in people who eat them.

Not content with the various forms in which the versatile soybean has nourished the Eastern world through the ages,

Western science and industry have extracted **soy protein,** spun it into fibers to resemble meat, treated it chemically to taste vaguely like meat, and ended up with a product that is neither one thing nor the other. Fortified with vitamins and minerals, and often doctored with artificial color and flavoring, frozen soy foods, with names like "meatless chicken," "meatless roast beef," "Wham" (fake ham), or "soysage," are sold to vegetarians who have a secret craving for meat. Textured vegetable protein (TVP) is another treated soy product, this one made to resemble hamburger, which it sometimes replaces and sometimes "extends" by being mixed in with the meat. None of these imitation corpses are of much interest to people who consider food preparation an art as well as a science.

Fortunately, real food is still to be had in abundant variety. In most cultures which survive on beans and grains, people's choice has been limited to the few varieties grown locally. We now have so many dry beans available, and we can draw from so many people's ways of cooking them, that we could eat beans every night for months and never have the same dish twice. Eating a variety of beans and grains is good nutrition, too, because each one offers a slightly different combination of vitamins and minerals.

EGGS

In the 1930s, when my husband was growing up in Detroit, the mailman used to deliver eggs mailed up from the Fretz grandparents' farm in Indiana. After their interstate train ride, these eggs were still fresher than the ones we buy in supermarkets today. They were also obtained from hens that were free to move about, and to use their beaks and claws as their nature demanded. What most amazes a younger generation, the eggs arrived intact. Any eggs sent by train today are sure to be scrambled on arrival, not just from rough handling but because today's factory-farm eggs are far more fragile. Besides thinner shells, today's eggs have paler yolks, watery whites, and less taste. One study found that they contain less vitamin B_{12} than the eggs of chickens allowed to feed in a more traditional way.

Nevertheless, eggs are still high in nutrients. Their major drawback is that they are also high in cholesterol. For this

155

reason the American Heart Association recommends eating no more than three eggs a week.

As healthy lacto-vegetarians demonstrate, vegetarians who eat enough grains, beans, and dairy products don't need eggs. However, they are a rich source of vitamin A, and of the protein, zinc, iron, and vitamin B_{12} most Americans get from meat. And vegetarians can afford an occasional egg better than meat eaters can. The average American takes in 600 milligrams of cholesterol a day, and the Dietary Goals recommend reducing this to 300 milligrams. One egg contains 250 milligrams, which doesn't leave room for much meat.

A good way to get the benefits of eggs without getting too much cholesterol is to mix an egg or two in with a grain or vegetable dish for a family meal. People who object to factory-farm eggs on humanitarian grounds can sometimes find eggs from free-ranging hens at farmers' markets or natural-food stores.

MILK AND DAIRY PRODUCTS

Like eggs, *milk* is rich in both the nutrients essential to health and the fats now associated with serious disease. Medical authorities no longer recommend whole milk for adults, yet nutritionists have recently called for more calcium in American diets. A sensible compromise is to drink skimmed milk. If you can't get used to the taste, try milk that is very low in fat (1 or 2 percent). You can also buy low-fat cottage cheese, yogurt, and ricotta cheese. Changing from whole milk to skimmed or low-fat not only reduces the calories and fat you take in; it also helps screen out the pollutants that tend to concentrate in the fat.

If you are not much of a milk drinker, three or four glasses a day might seem more than you can comfortably get down. But remember that a cup of yogurt or cottage cheese, or a mere one-ounce slice of cheese, will count as one glass of milk. Some of your milk quota might come from the cheeses on pizza or an Italian baked dish. The only nutrient you won't get from the substitutes is vitamin D, and you can substitute sunlight for that.

If you eat *yogurt*, remember that a cup of plain yogurt has fewer calories than a cup of yogurt with fruit preserves. You can always add your own fresh fruit at home, and for that matter

156

you can always add your own sweetener. At least you can control the amount. Mashed bananas make a good yogurt mix; so does honey with wheat germ, granola, or chopped nuts and raisins. My favorite yogurt mix is tahini with a few drops of lemon juice, a pinch of ground cumin, and no sweetener at all. When you buy plain yogurt and add your own extras, you are also avoiding the artificial flavor and coloring added to many flavored yogurts. (Some brands, such as Dannon, have no additives except for the sugar in the flavored yogurts.) Artificial colors don't have to be listed on dairy products, so you have to look for a label that says "no additives."

All sorts of magical health properties have been attributed to yogurt, most of them exaggerated. Dannon once made some cute commercials based on the findings that the residents of certain areas of the Caucasus, in the Soviet Union, live to an impressively old age. They also eat a lot of yogurt. However, doctors studying the groups tend to attribute their longevity to their vigorous, active lives, and to the fact that the elderly are respected and integrated members of their communities. Nevertheless, yogurt is a nutritious food, and it is enjoyed by many people who don't or can't drink milk.

A large portion of the world's adult population falls into the category of those who can't drink milk, or at least can't drink much at a time. It seems that through history, only northern Europeans and a few groups in Africa and Asia have kept dairy cows. The rest of the world did not drink milk past early childhood, and so their descendants have evolved without the enzyme needed to digest it. Without the enzyme, lactase, such people can't break down the milk-sugar lactose. Drinking more than a small amount of milk at one time is likely to result in stomach cramps, a bloated feeling, and possibly diarrhea. But lactose is partially broken down by bacteria in yogurt and cheese. Many (not all) people who can't tolerate much milk do eat yogurt and cheese without any trouble. In parts of Asia and Africa and around the Mediterranean Sea, people have traditionally enjoyed cheese or yogurt, often made with goat, sheep, buffalo, or even camel milk.

Cheese is not only a milk substitute; it can also be a meal substitute. When no one feels like cooking, a board of bread, cheese, raw vegetables, and fresh fruit can save the day. If you

have to buy cheese in supermarkets, make sure that it is "natural" and not "processed" cheese. The latter is really a mixture of different cheeses, with no character of its own, and usually with a lot of salt and artificial flavor and coloring added. Products labeled "cheese food" or "cheese spread" are even further from the real thing.

If you have any alternatives, such as a cheese store, ethnic grocery, or natural-food store, don't limit yourself to supermarket cheese. Instead of the familiar rubbery American Swiss cheese, try real Swiss Emmenthaler or Gruyère. If you like cheddar, look for Vermont, New York State, or Canadian white cheddar as a substitute for the salty, artificially colored bricks in the supermarket. Brie, a soft cheese from France, is a favorite at cheese parties. Goat cheese has an interesting tangy flavor. Some of these cheeses are too high in fat and in price to eat every day, but vegetarians can more easily afford them as a treat than meat eaters can.

Speaking of treats, ***ice cream*** and ***frozen yogurt*** should be considered just that. They are more nutritious than potato chips, candy, and most other snacks, but too high in sugar to be considered a basic food like regular yogurt. Most commercial ice cream is loaded with additives, including artificial flavor and color. (The ones that are not are better tasting as well.)

158

Frozen yogurt, like commercial granola, is a cross between health food and junk food, with the junk side dominant. And whether it is sweetened with white sugar, corn syrup, or honey, the nutrients per calorie are basically the same.

Without dairy products, teen-age vegans have to find some other way to get calcium, vitamin B_{12}, vitamin D, and sufficient protein and riboflavin. Many use fortified soy milk, or tofu and fortified yeast, with lots of leafy green vegetables.

VEGETABLES AND FRUITS

"How can you be a vegetarian when you don't even like vegetables?" The first reaction most new vegetarians get from their parents is disbelief. Remembering how hard it was to stuff canned peas or frozen spinach down their children's little throats, most parents fully expect that the kids will soon come back to meat, if only out of hunger. But if the kids take up natural fresh food at the same time that they give up meat, they might end up teaching their parents what their great-grandparents know about vegetables. Fresh vegetables, they learn, have taste and texture. Fresh vegetables might take a few minutes longer to trim and to cook than canned or frozen ones, but the difference in taste is well worth it. And for that matter, they needn't be cooked at all.

Vegetables can be eaten raw with dipping sauces, as in the French *crudités*. They can be stir-fried lightly and served crisp with a dash of soy sauce, as the Chinese have taught us. They can be cooked until soft in a meld of delectable spices, as the people in India like them. Or they can be steamed for a few minutes and eaten plain, as some natural-food purists prefer. Hot or cold, soft or crisp, tossed in a salad or smashed in a sauce, vegetables can add color, taste, texture, vitamins, minerals, and even a little protein to every meal.

If you have a local farmers' market in your area, it is worth a visit just to find out what fresh vegetables are like. In many communities, natural-food stores also carry local farmers' produce in season. Almost any produce market is likely to have more and fresher vegetables than what you can find in most supermarkets. (A produce market is just a store or stand that specializes in fresh fruit and vegetables.) But even if all your food comes from the supermarket, some fresh vegetables are available all or most of the year. They include carrots, cabbage, beets, broccoli, cauliflower, eggplant, lettuce, spinach, potatoes, sweet potatoes, zucchini, white turnips, mushrooms, celery, green peppers, onions, and garlic. There is no reason to buy any of these vegetables in canned, frozen, dried, or packaged form.

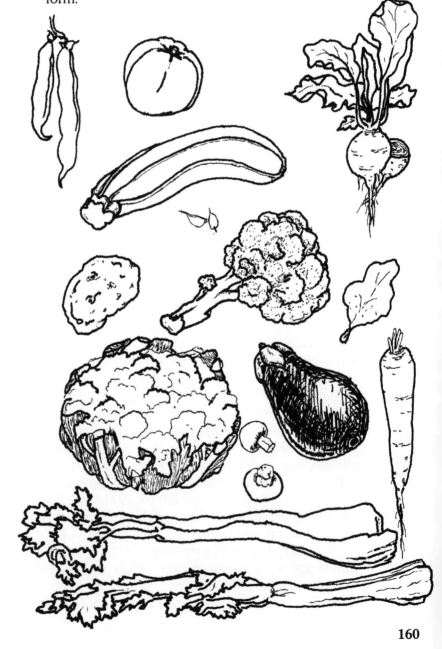

If there are no fresh-looking specimens of zucchini, mushrooms, or spinach to be found on the day you want them, get something that does look fresh and save your zucchini or mushroom or spinach recipe for another time. Some vegetables, such as squash, are more seasonal; but it's better to make squash a special fall and winter treat than to buy frozen mush in the summer when you could be eating other fresh vegetables instead.

While you are in the produce department, don't overlook the potatoes. Most Americans today think of potatoes either as fat-soaked french fries or as a side dish to a meat meal, covered with butter, gravy, or sour cream. But potatoes are well suited to any number of cooking and spicing arrangements. At one time in history the poor in Ireland lived on potatoes, which gave them carbohydrates, protein, vitamins, and minerals. And despite their unearned reputation, potatoes are not fattening. It's the butter, gravy, and sour cream that are high in calories.

Ideally, all vegetables are better fresh than frozen, but the "fresh" vegetables available are not always ideal. Frozen green beans are often superior in taste and vitamin content to the limp, wilted ones sometimes found in produce departments. If the "fresh" beans look dull and if they bend instead of snap, use frozen. Frozen peas are also a reasonable buy, especially where fresh ones are not often seen.

Of course, frozen foods are not always what they can and should be, either. The frozen food in your supermarket cases might have traveled for hundreds of miles to get there. Even when the trip is made in refrigerated trucks, packages are sometimes allowed to thaw during loading and unloading, or left to sit in broken-down freezers. To save money, stores sometimes set the freezer-case temperature at a level that does not quite keep the vegetables frozen. If the packages are misshapen or covered with white, frosty "snow," they have no doubt been defrosted and refrozen. If you get frozen green vegetables home and find them brown and dried out from defrosting, take them back. Only if customers complain will food dealers all down the line know what they can't get away with.

Canned vegetables are a less attractive alternative. Taste, texture, and vitamins are cooked out of them before canning. Then water, salt, and sugar are usually added. By reading labels you can find sugar-free canned vegetables, and in 1982 two

161

major companies came out with salt-free lines. Still, canned vegetables are only pale shades of their former selves. The only ones that are hard to pass up are canned tomatoes. Again, in an ideal world, fresh tomatoes are best. But most of the fresh tomatoes sold in supermarkets have been bred to pick and travel easily, not to taste good. For cooking, canned Italian-style tomatoes often have more flavor and certainly more juice.

Canned fruits are always soggy and usually glopped up with heavily sweetened syrup. So are many frozen fruits. Fortunately, you can always find some fresh fruit whatever the season. Fruits are good sources of energy, fiber, vitamins, and minerals. Either whole or chopped and mixed, fresh fruits make a delicious dessert that is lower in calories than the usual sweet course. Dried fruits mixed with nuts make a good high-energy snack to take along for hiking, biking, or other outings.

As for fruit juices, most of us do break down and buy them bottled or frozen. Home juicers are available, though, for those who prefer to make their own. The rest of us can only read the labels and hope that we are buying 100-percent fruit juice. (Unfortunately, the labels can be misleading. Some that say "no sugar" have corn syrup added, which amounts to the same thing.) Fruit *drinks* always have additives, usually artificial color, flavor, and preservatives along with large amounts of sugar and water.

Even without juicers, most of us can squeeze our own oranges. But if your family buys orange juice, whoever does the shopping should get the frozen concentrate rather than the ready-to-drink juice that comes in cartons or bottles. State inspectors in Connecticut and New York have found that the bottled and carton orange juice in grocery store cases lose about half of their vitamin-C content before they are sold. The frozen orange juice tested had not lost vitamin C.

CHAPTER
18

What You
Don't Need

T t's hard to talk about the trace elements and other nutrients you need in your diet without some mention of the additives and contaminants that don't belong there. With doctors warning against the saturated fat and other hazards in the American diet, consumers now question the whole range of chemicals added to processed foods. The more canned and packaged food and prepared foods we consume, the more thickeners, sweeteners, moisturizers, drying agents, preservatives, stabilizers, dyes, and artificial flavors we take in. FDA scientists have estimated that every year the average American eats about nine pounds of chemical additives other than sugar and salt.

As most of us realize, not all food additives are harmful. Reading labels, you will recognize the preservative ascorbic acid, otherwise known as vitamin C. Beta carotene, used for coloring, is the natural substance in orange vegetables that the body converts to vitamin A. But most additives, harmful or not, seem put in to benefit the people who make and sell the food, not those who buy and eat it.

Some additives are used as substitutes for more expensive real-food ingredients that customers are led to believe they are getting. Some can cover up distasteful smells or moldy appearance. Some might interfere with the absorption of vitamins and essential minerals. Some have not been sufficiently tested for safety. Others have actually been associated with cancer, birth defects, or other disorders in humans or laboratory animals.

Of all the additives used in food, probably the most suspect are the artificial coloring agents that have the least excuse for being there. Artificial coloring goes into soft drinks, imitation fruit drinks, cheap wines, baked goods, candy, gelatin desserts, puddings, potato chips, ice cream, cheese products, pet foods, sausages, vitamin pills, and other processed foods. Most of these dyes are derived from coal tars, and coal-tar dyes have caused liver damage, miscarriages, and cancer in laboratory animals. Coal-tar dyes have also been known to cause bladder cancer in workers exposed on the job, and they have been linked with behavior problems in certain susceptible children.

The risks from eating dyed foods might be small for any one individual; but is getting deceptively attractive food worth any risk at all? Most consumers, as surveyed in a 1976 Gallup poll, say no. And consumer advocates worry about the cumulative effects of taking in many little bits of dye over the years. As the labels on artificially colored foods do not always specify what kind of coloring is added, the only sure way to avoid coal-tar dyes is to stay away from any food that lists "artificial color" or "U.S. Certified Color" on the label. Even then, dairy products, alcoholic beverages, and some other processed foods don't have to list color additives at all.

It might seem reasonable to take the phrase "U.S. Certified" as assurance that an additive is safe, and the laws on record are reassuring. The Food Additives Amendments passed by Congress in 1958 and 1960 allow the FDA to outlaw dangerous food additives. One part of these amendments, known as the Delaney clause, states that "no additive shall be deemed to be safe if it is found to induce cancer when ingested by man or animal." But the Delaney clause has proved difficult to enforce.

At the time the Food Additives Amendments were passed, certain ingredients in common use were put on a list labeled Generally Regarded as Safe (or GRAS, for short). However, few of them had been tested for safety. All additives put into use after 1958 were to be tested for safety before approval. But as the FDA did not have the time or the money to test all new additives, it was often the companies who did the testing and decided whether an additive was safe.

Some additives were later tested by the FDA and taken off

the list. But in some cases where color additives were banned, the food companies simply switched to other, related substances. In 1976, a dye called red dye number 2 was banned because it had caused cancer in laboratory animals. As a result, foods previously colored with red number 2 now use a similar dye called red number 40. But red dye number 40 is illegal in several other countries, including Canada, for the same reason that red number 2 was banned here.

When consumer groups pressed for more vigorous enforcement, the FDA agreed to review the existing studies on all ingredients. In 1981, FDA scientists again declared most GRAS items safe, but recommended restrictions on salt and certain starches used for thickening. They also said that the preservatives BHA and BHT needed further testing. Artificial colors, which the FDA considers in a different class from the GRAS ingredients, were not reviewed for the 1981 report. Neither were accidental contaminants, such as pesticides and PCBs, which are not regulated by the FDA at all.

Dyes, PCBs, and other questionable substances are now so widespread in food that people have come to feel helpless against them. As more and more chemicals in food are associated with cancer, more and more people have adopted the attitude that "everything causes cancer, so you might as well eat what you like and take your chances." In fact, however, one public-interest organization, the Center for Science in the Public Interest, has pointed out that most tested chemicals are not dangerous and do not cause cancer even in large doses. In 1969, National Cancer Institute scientists tested 120 pesticide chemicals they thought might cause cancer. In their animal studies, only 11 of the 120 did cause cancer. So it should be possible to avoid the ones that do.

AVOIDING FOOD POLLUTION

Becoming a vegetarian already rules out the hormones, added nitrites, and antibiotics found in meat. Vegetarians also avoid the high concentrations of pesticides and PCBs in meat and fish. As for dairy products, drinking skimmed or low-fat milk instead of whole milk, and uncreamed rather than creamed cottage cheese, cuts way down on one's intake of these same substances.

You can cut down further on pesticides by peeling or scrubbing fruits and vegetables to remove any spray that might be clinging to the skin. Scientists with public-interest groups also recommend scrubbing or peeling apples, green peppers, and cucumbers to get rid of the wax coating these fruits and vegetables are sometimes given for the sake of appearance. This is a tradeoff, because vitamins also tend to concentrate near the surface. However, on a proper diet, none of us have to count our vitamins that closely.

Scientists associated with the Environmental Defense Fund advise staying away from all artificially colored foods and all diet foods and soft drinks containing saccharin. They warn against junk foods such as potato chips, and prepared foods such as frozen pizzas, TV dinners, and dessert mixes. All these foods are likely to contain artificial colors and flavors. As dairy products don't have to list additives, it is safer to buy yogurt and ice cream that specify "no additives" and "no artificial color" on their containers.

TAKING ACTION

In the end, though, there is only so much that an individual can do alone. Acting separately, consumers have some control over their own diets but little effect on what goes into the common food supply. That sort of control requires organized action.

As a first step, people who complain that "something should be done" are often urged to make these feelings known to their government representatives. The food industry pays full-time lobbyists to convince Congress members and regulatory officials of their side of any issue that arises. What's more, many regulatory officials have worked for the very companies they are supposed to regulate. When their four- or eight-year stints with the government are over, many return to these companies in still better jobs. A 1969 congressional study found that thirty-seven of forty-nine recently retired FDA officials went on to top jobs in the food industry. These prospects make them reluctant to oppose food-company interests. Public-interest groups of the 1960s and 1970s hoped to balance such ties with pressures for action in the consumer's interest. But hope for a balance faded in 1981, when a new administration came into office promising to free business from government regulation.

166

In 1981, environmental-protection posts were filled with industry representatives who had fought environmental protection measures in the past. Secretary of Agriculture John Block, a former hog farmer, declared that his department should not be concerned about food safety. The man Carol Tucker Foreman had replaced as Assistant Secretary for Food and Nutrition returned to the department, after sitting out the Carter years as director of a meat-producers' lobbying group. In related areas, the Federal Environmental Protection Agency moved to ease restrictions on air and water pollution. Still, environmental organizations reported a surge of new members. As one group's newsletter explained, "It's clear that our work is more necessary than ever. As the going gets tough, consumers come to realize that letter-writing campaigns have to be backed up with action on other fronts." Groups such as the Environmental Defense Fund have the legal and scientific expertise that such action requires. Through newsletters, they also keep members posted on upcoming decisions that letters to lawmakers might affect.

These public-interest groups have long been responsible for many of the consumer protection measures that were established. One such organization is the Health Research Group, established by consumer-advocate Ralph Nader's Public Citizen organization. To show the need for organized action, the HRG's founder, Dr. Sidney Wolfe, made a list of twenty-six cases in which the FDA or the Environmental Protection Agency finally banned a cancer-causing substance. In only four cases did the government agency act on its own initiative. Twenty-two of the twenty-six actions were initiated by independent public-interest groups or by labor unions concerned about workers' on-the-job exposure.

More and more, government officials are declaring that environmental laws must compromise between risks to health and costs to industry. This is called balancing risks and benefits. What consumer advocates fear is that the public will take the risks while the companies reap the benefits. Government and industry spokespeople maintain that tighter controls on industry will end up costing the public in lost jobs and higher prices. But as John B. Oakes pointed out in the *New York Times,* figures from the 1970s show that pollution-control laws actually create jobs. In addition, says Oakes, such legislation could save Americans as much as twenty-two billion dollars a year in medical bills and other indirect costs.

The more people learn about corporate pressures and government response, the more discouraged and cynical they may become. According to a 1980 Harris poll, most Americans now believe that their opinions don't count with the people in power. They feel that the people running the country don't care about the ordinary citizen. Eighty-four percent of the people polled feel that "special interests get more from the government than the people do." These beliefs are associated with a feeling of powerlessness that makes citizen action seem futile.

Other Americans still have faith that our government officials are doing their best and the authorities can be trusted to make the right decisions. They think that where complicated scientific questions are concerned, the average person just has to take the word of the experts.

These two attitudes might seem directly opposite. But in fact they have the same effect. In both cases the people are sitting back and allowing the special interests to have their say unopposed. The trouble with taking the word of the experts is that every side has its experts. Experts paid by a chemical company might reach different conclusions from experts working for a consumer group. Hard as it is, we have to learn to choose among experts, and to act on our choices.

PUBLIC-INTEREST ORGANIZATIONS
CONCERNED ABOUT FOOD LAWS AND SAFETY

Environmental Defense Fund
1525 18th Street, NW
Washington, DC 20036

Health Research Group of Public Citizens, Inc.
2000 P Street, NW
Washington, DC 20036

Center for Science in the Public Interest
1755 S Street, NW
Washington, DC 20009

(CSPI is a good source of inexpensive information on food and materials for nutrition action programs. Send for its free list.)

The Search for Organic

☐ In 1977, a California food and drug inspector visited the warehouse of a company that supplied "eggless mayonnaise" for total vegetarians and people allergic to eggs. The inspector found employees steaming off the labels from jars of a regular commercial mayonnaise (containing eggs), then substituting their own labels.

☐ In 1971, the Consumer Protection Department of the state of Connecticut tested seven foods that the sellers claimed were "organically grown." Residues of pesticide spray were found on six of the seven.

☐ In 1979, a newspaper investigating apple juice sold in super-markets and natural-food stores found large amounts of added sugar and corn syrup in most brands. Some had labels claiming the juice was "all natural" and had "no sugar added."

☐ That same year, TV interviewers and camera crews visited two of the leading natural-food stores in Los Angeles. On camera, the store personnel asserted that the vegetables in their bins were organically grown and free of pesticides. Then the TV reporter announced that he had just had the same vegetables tested and found pesticide levels equal to those in supermarket produce.

☐ In New York City, the owner of a natural-food store was seen buying produce in a nearby supermarket, then selling it for twice what he had paid.

☐ In almost every state, customers have run into natural-food-store owners who didn't know or care where their "organically grown" produce came from. In numerous cases, sincere natural-food-store owners have been shocked to discover how few of their suppliers could guarantee pesticide-free food.

Throughout the 1970s, shoppers were polled on numerous occasions by government, industry, and consumer groups. In all surveys, most people thought natural foods were superior, and about half said they would pay more for foods labeled "natural." For these gullible shoppers, supermarkets fill their shelves with nonnutritious, artificial concoctions labeled "natural."

Some time in the early 1970s, a cartoon in *The New Yorker* magazine showed a farmer couple selling produce at a roadside stand. The man was saying to his wife, "If they want organic, it's organic."

As there is no legal definition for "organic" food, the man had the right to use the term as he pleased. Chemically, all food is organic in the sense that it contains carbon. Most people, though, expect "organic" food to be grown without synthetic chemical fertilizers and pesticides. "Natural" is usually thought to mean free of excess processing and artificial additives. In 1980, the Federal Trade Commission proposed banning the term "natural" in advertisements and commercials for processed foods or foods with additives. The next year, a new FTC chief dropped the restrictions. The Food and Drug Administration, which regulates the wording on labels, also refuses to restrict the use of "natural" or "organic." The FDA claims that legal definitions would not be worth the cost of enforcement. Besides, says the FDA, such a distinction implies that "organic" or "natural" food is better and safer than other food. And how could the FDA imply that the additives and pesticide levels they allow in commercial foods are unsafe? So, as things stand, consumers are at the mercy of anyone who wants to get more money for food by calling it "organic" or "natural."

It has often been said that the only way to make sure you get organically grown food is to grow it yourself. Otherwise, you just have to take the word of the seller. Consumers are often advised that stores selling "organic" food should be able to furnish written certification that their foods are pesticide free and additive free. However, none of the stores that I have

170

checked in New York and New Jersey actually have such documents. Most claimed that they could get them but backed down when I pressed them to do so.

I spoke to one natural-food-store manager with experience buying produce in California. He went out to the farms himself, and from sounding the farmers personally, he found some he felt he could trust. But he admitted having suspicions about a lot of the stuff sold in his New York store. "If our suppliers tell us it's organic, we sell it as organic," he told me. "That's what the customers ask for, and nine out of ten don't even know what they mean by the word.

"When you buy from a distributor, you just have to take the guy's word for it. And believe me, there's a lot of cheating in the business. Even if you ask for certified proof, it doesn't mean a thing. No government agency issues any kind of certificate. Regional organic-farmers' associations do, but what do they mean? A farmer might grow one little patch to qualify for certification, but when he sells to a distributor you know all that produce didn't come from that one little patch. *Organic Gardening and Farming* magazine issues certificates to organic-growers' associations, but the magazine allows the associations to do their own testing. That makes the magazine's seal of approval no better or worse than the growers'."

All this does not mean that organically grown food is impossible to find. Many small farmers do use natural methods, and their numbers are growing as artificial pesticides prove less and less effective. But there is no easy way to find them, other than getting to know and trust the store buyers, who in turn get to know the farmers. Finding a natural-food store that sells local produce might be a first step.

With packaged foods, there are some brand names that have a reputation for dealing in "organic" and "natural" products. Arrowhead Mills products contain no additives, and their labels state that the foods were grown without the use of chemical pesticide or artificial fertilizer. Erewhon products contain no additives, and their labels use the word "organic." However, when I wrote to the company for their explanation of "organic," I received no answer. Arrowhead Mills, on the other hand, sent me lab reports and a detailed answer. Chico-San rice, according to their ads, is grown on the company's own farms without chemical fertilizer or pesticides.

171

With any brand of packaged foods, in supermarkets or natural-food stores, it pays to read the labels. The words "natural" and "organic" mean nothing; but if the label states specifically that there are no additives or pesticides, the company can be legally held to the claim.

Is eating organic food worth all this trouble, not to mention the extra cost? Independent investigators have found no nutritional difference between organically grown and chemically fertilized food. Nevertheless, many people are concerned about chemical fertilizers' long-term tendency to deplete the soil of trace minerals not supplied in the fertilizer. In an age of dwindling fuel supplies, many are becoming alarmed at the amount of energy it takes to produce synthetic fertilizer. More and more people are starting to worry about the pollution of our water supply from pesticide and fertilizer runoff. Former U.S.D.A. scientists who once scorned organic methods now see the need for farmers to reduce their reliance on chemicals. Consumers who share these environmental concerns prefer to eat organically grown food on principle, whether it helps them personally or not.

As for pesticides and additives, we have seen that some additives and many pesticides can cause serious health problems in workers and others exposed to high doses. The only argument is whether the levels now permitted in food are risky enough to offset the benefits claimed by the food industry. People who prefer to play it safe believe that uncontaminated food is worth tracking down.

It is also worth shopping in natural-food stores, just as long as you don't leave your supermarket skepticism behind. The terms "health-food store" and "natural-food store" have as many meanings as the terms "organic food" and "natural food"; but I tend to think of stores that deal mainly in fresh whole food, with a variety of beans and grains and vegetarian items, as natural-food stores. They may or may not try to stock organically grown food. The ones that deal in pills, miracle health products, fad-diet aids, and unconventional cancer preventives are usually called health-food stores.

But when push comes to shove, even the worst type of health-food store might be the only place in town that carries whole-grain foods, organically grown or not. This isn't as true as it once was, because when natural-food stores started to make money, the supermarkets realized that they, too, could benefit from selling whole foods. But in some areas the natural- (or health-) food store is still the only source of whole-wheat spaghetti, bulgur wheat, tahini, miso, tempeh, tofu, and a lot of other real foods that people in other countries have been eating for hundreds or thousands of years. Some natural-food stores carry eggs and milk from humanely treated animals. And some people buy their yogurt, bread, ice cream, or cheese at natural- food stores simply because the brands they carry taste better than the brands sold at supermarkets. But whatever the store, be it Super Mart or Nuts to You, consumer awareness is in order.

Carbohydrate Power: The Vegetarian Jock

O kay, so it's established that most people can get along fine on a vegetarian diet. But doesn't it stand to reason that athletes need meat to keep up their strength and stamina? And that growing athletes need extra protein to build up their muscles?

It might seem reasonable, but in fact that kind of reasoning makes no more sense than our primitive ancestors' habit of eating the hearts and ground-up teeth of lions. Their reasoning was that by ingesting the tough or "hearty" organs they could also take in the animals' courage and strength. By the same reasoning, athletes throughout history have believed that meat, being muscle itself, was a logical source of muscle power. By the 1860s, when the Oxford rowing crew in England stoked up on bread, beer, and undercooked beef and mutton, it was known that muscles and meat were made up of protein. The practice seemed to have scientific support.

Then in 1865, two German scientists went mountain climbing. By measuring the nitrogen in their urine throughout the expedition, they found that the extra exertion did not use up extra protein. These findings were soon confirmed by other experimenters. Their conclusion that muscle exertion uses carbohydrate, not protein, is now regarded as a landmark in nutrition history.

In 1907, another now-famous study at Yale University put

forty-nine men through a series of exercises and found that the vegetarians among them had more than twice the endurance of their flesh-eating counterparts. Since then, countless studies have confirmed these early findings. Scientists and sports doctors now agree that strenuous muscle work is fueled by carbohydrates; that strong muscles are built up by exercise, not extra protein; and that a high-protein diet does not improve athletic performance. What's more, it doesn't matter whether the protein you do get comes from animals or plants.

Of course, this doesn't mean that protein is unimportant. Normal amounts of protein are required for building all body tissue, including muscle. We should also remember that teenage athletes, like other teen-agers, need more protein per pound than adults do. But beyond these normal requirements, more protein does not make more muscle. Only exercise develops muscles.

Why, then, have coaches continued to order steak for their players' pregame meals? Mainly because psychological associations die hard, and the macho image of meat eating has been deeply ingrained. Recently, though, after an information lag of more than a hundred years, the message has been getting through. Sports-medicine authorities are convincing coaches that the fat in steak is especially hard to digest and can cause cramps if it is eaten within a few hours before any heavy exercise. And instead of increasing strength or endurance, extra protein can increase the need to urinate. Nobody needs this in the middle of a game. Worse, doctors warn that high-protein diets can be hard on the kidneys.

If not steak, what are today's athletes fed before a match? At the 1980 Winter Olympics, it was lots of pasta. John Scanlan, who ran the food operation for the games, brought in 16,800 pounds of spaghetti and macaroni. This amounted to 12 pounds of pasta for each athlete there. The reason was pasta's high carbohydrate content, which made it an excellent fuel for all that strenuous activity. For breakfast it was more carbohydrates. USA's Eric Heiden, who won five gold medals in speed skating at the Winter Olympics, told reporters that his breakfast on gold-medal days consisted of corn flakes and raisin toast. Hanni Weizel from Liechtenstein, a double gold medalist in women's skiing events, also had corn flakes for breakfast. True, commercial corn flakes aren't the most nutritious of breakfasts.

175

But this choice shows how the athletes rely on carbohydrates before a contest.

In Boston restaurants on the eve of the Boston Marathon, pasta and pizza are the order of the day. The reason, again, is pasta's carbohydrate power. And in 1980, after eighty-three years of serving beef stew to runners who complete the race, Boston Marathon officials switched to yogurt and fruit-and-nut bars. According to four-time marathon winner Bill Rodgers, "The more you run the more you will want carbohydrates." In his book, *Marathoning,* Rodgers says that "most of the top runners eat large amounts of carbohydrates. . . . Carbohydrates I like are rice, macaroni with cheese, and potatoes. I eat fruits, vegetables, breads, and fruit juices. I also eat so-called junk foods." Among the "junk foods" that Rodgers mentions are pizza and muffins, two good high-carbohydrate foods.

In recent years, it seems that carbohydrates have just about taken the place of proteins as a magic muscle food for athletes. Swimmers, runners, and other athletes at all levels have taken up a practice called carbohydrate loading. The idea is to pack the muscles with carbohydrates just before a big event. First, the athletes exercise strenuously to empty the muscles of the stored carbohydrate glycogen. Then, for three days, they load up on starchy carbohydrates such as spaghetti, rice, bread, and potatoes. In the original plan, a three-day protein and fat diet came before the exercise and the three-day carbohydrate phase. But many athletes found the first phase unnecessary, and sports doctors warned that it could cause kidney damage. Now the exercise and carbohydrate phase alone is in favor.

What do the experts say about all this spaghetti stuffing? Some of the biggest names behind carbohydrate loading have been Dr. David Costill, a leading sports nutritionist at Ball State University in Indiana; Dr. James Counsilman, prominent University of Indiana swimming coach; and Dr. Norman E. Ruddy, medical advisor to America's Davis Cup tennis team. They recommend the practice only for infrequent, special events, and other well-qualified sports doctors consider such deliberate last-minute loading unnecessary at any time. However, no specialist today recommends loading up on meat. In university physical-education departments, the steak-for-strength kick is an idea whose time has come and gone.

Of course, you can still find entire pro football teams eating

176

steak and playing well. Some coaches still go along with the practice for "psychological" reasons. But if you're looking for vegetarian models, you can find them in every sport. In basketball, before he left the game with a foot injury, there was Portland Trailblazer Bill Walton, whom *Sports Illustrated* magazine proclaimed the world's best all-round basketball player. And Walton is no fluke in basketball. When he was playing, two of Walton's teammates and three Cleveland Cavaliers were also vegetarians. In baseball there is St. Louis Cardinal Jim Kaat, who gave up meat in the 1970s and continues pitching to men half his age after a quarter-century in the major leagues. Rodger Doyle, in *The Vegetarian Handbook,* adds a football player (Oakland Raiders linebacker Chip Oliver) and a record-holding weight lifter (Australian Alexander Anderson) to the list of vegetarian athletes. Tennis pro Peter Burwash is so enthusiastic about his meatless diet that he has founded an international organization just for vegetarian professional tennis players. Vic Sussman, author of *The Vegetarian Alternative,* has even come up with a vegetarian marine: Captain Alan Jones, who runs 100 miles a week and set a world record with 17,003 continuous sit-ups.

Every vegetarian's brag list includes Paavo Nurmi, the "Flying Finn," who set twenty world running records between 1920 and 1932. Amby Burfoot, another vegetarian runner, won the Boston Marathon in 1968. In 1956, a good year for vegetarian swimmers, Bill Pickering of Great Britain swam the English Channel in record-breaking time, and seventeen-year-old Murray Rose of Australia won three Olympic gold medals. And for overall achievement, the Vegetarian Cycling and Athletic Club of Great Britain is famous for the number of records its members have set in a variety of sports, including wrestling.

Of course, for every vegetarian athlete you can come up with ten carnivorous counterparts. Turning from steak to sprouts won't turn you into a winner, and going vegetarian might not make a whit of difference to your performance. But the list of vegetarian achievers does confirm what informed nutritionists have known for decades: You don't need meat to win, or to keep on winning year after year.

CHAPTER
21

Fighting Fat: The Vegetarian Weight Watcher

When most people think of weight-reducing diets, they almost automatically think "high protein, low carbohydrate." And when they think of vegetarian food, they think "starchy carbohydrates." But the first of these associations is more a result of fad-diet advertising campaigns than of real knowledge. And we already know that starchy carbohydrates are good, nutritious foods. Once you understand a few basic facts about calories and carbohydrates, it is clear that a sensible vegetarian diet is one of the best ways to lose weight.

First, let's get straight just what a calorie is. It is not a thing or even an amount of fat, but a metric unit that is used to measure heat energy. When the word is used in connection with dieting, it refers to the amount of energy provided by a particular food. It can also measure the amount of energy your body uses to keep warm, to grow, and to move around. What does all this have to do with fat? Very simply, fat is the form in which your body stores the energy it does not use. Whether you gain or lose weight, then, depends on whether you take in more or fewer calories than you use.

Now for those facts:

☐ Ounce for ounce, carbohydrates contain no more calories than do proteins. But fats have more than twice as many calories as do carbohydrates or proteins.

☐ No food is pure protein or pure carbohydrate. As we know, beans and rice contain both, which is as it should be in a healthy diet.

☐ If you don't get enough carbohydrates, the protein you get will be broken down and used for energy. As protein, it is wasted. In effect, then, a low-carbohydrate diet can deprive your body of protein.

☐ Meat is not all protein. Most high-protein meat diets are actually protein and fat diets. For this reason a five-ounce steak, even with the outer fat layer trimmed off, contains more calories than a five-ounce serving of macaroni and cheese. Look it up.

☐ A one-ounce slice of lean, trimmed roast beef (and that would be a very thin slice) contains about sixty calories. With fat, it might well have twice that many. A one-ounce slice of whole-wheat bread (a normal slice) also contains sixty calories.

Does this mean that you could lose more weight on a bread diet than you could on meat? Ounce for ounce, yes. In an experiment at Michigan State University, a group of slightly overweight young men lost weight when bread was added to their meals. Each of the dieters ate twelve slices of bread a day. They lost an average of 12.7 pounds in eight weeks. The diet worked because the bread filled them up so they ate less of the more fattening foods.

Of course, an all-bread diet is no more to be recommended than an all-meat one. But a varied vegetarian diet based on grains is both healthy and effective. A reducing diet in *Laurel's Kitchen,* which is listed with the suggested readings at the end of this book, gets over a third of its calories from whole-grain bread and cereal. Also on the diet are dried beans, skimmed milk, peanut butter, seeds, cooked vegetables, green salad with dressing, and oranges. You've probably noticed that this isn't much different from the normal vegetarian diet that nutritionists recommend for everyone. Weight watchers simply cut out extra fat and cut down on their portions. This makes sense because a diet that leaves out certain classes of foods, or cuts down too far on all foods, is likely to leave you short of energy, protein, and other nutrients.

Another problem with extreme or unusual diets is that they reduce your chances of keeping off the pounds you lose. Most people who go on unrealistic semistarvation diets are so happy

179

to get off them that they go right back to the bad habits that made them fat in the first place. In most cases, simply replacing whole milk with skimmed and soft drinks with fruit juice, and giving up sugary desserts and greasy snacks, will slowly but surely take off fat and keep it off. (The calories in fruit juice can add up, too, though. Try plain old tap water when you are really thirsty.) It's not a good idea, though, to substitute diet soft drinks for those with sugar. As Chapter 11 explains, sugar substitutes aren't much help in losing weight and might have dangers of their own.

Replacing meat with beans and rice is just another way to cut down on fatty foods. Of course, if you are a problem overeater, just giving up meat won't automatically solve your problem. The secret with all these replacements is to avoid substituting extra helpings of permitted foods for those you give up.

Besides the one in *Laurel's Kitchen,* another good vegetarian diet has been developed by the Seventh-day Adventist Dietetic Association. Like "Laurel's," it, too, is made up of grains, legumes, eggs, milk, vegetables, greens, and citrus and other fruit. A vegan version omits the eggs and substitutes fortified soy milk for cows'. Many non-Adventists took up this plan when it was recommended in the *Consumer Guide* book, *Rating the Diets.* The *Consumer Guide* is an independent service that advises shoppers on products and programs. For this book their researchers surveyed scientific studies and expert opinion, then ranked all the popular diets on a scale of four stars to none. To be recommended, a diet had to be effective (that is, really help people lose weight), and it had to be safe (free of any harmful effects). The Seventh-day Adventist diet got a top, four-star rating on both counts.

Diets that were high in protein and low in carbohydrates were ranked lower by *Consumer Guide.* Some were at the bottom of the list. Overall, these diets were judged less effective because they tend to be high in animal fat, and less safe because they can cause weakness, fatigue, and kidney problems. Not all vegetarian diets were approved. One has dieters eating nothing but vegetables except for a half cup of cereal and a half cup of milk a day. It was judged one of the worst plans because of its low protein content. However, the *Consumer Guide* gave a general endorsement to what they called a "planned" vegetarian diet, such as the Seventh-day Adventist program.

Whatever diet plan you follow, you should be aware that teen-agers need extra calories (and extra protein) just for growing. Following a diet made for adults might not give you enough. For example, where many adult women on reducing diets can get by on 1,200 calories a day, teen-age girls are cautioned not to go below 1,500. (Normally, teen-age girls can handle over 2,000 calories, and boys average closer to 3,000.) At the right level, you can lose about a pound a week without endangering your health or feeling dragged out.

But what you eat is only part of the picture. As we've said, the number of calories you need to maintain any given weight depends on the number you use. And the number you use depends to a large extent on how physically active you are. And that brings us to the other side of the weight-losing equation.

Would you believe that high-school girls who are overweight eat less than those who aren't? That was the finding of Jean Mayer, who studied a group of fifty-six girls. Twenty-eight were overweight and twenty-eight were of normal weight. The important difference was that the thinner girls were more active. In another study of younger children, Dr. Mayer found the same pattern. The overweight children ate less but also spent far less time in physical activity. He also found that the fat kids usually started to gain too much in late fall and early winter. Why? Because this was the time that they stopped playing outdoors and began to hole up in front of the TV.

On the whole, says Dr. Mayer, Americans are getting fatter but eating less than they did a few generations ago. The reason is that back in 1900, more people did more physical work. So the best way to lose weight, with or without dieting, is to exercise. Besides burning up calories, exercise also helps regulate your appetite. It doesn't make you eat more, as many nonexercisers believe. Dr. Mayer advises an hour a day of steady, vigorous exercise on work or school days, and three hours on weekends. He suggests doing something you enjoy, such as tennis, swimming, or running. That way you are more likely to stick with it.

If you are already thin, exercise won't make you skinnier. It will probably shape up your body and make you look better, without adding fat. Similarly, if you are already thin, giving up meat need not make you skinnier. Simply substitute the same number of calories from nonmeat foods.

181

CHAPTER
22

Feeding Fido:
The Vegetarian Pet

The vegetarian *what??* We've already talked about whether people are or are not built to be carnivores. We have agreed (I hope) that the important thing is not the shape of our teeth or the length of our intestines, but how we use our human abilities to make our own rational and ethical choices. But if we ask the same questions about our pets, we have to admit that cats and dogs *are* naturally carnivorous. Their bodies are built for that way of life. Their ancestors and cousins in the wild get their nourishment by killing and eating other animals, and this generally works for the overall good of all species involved. Furthermore, when it comes to making choices, cats and dogs have no concept of morality and no tender feelings for the creatures who must die so that they can eat. Outlawing meat for your pet, then, is not respecting the animal's choice but forcing your own choice on it. Even then, you might have a hard time keeping your dog away from the bones in your neighbors' garbage or your cat from stalking birds or mice.

Still, many vegetarians feel justified in applying their own principles to their pets' diets. After all, opening a can of Arfo is not contributing to the balance of nature. It might be supporting practices that are just as cruel as the abuses suffered by cows and chickens raised for human consumption. For example, animal lovers have been shocked by the treatment of the wild mustangs that roam on public land in several of our western states. Ranchers complain that the horses compete with sheep and cattle who graze on the same government-owned land. As a result, the horses have been systematically poisoned, trapped, shot from airplanes, roped and dragged behind trucks, and brutally rounded up. Once removed, many have been sold to pet-food companies for meat. Today such practices are outlawed, and excess horses are humanely rounded up and offered to private families for adoption. Still, a few underground dealers have managed to "adopt" large numbers of mustangs, then sell them off for slaughter. And the fate of unadopted horses is currently uncertain. For this reason, mustang sympathizers are still leery of canned dog food.

Nevertheless, anyone switching a pet from commercial food to a meatless diet should be aware of the risks. Cats' and dogs' nutritional needs are not the same as ours, and cats' are not the same as dogs'. Both dogs and cats need more protein per pound than we do. Kittens and puppies need many times more. Cats need many times as much as dogs do. Without meat, cats risk going blind from a deficiency of taurine. To make taurine, they need substantial supplies of the amino acid methionine. Both cats and dogs also require more fat in their diets than we do, and it is thought that cats might have a specific need for arachidonic acid. This fatty acid is found only in animal fat.

Dogs and cats, especially young growing ones, also need several vitamins and minerals. Dr. Richard Pitcairn, who writes the "Healthy Pet" column for *Prevention* magazine, reports that cats need six times as much calcium as we do. Dogs need sixteen times as much. Cats also need a preformed source of vitamin A, which is present only in meat and animal products.

(Unlike humans, cats can't make vitamin A from carotene.) At the same time, too much of these nutrients in unbalanced supplements can cause poisoning, growth problems, or bone deformities. Pet-food companies, however, pay animal nutritionists to work out formulas that provide them all in the right proportions.

The makers of canned pet foods also go to a good deal of trouble to make their mixtures of meat and other ingredients look like hamburger or beef stew—not that the animals care, but because it makes the owners feel that they are giving their pets a tastier meal. By the same reasoning, vegetarians might feel okay about giving their pets the dry meal or kibble that comes in sacks and doesn't look at all like meat. Dry dog food is in fact made up mostly of vegetable products, as this is cheaper for the companies than using meat. Dry dog food also happens to be cheaper for consumers. What's more, authorities agree that it is better for Fido or Pippa or Mr. Arf than the more expensive canned food or fake burgers that appeal to some pet owners. In *The Dog and Cat Good Food Book,* vet Terri McGinnis has just one reservation: Dry food can be too dry. If the cat-food label shows less than 10 percent fat content, or the dog food less than 8 percent, she recommends adding a tablespoon of vegetable oil to every four-ounce serving of kibble.

But yes, if you check the labels, you will find that dry dog food does have some ground bone, meat, and meat fat mixed in with the other ingredients. Dry cat food has even more animal parts, usually chicken by-products and ground fish. If you can't accept this, you can keep a healthy lacto-ovo-vegetarian dog with some care and a little help from your vet. (We'll talk about cats later.)

Just what do you feed a vegetarian dog? Most plans call for a cooked egg, a cup of whole milk, and one or two tablespoons each of vegetable oil and nutritional yeast at every daily meal. The yeast supplies B vitamins, and the oil helps meet the dog's need for fat. Some adult dogs have trouble digesting milk, but without meat they might need it. If milk gives your pet diarrhea or other digestive problems, wait until he or she is back to normal and then try yogurt or creamed cottage cheese. If this doesn't work, your vet might recommend a fortified soy milk. (For new puppies and kittens, there are special formulas designed to take the place of mother's milk.)

184

To these basics, vegetarian dog owners add moistened bread and leftover or specially cooked cereal, beans, and vegetables. Some advise mashing as well as cooking the beans and vegetables, as dogs and cats can't digest vegetables the way we can. (In the wild, they get them at least partly predigested by their prey.) Remember, though, that vegetables are extras for dogs and cats. A diet of *all* leftovers, from vegetarian meals that are perfectly good for you, probably won't fill your dog's higher protein and fat needs. It almost certainly won't be enough for a puppy, or for a cat or kitten. Leftovers also turn out to be expensive. Consciously or not, families usually start buying more groceries to feed that extra mouth, or buying lunch for themselves instead of eating their own dinner leftovers. Buying kibble for the canine family member is a lot easier and cheaper.

As you have probably guessed already, meatless diets for cats are usually not recommended. We've seen that cats need even more fat and protein than dogs do, and they might need other substances that only meat can supply. Many cat owners claim that their pets thrive on vegetarian diets. These consist of wheat germ, oats, soy protein, beans, lentils, yeast, milk, cheese, eggs, cooked nuts, and chopped vegetables.

On the other hand, Dr. McGinnis says that meat, fish, eggs, and dairy products should make up 75 percent of a cat's diet. According to Dr. Pitcairn, a vegetarian himself, cats should have meat or fish twice a week and cod-liver oil daily. The vets I talked to at The Cat Practice in New York City also believe that meat is necessary. One staff member there told me that he, too, is a vegetarian, but he recognizes that "cats are carnivores, and that's that."

With all these experts advising against vegetarianism for cats, it would seem safer to feed them some meat. A cautious pet owner would probably not put too much faith in what scientists call the "anecdotal evidence" of vegetarian cat owners. Who knows how long the cats will thrive? Or how many supplement their diets with birds and mice on the sly? Or whether yours might be the one who turns up with a deficiency? Do your cat a favor and wait until a controlled, long-term study backs up the anecdotes. Or think about getting a rabbit or hamster, who will thrive on vegetables.

Macrobiotics: The Vegetarian Fringe

L ife is simple for an infant, who seems to find total happiness in a meal of warm milk on a warm lap. Our problems become more complicated as we grow older, but some of us still seek to solve them all with a magic diet. Health-food stores abound in books and pamphlets promoting mythical vitamins, mega-doses of minerals, special formulas, simplified or complicated diets, or even fasting in a prescribed manner. Following their programs, the authors claim, can bring you better health, longer life, more energy, a sense of well-being, or even spiritual peace.

Throughout the long history of food fads, the most extravagant claims for a product or diet have been the least likely to hold up. Yet it is usually the sweeping claims that win the most fervent following. People have wasted away on bizarre diets, sure that sticking with the regimen represented their only hope for recovery. Like other true believers who feel that the Word has been revealed to them, food zealots only become defensive when their programs are questioned. If they feel better after switching to a miracle diet, they give credit to the diet. If they feel worse, they have a ready-made explanation. Years of bad eating, they believe, have built up poisons in their systems. Good eating is now flushing these poisons into their bloodstreams. Sticking with the diet will eventually flush them out.

Macrobiotics is one system of eating that has attacted both

establishment outrage and flocks of true believers. Some macrobiotic eaters have wasted away on brown rice; others have flourished on a delectable variety of natural foods. The system has been attacked in medical journals for causing disease and death, but hailed in the *New York Times* for being sane and wholesome. One doctor called it a "killer" in 1971 and "healthy" in 1978. Several people, including a conservative medical doctor, say they have been cured of cancer by following a macrobiotic diet. Other doctors maintain that this fake cure only keeps people away from conventional treatment that could save their lives.

What is macrobiotics, anyway, and where did it come from? It has been called a vegetarian diet, but most vegetarian leaders go out of their way to condemn it. Its founders called it "Zen Macrobiotics" and claimed it was the traditional diet of Zen Buddhist monks, but today's Zen Buddhists say there is no connection between Zen and macrobiotics. The macrobiotic system uses certain ancient Oriental beliefs as a starting point, but most of it seems to be the invention of a twentieth-century Japanese named George Ohsawa.

The term "macrobiotics," according to Ohsawa, is based on the two Greek words *macro* and *bio,* which he translated to mean "great life." The system itself, he maintained, was based on the ancient Oriental concept of yin and yang, the two basic forces at the heart of all reality. According to this ancient Chinese philosophy, everything in the universe is guided by two opposite but complementary forces. Yin is the passive female force. Yang is positive, active, and masculine. In Chinese folk medicine, health depends on maintaining a proper balance between yin and yang within the body.

For Ohsawa, striking the right balance was all a matter of eating the right foods. He set up a "macrobiotic table of foods," which listed all foods in order from very yin to very yang. The most yin foods, according to him, are sugar, potatoes, tomatoes, eggplant, and most fruits. Meat, however, is very yang. Diseases, he says, are caused by extremes of one or the other in the diet. His list of yin diseases ranged from cancer, diabetes, and heart disease to dandruff, baldness, and bedwetting. To avoid them, people should avoid very yin foods.

As for what people *should* eat, for Ohsawa that pretty much boiled down to one "principal food," brown rice, which was supposed to contain a perfect balance of yin and yang. This was the most controversial part of Ohsawa's program. He didn't tell people to suddenly stop eating everything but brown rice, but he did set that up as a goal to work toward. To climb the ladder from the "lowest" to the "highest diet," followers should gradually give up the less balanced foods. First salad, fruit, and dessert should be eliminated, then meat, and finally vegetables. At last the dieter reached diet number seven, the ultimate diet. Through this he might also hope to attain the highest levels of physical, mental, and spiritual well-being. Diet number seven consisted of nothing but cereal foods, preferably brown rice, with a little sea salt and sesame seed sprinkled on top.

It might be hard to understand why so many people took these ideas seriously. Undoubtedly, Ohsawa's timing was right. He came to America in 1960, a time of growing interest in more authentic forms of Eastern philosophy. The word "Zen" in his book title, *Zen Macrobiotics,* attracted young people who saw the spiritual values in Zen Buddhism as an alternative to the materialism they were rejecting in our own culture. Some of the same people were becoming fed up with the so-called American way of eating, which was not traditionally American at all but a result of food-industry practices that had been creeping up on us for decades. Ohsawa was an early enemy of refined and "industrialized" foods, and that appealed to young people committed to living naturally. Finally, these attitudes probably combined with an all-too-human longing for someone to come along with all the answers.

Whatever the reasons, by the mid 1960s, thousands of American young people were following Ohsawa's system and working their way up his ladder. One of these new macrobiotics was a twenty-four-year-old woman in Clifton, New Jersey. In February 1965, Beth Ann Singer went on Ohsawa's brown rice diet. She grew weaker and weaker but refused to see a doctor. "Be your own doctor," Ohsawa had written. By November she was dead. A New Jersey grand jury that investigated the case found the cause of death to be starvation due to her brown rice diet. The jury also blamed macrobiotics for several other cases of severe malnutrition.

After this one macrobiotic death made headlines, more bad publicity followed. Doctors warned against the diet in medical journals, blaming it for scurvy, anemia, protein deficiency, calcium deficiency, kidney failure, and starvation. The only actual case they could cite was Beth Ann Singer. Nevertheless, the charges were repeated in an article in the *Ladies' Home Journal,* later reprinted in the *Reader's Digest.* The article, written by a well-known Harvard University nutritionist named Dr. Frederick Stare, was dramatically titled "This Diet Can Kill."

Following all this furor, macrobiotic leaders began to play down the all-brown-rice diet. The newer macrobiotic books, though still based on yin and yang, recognized that there are such things as vitamins and minerals. From the movement's cookbooks and restaurants emerged a macrobiotic cuisiné for gourmets, blending the Japanese influence into the new health-food melting pot. Prominent people in the arts became macrobiotic and seemed to thrive on the diet. In July 1978, the *New York Times* interviewed several people who said they had been macrobiotic for years and felt much better than before. Most ate whole grains, beans, certain vegetables, and some fish and fruit. Red meat and eggs were out of bounds, and bread and dairy products reserved for special treats. To them, macrobiotics was basically a matter of achieving a proper yin-yang balance among the foods they ate. All of them disowned the all-brown-rice diet, but they still considered Ohsawa's yin-yang balance a key to health and happiness.

The same *New York Times* article also pointed to a Harvard Medical School study of the macrobiotic community in Boston. The Harvard doctors found that people who follow the macrobiotic diet have lower than average blood cholesterol levels and blood pressure. Both "lows" are definite health advantages. Dr. Stare, the same nutritionist who had warned that the diet "can kill," was now quoted as saying "the macrobiotic diet as we've known it for the past three or four years is a healthy one, not much different from a typical vegetarian diet. And you know as well as I do that meat isn't necessary." It seemed that Dr. Stare's original warning had been directed against the all-brown-rice diet, which the new macrobiotics no longer endorsed.

It certainly seemed that macrobiotics was having the last laugh. Many experts now agree with Ohsawa's advice against refined and "manufactured" foods, sugar, dyed foods, alcohol, and tobacco. As the *New York Times* declared, the current macrobiotic diet is "closer to the Senate Dietary Goals than the typical American diet high in sugar, processed foods, and animal fats."

So that settled it, right? Not quite. Just when readers of the *New York Times* were deciding that macrobiotics had either cleaned up its act or been misunderstood all along, another study was going on in Boston. The results were published in the February 1979 *American Journal of Diseases of Children,* another publication for doctors. Dr. Johanna Dwyer reported finding "multiple nutritional deficiencies" and several cases of rickets due to vitamin-D and calcium deficiency among strict vegetarian macrobiotic children. (No cases were found among vegetarian children who drank milk.) One baby had died, and Dr. Dwyer blamed the death on the strict macrobiotic diet.

Once more, doctors warned that the macrobiotic ban on fruits and dairy products could cause vitamin and mineral deficiencies, especially during the growing years. They still objected to the macrobiotic practice of drinking very little water, and none at all with meals. This "rests the kidneys," Ohsawa wrote. But doctors say it has the opposite effect. Too little liquid can lead to painful kidney stones and serious kidney damage. Dr. Stephen Appelbaum, a psychiatrist studying alternative cancer therapies, tried the diet himself and reported that after eighteen months he was fifteen pounds underweight and generally weaker and less energetic than before. He found that he needed more sleep and was able to do less work.

Most of all, doctors protest the macrobiotic doctrine that all disease is caused by eating too much yin or yang and that the only real cure is a change in diet. Ohsawa's successor, Michiu Kushi, still preaches that treating diseases, as doctors do, is only treating symptoms. His remedies might be harmless, but they can keep people from seeking needed medical care. In a few well-publicized cases, there seems to be no doubt that cancer patients have made amazing recoveries on macrobiotic diets. However, the leaders will not say how many patients have tried the diet without being helped. As for those who did recover, most doctors attribute their cures to the power of faith. "We still don't know how profoundly our mental attitudes can affect our health," one doctor said. "The shrine at Lourdes is full of crutches left behind by cripples who came seeking miracles and walked away healed. Maybe one man's miracle is another man's macrobiotics."

And so it goes. The arguments for and against the diet will probably continue as long as there are people who call themselves macrobiotic. But who of all these doctors and dieters is to be believed? The answer is, probably, all of them. If there is one accurate definition of macrobiotics, it might be the one given to a friend of my son. David went macrobiotic in high school, but after a few years without meat, milk, eggs, fruit, much liquid, and a whole list of vegetables, he was skinny and weak and seemed to be just dragging himself around. Finally he went for help to the macrobiotic center in Boston. There, as I'm told, he was advised that "macrobiotics means many things to many people. For you right now, it means eating whatever you want, whenever you want, and as much as you want."

As David was lucky enough to discover, today's macrobiotic leaders try to adapt Ohsawa's teachings to individual needs. Followers who do the same, at least the adults among them, can enjoy a wholesome natural diet. But young people still read Ohsawa's books and follow his advice without having anyone tell them that "macrobiotics means many things to many people." Kushi's own books draw the same crackpot connections between foods and diseases. (Crossed eyes, Kushi says, are caused by too much inward-turning yin foods, whereas expansive yang foods cause the eyes to turn out. If one eye turns out and one in, the patient has eaten too much of both extremes.)

Followers of the macrobiotic regimen often refer to the "magic goggles" or "magic glasses" of yin and yang. This is probably the greatest danger of the macrobiotic mystique. Like the magic glasses of any other total system, these tend to reduce everything in life to a simple formula and to screen out all evidence that doesn't fit the formula. Just as serious as their effect on health, magic glasses can prevent their wearers from trying out different ways of looking at reality. When that happens, magic glasses have become blinders.

PART
 4

Vegetarian Cooking

CHAPTER

24

Getting Started

Y ou don't have to do a lot of cooking to prepare a vegetarian meal. You can make a main dish of canned lentil soup, frozen lasagna, or instant soyburgers and still be at least as well off as people who live the same way on hot dogs, canned hash, and frozen beef pie. But vegetarians who enjoy food and like to experiment have a world of meatless cooking to choose from.

This book can only offer a glimpse of the ethnic traditions and new ideas available to vegetarian cooks. The possibilities range from tempeh, the Indonesian soy food unknown here ten years ago, to pasta dishes, well known to nonvegetarians because they weren't adopted here as substitutes for meat; they simply attained perfection without it. If this sampling induces you to look further into Chinese, Indian, Mexican, or Italian cooking, you can get the advanced course straight from the experts by checking out of your library some of the ethnic classics recommended in the cookbook section at the end of the book.

My first step in narrowing this down was to limit the list mostly to main dishes that you can use as alternatives to meat meals. You might find it odd that there are no recipes for desserts or sweets included, but for me that was the easiest category to eliminate. The first reason is entirely personal: Except for ice cream once in a while in the summer, my family does not eat sweets and does not miss them. We would rather have a second helping of lentil soup or spaghetti sauce than a slice of cake or pie. Secondly, even if I haven't persuaded you to do it our way, you'll have no trouble finding dessert recipes. Most cookbooks for young people have more sweets and snacks than anything else.

Other items you will not find here are soyburgers, bean cutlets, or any such meat analogs, as they are called in the industry. If you really don't want to eat meat, why eat fake meat? Also missing are health-food supplements that have no place in any culture's natural diet. Nutritional yeast, for example, is a healthful additive and any readers who doubt the adequacy of their diets should feel free to sprinkle it on whatever real or junk food they do consume. But nonmeat diets can be healthful without such fortifiers.

ON SHORTCUTS VS. STARTING FROM SCRATCH

At some time or other everyone who cooks on an everyday basis has to make some compromises between starting from scratch for better flavor, texture, and nutrition and using some prepared items to save time. Where you draw the line will be up to you. Where these recipes call for a tomato sauce, an appropriate recipe is given; but you can always substitute a commercial spaghetti sauce. I recommend using dried beans and chick peas because they are cheaper than canned ones, have more texture, and are uncontaminated by lead and additives. But for those who choose to use canned beans, equivalent amounts are given on page 210. On the other hand, I don't include any piecrust recipes. You can buy a frozen piecrust at the supermarket (consider it just an edible package) or you can find a recipe in any standard cookbook. Crusts from whole-wheat flour are favored by nutrition-conscious vegetarians but are harder to make, which could discourage beginning cooks. Again, it's up to you.

Vegetarians also differ in their strictness about optimal nutrition. Two of these recipes call for cream and butter, which health-food purists wouldn't touch. I feel that these foods should be used sparingly, but needn't be banished altogether.

For those who have never done much cooking, some of these recipes might seem long. This is partly because I have tried to go into enough detail so that beginners will know exactly what to do. But it is also true that some of the dishes take time to prepare. They are not tricky or difficult, but the chopping alone can get to be a job. Nevertheless, I feel that the results justify the effort, and I am confident that once you get into cooking, you will enjoy the process as well. You might want to save the more time-consuming dishes for occasions when you have a partner—a friend or family member—to work with you. We usually cook together in our family, which we feel makes the job easier and more fun than taking turns. If you are cooking for yourself alone, you can often make enough for two or more servings when you do have the time, and reheat left-overs when you don't. Some dishes can be partly prepared in advance, then finished one serving at a time.

The following chapters are designed to give you some basic cooking methods, a few special recipes, and some ideas for variations. The variation ideas are less precise than the basic recipes; the idea is to be flexible. Once you've tried some of these, you'll be ready to try other variations of your own. Not every departure from a recipe will turn out equally well, but then that is what makes cooking an adventure.

SPECIAL EQUIPMENT FOR VEGETARIAN COOKING

Cast-iron skillet: I wouldn't want to say that you can't be a vegetarian cook without a cast-iron skillet, but if any piece of equipment can be labeled essential, this would be my nomination. This durable old-fashioned frying pan is excellent for holding and distributing heat, and it also boosts your iron intake. The size labeled 'twelve-inch (actually it measures ten inches across the bottom) is best for family cooking; a smaller one would be handier for cooking one portion at a time. Iron pots do rust, so they should be cleaned and dried right after the meal. Also, acidic foods such as tomato sauce should not sit around in iron pots *after* the heat has been turned off, because they might pick up an iron flavor.

Some cooks insist that iron skillets should never be washed, but I have never had any trouble washing mine by hand. The trick is to dry it right away. If an iron skillet does begin to rust or discolor, simply spread some oil on the surface, heat it on

197

the stove until the oil begins to smoke, and then (when you can handle it) wipe with a paper towel until all the oil is absorbed. New iron pots that are not precured should have this treatment before they are used.

Vegetable steamer: Also on the "must" list, this collapsible metal basket sits over a small amount of water in a covered saucepan. The water should not come up past the bottom of the steamer. Steamers cost under five dollars and go a long way toward preserving the flavor and nutrients in fresh or frozen vegetables.

Four-sided hand grater: This is for grating, shredding, or thin-slicing vegetables, cheese, and some spices.

Chopping tools: Vegetarian cooking involves so much chopping of onions, peppers, carrots, and other vegetables that it is important to invest in good-quality cutting knives. Paring knives have many uses, but for heavy chopping an eight-inch or even ten-inch blade is more efficient. Both the French chef's knife and the cleaver, which is similar to the Chinese chopping knife, are useful. Chefs used to recommend carbon-steel blades rather than stainless, as they can be sharpened to a finer edge, but today's top-quality, high-carbon stainless blades are very good, too. We use some of each. Nonstainless carbon blades will rust, so they should be wiped right after using, washed by hand, and not allowed to sit in a wet sink. In good strong knives, the metal from the blade extends straight through the length of the handle.

198

Remember, too, that the best knives will not cut if they are not kept sharp. There are all kinds of fancy electrical sharpeners, but a plain carborundum stone works well. This tool costs less than a dollar at any housewares department, and it is not a big job to slap a knife up against it every now and then.

Speaking of fancy machines, if your family has a food processor, go ahead and use it to cut down your chopping time. But cooks have chopped for centuries without them.

HOW TO CHOP WITH A KNIFE

Onions: Cut off the ends and peel the onion, then cut it in half lengthwise and put the halves on a cutting board, flat side down. For each half, first hold the knife parallel to the board and make some lengthwise slices, cutting toward the root but not all the way through. (You don't want the onion to fall into pieces yet.) Then hold the knife so the blade faces down toward the onion and again slice lengthwise, up to but not through the root end. Finally, with the blade still facing down, make crosswise slices. The onion will now fall apart as you go.

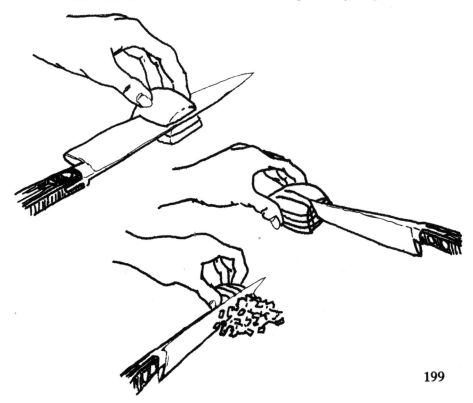

199

Zucchini and fat carrots can be chopped in essentially the same way.

Green bell peppers: Wash pepper and remove the stem. Cut the pepper in half, and remove the seeds and white inner membranes. Cut the halves into thin strips, then bunch the strips and cut crosswise.

Garlic: Remove a clove from a head of fresh garlic. Smash it flat with the side of a cleaver. Then discard the peel and slice the fibers crosswise.

Caution: When holding the vegetables to be sliced or chopped, make sure the tips of your fingers are tucked back so that they are not sliced, too.

ON INGREDIENTS

Parsley: Use fresh parsley, preferably the broadleaf Italian kind, which has more flavor.

Garlic: Any dish worth cooking is worth chopping garlic for; and once you get used to fresh garlic you will prefer it to the powder. Worse than garlic powder are garlic salt and other salt-seasoning combinations. Why pay for a manufacturer to mix them together when you can choose your own fresh combinations to suit each dish?

Peppercorns: Buy whole peppercorns and grind your own pepper as you use it. You will notice the difference in freshness and find that pepper actually has flavor.

Nutmeg: Whole nutmeg is best. Keep it in a closed jar and grate what you need as you use it.

Ginger: You guessed it. The powdered ginger you find on supermarket spice shelves is nothing like fresh ginger, which is stocked in the produce department. This knobby, tan-colored "root," actually a rhizome, or underground stem, is also sold in Indian and Oriental groceries. It can be kept in plastic in the refrigerator and chopped or grated just before using. A one-inch cube of ginger makes about one tablespoon chopped.

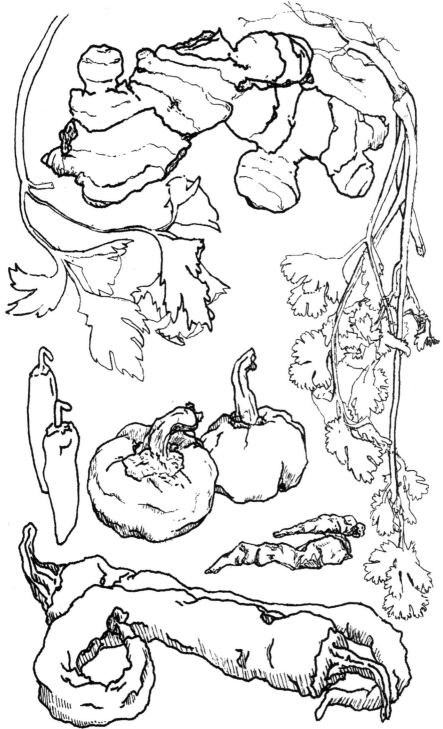

Basil, oregano, thyme, sage, and rosemary: Fresh basil is delicious but generally available only in late summer. Otherwise, unless you grow your own, you will probably have to buy these herbs dried. But try to get the dried leaves rather than the powdered form. They taste fresher, especially if you rub them between your hands just before using.

Ground cumin, coriander, and turmeric: These aromatic spices are used in both Indian and Hispanic dishes. They can be found in ethnic markets and some supermarkets. (They are also the main ingredients in curry powder, a sort of all-purpose imitation of the many different spice combinations that Indian cooks mix up for each dish.) Try to buy small quantities at a time to ensure freshness, and keep these and other spices in sealed jars.

Tahini: This spread, made from sesame seeds as peanut butter is made from peanuts, is sold in natural-food stores and Middle Eastern markets.

Soy products: Tofu, tempeh, miso, shoyu, and tamari are all explained in the section on soybeans, pages 152–5.

Fresh coriander, also called cilantro or Chinese parsley: This leafy plant looks like Italian parsley except that it comes with roots attached. Use only the leaves, and wash well. This herb gives a distinctive flavor to Mexican bean dishes and Oriental vegetable dishes. There is no substitute.

Chile peppers: Hot chile peppers are used in the foods of Mexico, the Caribbean, India, China, and southern Italy. Worldwide, there are about two hundred varieties of chile peppers, each with its own distinctive flavor. Serranos and jalapeños are among the better-known Mexican chiles. In many parts of this country, however, we are lucky to find one or two kinds of fresh hot green peppers, usually just called "hots" or "chiles."

Because the "hotness" of fresh chiles varies greatly, no recipe can tell you how much to put in. To test a chile, remove the seeds (the hottest part); then, with a glass of water handy, put a tiny sliver of pepper on your tongue and taste before swallowing. (Some peppers seem to burn the tongue, others work on the throat.) And be sure to wash your hands before wiping your eyes! If the pepper seems very hot, add only a very small amount at a time until you get used to cooking with chiles. If it's not hot enough, throw in some or all of the seeds. If you can't buy fresh chiles, or if the ones available are duds, canned Mexican chiles are worth using. Powdered cayenne pepper or dried red-pepper flakes will also make a dish "hot," but will not have the flavor of fresh or canned chiles.

ON COOKING WITH OIL

Many of the recipes included here call for cooking in vegetable oil. Safflower oil, corn oil, and peanut oil are all good all-purpose oils with mild flavors. It is also good to keep some of the richer-tasting olive oil on hand to flavor Italian dishes and salad dressings. The Chinese also add a little sesame oil to stir-fried dishes for its special nutty flavor.

When frying or deep-frying with oil, be sure to use caution. Handle the food with tongs and avoid leaning over the pot. (If you wear glasses, so much the better.) Never splash water on cooking oil; it will spit back. Much oil is required for deep-frying, but it can be reused two or three times. Wait for the oil to cool before handling it, then line a funnel with a coffee filter or cheesecloth and pour the oil through the funnel into a jar or bottle.

It is important to keep the oil at the right temperature when cooking. To test the temperature, drop a tiny bit of water onto the oil. If it sizzles, the oil is hot enough to add the food. Do not crowd the pot with food, or the oil will not stay hot. On the other hand, never let the oil get hot enough to smoke.

To *sauté* chopped vegetables is to cook them in a frying pan in a small amount of oil or butter until they are soft and clear but not browned.

HOW MANY OUNCES IS A MEDIUM EGGPLANT?

Some beginning cooks have anxiety attacks trying to figure out whether the size of the vegetables in their refrigerators matches up with the recipe's call for one medium carrot, two small zucchini, or whatever. The more experience you have with vegetables, the more you'll be able to estimate, for example,

203

whether the one large zucchini you have is about equal to two small ones. Meanwhile, don't panic. None of the recipes in this book are so delicate that a little more or less of any one vegetable will spoil the balance.

BEFORE YOU BEGIN

It is a good idea to read through the entire recipe before you go shopping for ingredients and again before you start to cook.

Have all chopped ingredients and spices measured out and ready to add before you start cooking.

You are not doing anyone a favor by preparing your own meals or the family meal and leaving a kitchen full of dirty pots and dishes. It saves work for yourself later to clean up as you go along. If you are preparing a meal that must be assembled first, then cooks untended for twenty minutes or more, use that time to get a start on the dishes.

Get in the habit of tasting as you proceed. Be conservative at first with salt, chiles, and seasonings, allowing time for the flavors to be absorbed before adding more.

CHAPTER
25

Basic Grain
and Bean Cooking

•REAL WHOLE-WHEAT BREAD

The best way to learn to make bread is to go through the process with someone who knows how. For a whole course in one book, try the *Tasajari Bread Book,* which describes the process in detail. This recipe follows the general method laid out in that book. It's a hearty, substantial whole-grain bread. Don't expect it to turn out light and fluffy. It takes 6 or 7 hours to make, but most of that is waiting time you can use for other purposes.

7–8 cups whole-wheat flour
1½ tbsp active dry yeast
3 cups warm (not hot) water
⅓ cup blackstrap molasses

1 tsp salt
⅓ cup corn or safflower oil
½ cup soy flour

To test the water temperature, splash a few drops against the inside of your wrist. It should feel neither hot nor cold. Pour the water into a large slope-sided bowl. Stir the molasses into the water. Sprinkle the yeast on top. In a minute or two you will see a mass of bubbly froth rise to the surface.

Then shake in 4 cups of whole-wheat flour, a cup at a time. Stir thoroughly after each cup, using a wooden spoon. Then give the mixture 100 strokes with the spoon. Form into a ball.

205

Cover the bowl with a damp dish towel. Put the dough in a warm place (about 100°F), such as an oven with a pilot light. Let rise for 45 minutes, or until it more or less doubles in size. This is the "sponge."

Add the salt and oil to the "sponge." Stir it in gently, folding the batter in toward the center as you stir. Shake in the remaining flour a cup, then ½ cup, at a time. Continue to stir. Be careful not to break the fibers in the dough. When thoroughly mixed, the batter should end up fairly dry on the surface and should come away from the sides of the bowl as you stir. This usually takes about 3 cups but might need more.

Rub a little flour onto a wooden countertop or a large wooden board for kneading. To knead, push the heels of your hands into the bread and push down and away from you until the end nearest you starts to rise off the surface. Rotate a quarter turn, fold the dough in half toward you, and push again. Continue for 5 or 10 minutes. If the surface becomes sticky, rub some more flour on. While kneading, the dough should always look smooth. If breaking or stretching fibers appear, you are being too rough.

After the first few minutes start sprinkling the soy flour on the wooden surface and kneading it in. Continue until the dough is fairly dry and springs back rather quickly when you press it with your thumb. (You might not use all the soy flour.)

Coat the mixing bowl with oil and rub the dough in the oil. Turn so the creased side is down and cover again with a dampened towel. Return to the warm spot for another 45 minutes until the dough doubles in bulk. Then punch it down by repeatedly pushing your fists firmly into the dough until it collapses or falls back. Re-cover and return to the warm spot for another 45 minutes, until it doubles once more.

Punch down again and divide the dough in two. Let sit for 5 minutes. Then knead each piece for 5 push-turn-fold sequences.

Coat 2 bread pans with oil and push each loaf into a pan. Make 3 slashes on the top of each. Let the loaves rise in the pans for about 25 minutes, until they have risen about an inch above the pans.

Bake in a preheated 425°F oven for 15 minutes. Reduce heat to 350°F and bake for another 35–40 minutes. Remove from pan and tap the bottom. If it feels hollow, it is done. If you are not sure, slice it down the middle. If it's still doughy inside, return to the oven until done.

Note: For a crustier loaf, but one that is not as conveniently shaped for sandwiches, bake the loaves on oiled pizza pans or cookie sheets instead of in bread pans.

• HOW TO COOK RICE
Portions
When rice is used as a side dish, start with 1 cup of uncooked rice for 4 people. For a rice and bean meal you might use twice that much: about ½ cup rice per person.

Method I
For every cup of rice you are using, bring 2 cups of water to a boil in a large, heavy saucepan. Without stirring, add the rice and ½ teaspoon salt. When the water returns to the boil, turn the heat to low. Cover the pot and continue cooking without lifting the lid. White rice takes 20 minutes to cook and brown rice takes 45 minutes.

When the allotted cooking time is up, remove the pot from the heat and let stand, still covered, to make sure that all the water is absorbed. This will take another 5 minutes for white rice, 10 or 15 for brown.

Method II
For every cup of rice you are using, heat 1 tablespoon oil over medium heat in a large, heavy saucepan. Then add the rice and salt and cook for about 3 minutes, stirring. Cook until the rice turns clear and then dull. (White rice will turn clear and then chalky white. Brown rice will also turn shiny, then dull.) Do not let brown.

Add 2 cups boiling water. Do not stir. Cover the pot, turn heat to low, and continue cooking according to the timing given in method I.

This method keeps the rice kernels from sticking together during cooking and makes a fluffier, less "starchy" rice.

• VEGETARIAN RISOTTO
Risotto and pilaf are names for rice-based dishes that can be as simple as rice with onions or as complete as a balanced full

meal. To make risotto, follow method II for cooking rice but add an extra tablespoon of oil. Before adding the rice, sauté about ¼ cup finely chopped onion until it is soft and clear but not brown. Then add the rice and proceed as in method II.

Variations

The amounts given here are for 1 cup of dry rice. For an ample main dish for one person, use ⅓ to ½ cup of rice and cut all other ingredients in half.

☐ Chop up to ¼ cup of carrots and celery and sauté along with the onion.

☐ For flavor, add a bay leaf, 2 or 3 sprigs of parsley, ⅛ teaspoon thyme, ¼ teaspoon salt, and a shake of pepper before cooking the rice.

☐ Begin with any or all of the above variations. When the rice has cooked, stir in ½ package thawed frozen peas and ¼ cup freshly grated Parmesan cheese. Re-cover and let sit 5 to 15 minutes, until peas are heated through.

☐ Follow the above variation but use 2 tablespoons pine nuts instead of the peas.

☐ For a vegan alternative, mash 4 ounces of tofu and add it to the rice in place of the peas and Parmesan. Season with ½ teaspoon curry powder, or make your own curry using small amounts of powdered cumin, coriander, and turmeric.

☐ After you sauté the onion, stir in ½ teaspoon curry powder or a mixture of powdered cumin, coriander, and turmeric. Then add the rice, with 2 tablespoons sunflower seeds. When the rice has cooked, stir in 2 tablespoons raisins. Re-cover and let sit 15 minutes. (This is best with brown rice.)

•BULGUR WHEAT

For each cup of bulgur wheat you are using, bring 2 cups of water to a boil and add the wheat and ¼ to ½ teaspoon salt. Turn heat to low, cover, and cook 15 minutes. Remove from heat and let stand, covered, another 10 minutes. This amount serves 3 or 4 for a side dish, 2 as the basis for a full meal.

Bulgur wheat goes well with chick peas or with lentils. You can also make a bulgur pilaf using any of the ideas given for risotto above. For other recipes using bulgur wheat, see the tofu ideas on page 212, the bulgur-stuffed peppers on page 224, and the tabouli salad on page 246.

•MILLET

Cook millet for 15 minutes as you would bulgur wheat. Or, mix a small amount of millet into bulgur wheat or brown rice to give the grain a nuttier texture.

•CORN BREAD

1½ cups stone-ground cornmeal	2 tbsp honey
½ cup whole-wheat flour	1 egg, beaten
1 tsp salt	2 tbsp vegetable oil
2 tsp baking powder	1½ cups milk

Preheat oven to 425°F.

Mix the four dry ingredients in a large bowl. Mix the four wet ingredients and stir them into the dry. Using a rubber spatula, turn the mixture into a greased 8-inch-square baking pan.

Cook 20–25 minutes.

Variations

☐ Before baking, stir in a cup of grated cheddar cheese *or* a grated carrot.

☐ If you prefer a sweeter corn bread, use 4 tablespoons honey instead of 2.

•HOW TO COOK DRIED BEANS

Navy, pea, great northern, Michigan, kidney, pinto, garbanzo, pink, red, or black: Whatever the bean and whatever the sauce you eventually mix in, the basic preparation is the same.

Portions

For a rice and bean meal, 1 pound of beans will serve 4 hungry people. In soups and other combination dishes, 1 pound of beans will feed 6 people. (One pound of dried beans measures about 2¼ cups and makes about 6 cups of cooked beans.)

Preparation

1. Rinse the dried beans in a colander and pick out any foreign

209

matter such as small pebbles or chunks of dirt. Put the beans in a large pot. Flameproof earthenware is best, but any large cooking pot will do. Add 3 cups of water for every cup of beans. (For 1 pound of beans, add 6 cups of water.)

2. Bring to a boil and cook uncovered for 2 minutes. Remove from heat. Cover the pot and let sit for one hour.

3. When the hour is up, return the pot just to a boil, then turn the heat to very low and cook until tender. Add more water during cooking if needed to keep the beans just covered. Do not add salt until the end of the cooking period.

A Note on Soaking

If it fits your schedule better, you can put the beans in water before leaving for school in the morning and cook them that evening. You then skip step 2.

If you are afraid that beans will give you gas, soak them for several hours in about a gallon of water per pound. Discard the water and add 6 cups of fresh water to cook.

Today's beans don't have to be soaked at all, but they will cook faster if they are. Also, unsoaked beans tend to separate from their skins during cooking.

Lentils and split peas do not need presoaking of any kind.

Bean Cooking Time

Cooking time varies. You just have to test the beans to decide when they are done. Some cooks blow on a bean, and if the skin comes off they know the beans are done. These are very approximate cooking times:

lentils	30–45 minutes
white beans	1½ hours
black beans	1½ hours
kidney beans	2 hours
soybeans	3 hours
chick peas (garbanzos)	3 hours

Canned Beans

Several recipes in this book call for cooked dried beans. If you choose to use canned beans for convenience, use 3 cans to equal 1 pound dried beans. One can equals 2 cups of cooked beans. But remember, dried beans cost less than canned ones, take up less storage space, have a better texture, and are not contaminated by lead, salt, or other additives.

•IDEAS FOR SEASONING BEANS

If you are cooking for yourself alone, you can cook ½ pound or a pound of beans ahead of time and refrigerate them. Each night, reheat one serving and eat it with bread, rice, corn bread, or tortillas. A salad or green vegetable completes the meal. You can add seasoning to the beans when cooking them, or when reheating. The amounts of vegetables and seasonings given below are for 1 pound of beans. For seasoning single servings, start with very small amounts of spices, then gradually add more to your taste. You will soon get to know how much seasoning you like.

A basic sauce for beans:

In 2 tablespoons oil, sauté 2 minced garlic cloves and 1 medium onion, chopped. Add 2 to 4 tablespoons tomato paste *or* 1 cup fresh or canned tomatoes *or* ½ cup tomato sauce. Stir this sauce into the cooking beans. Add 1 or 2 teaspoons salt after the beans have cooked.

You can vary what you add to the basic sauce, before stirring the mixture into the beans.

For white beans (navy, pea, great northern, Michigan, or Italian), *add 1 teaspoon dried thyme, ½ teaspoon dried sage, 1 bay leaf. Just before serving, add ¼ cup chopped parsley.*
   Or
1 teaspoon dried mustard, ⅓ cup molasses, and, when the beans are cooked, 1 teaspoon vinegar. To make old-fashioned New England-style baked beans, add this mixture to the cooked beans with the onions, garlic, and tomatoes. Then bake, covered, in a 300°F oven for 2 hours. If the beans are still soupy, remove the cover and cook another ½ hour, or until the liquid is absorbed.

For black beans, *stir 1 teaspoon ground cumin into the oil and onions before adding the tomato paste or sauce. Or use ½ teaspoon each ground cumin, coriander, and turmeric.*
   Or
Skip the basic garlic-onion-tomato sauce. Cook the beans plain. Then, just

before serving, stir a little ground cumin and some yogurt into the beans.

For kidney beans, *stir 1 tablespoon chile powder and one teaspoon ground cumin into the oil and onions before adding the tomato paste or sauce. When the beans are cooked, preheat the oven to 350°F. Drain the beans well and put them in a casserole or baking dish. Sprinkle some shredded cheddar cheese over the top. Bake for 20 minutes. If the cheese has not yet melted, put the baking dish under the broiler for about 2 minutes.*

Small Red Beans, Nicaraguan Style

Cook the beans plain and drain off the water. Then, for each cup of dry beans, chop a small onion and half a green pepper. Sauté the chopped vegetables in oil. (Nicaraguans use coconut oil.) Add drained beans and cook until you no longer see water. Add an equal amount of cooked rice. Mix and cook, stirring, for 5 or 10 minutes. Serve with cubed cheese, preferably Mexican white cheese, and taco sauce (or use the *ranchero* sauce on page 242).

Bean Soups

Some of the bean-cooking ideas suggested above can also be used for bean soup. Basically, you just use more water—about 8 cups, instead of 6 cups, for a pound of beans. You might also want to chop more vegetables, such as a carrot, a stalk of celery, and a green pepper, to sauté with the onions and garlic.

White-bean soup can be seasoned with the thyme-sage-bay leaf-parsley combination suggested above. For a smooth, thick soup, mash about a third of the cooked beans in a blender or food processor. Return to the pot, stir, and serve.

For black-bean soup, season with ½ teaspoon each ground cumin, coriander, and turmeric. Just before serving, add ½ cup lemon juice or a few tablespoons of rum or sherry wine.

For our family's favorite bean-soup recipes, see lentil soup on page 222, and minestrone on page 225.

• COOKING WITH TOFU

The soybean curd called tofu comes in two basic forms, firm and soft. Most fresh tofu sold floating in water is "firm" tofu, though it might seem soft until you see "soft" tofu. For frying or deep-frying, buy firm tofu if possible. Dry the tofu between layers of a terry-cloth towel. If you have time, cover the towel with a breadboard or heavy book and let sit for an hour or more before cooking. Before frying or deep-frying, read the directions for cooking with oil on page 203.

All these recipes are for one person.

Stir-Fried Tofu

Cut a 4-ounce square of tofu into ½-inch cubes before drying. Heat 1 tablespoon vegetable oil in a small skillet. Add ½ teaspoon minced garlic or ½ teaspoon fresh-grated ginger root, or both. Fry, stirring, about 2 minutes. Add the tofu and cook, stirring, until golden brown—about 1 or 2 minutes. Remove and drain on paper towel.

Marinated Tofu

Cut 4-ounce square of tofu into 6 to 8 slices and pat dry. Dip the slices in tamari or shoyu and let stand 1 hour. Then coat each slice with flour. Bring a small skillet to medium heat and add enough oil just to coat the bottom. Add the tofu and grill, about 2 minutes on each side.

Deep-Fried Tofu

Cut 4-ounce square of tofu into about 6 slices before drying. Heat 2 inches of oil in a wok or small skillet over medium-high heat. Drop in the tofu slices one by one. Never have more than 2 or 3 slices in the oil at one time, as crowding will cool the oil and prevent browning. The slices will float to the top of the oil after a minute or two. When they are a light golden brown on both sides (another minute or so), they are done. Remove and drain on paper towel.

Tofu "French Fries"

Cut the tofu squares into french fry–sized sticks. Coat with flour and deep-fry as above.

All these fried tofu dishes can be served with brown rice, tamari or shoyu, and a steamed or stir-fried vegetable.

Other Ways to Use Tofu

Soft or firm tofu can be used for these dishes, and it does not have to be dried:

☐ Crumble up some tofu and stir-fry with vegetables and tamari. Serve with rice for a complete meal.

☐ Mash some tofu with a little tamari or miso paste and stir it into cooked brown rice or bulgur wheat. With a tossed salad or a steamed green vegetable, this makes a complete quick meal for one person.

☐ Cut tofu into small cubes and sprinkle into a tossed salad.

☐ Blend tofu with yogurt or tahini in a salad dressing (pages 249-50).

☐ Other recipes for tofu are given on pages 220 and 255.

●TEMPEH

Soy tempeh, described on page 153, can be fried or deep-fried like tofu and has a more interesting flavor in itself. It is good cut into strips and grilled, with a little lemon juice and tamari sprinkled on just before serving. Another good way to season tempeh is to rub the slices with ground coriander and minced garlic before frying. Or, cut it into cubes or shreds and stir-fry with a vegetable.

To avoid using oil, you can broil seasoned or unseasoned tempeh. Put the strips on a broiler pan close to the flame and cook at 550°F for two minutes. Turn the pieces over and cook for one minute.

Serve with rice and tamari.

CHAPTER
26

Beans and Rice and Other Grain-Legume Recipes

•CUBAN BLACK BEANS WITH RICE

Cuban-style black beans and rice has become a classic vegetarian meal, although in truth Cubans traditionally cook a ham bone in their beans or cut up a slice or so of ham in the *sofrito* (a spicy fried tomato sauce). This makes the dish a good one for people who simply want to eat less meat or to phase it out gradually. However, if you've already kicked the meat habit, you'll find this hearty meal sufficiently flavorful without it.

1 lb (or 2 cups) dried black beans

Cook the dried beans about 2 hours according to the directions on pages 209–10. While the beans are cooking, make the *sofrito* mixture and stir it into the beans. Cook, stirring occasionally, until the beans are done.

Just before serving, stir in the vinegar. Arrange the pimento strips in a crisscross pattern over the beans.

Sofrito

2 tbsp oil
1 large or 2 medium onions, chopped fine

1 large green bell pepper, chopped fine
2 large cloves garlic, minced

½–1 tsp hot chile peppers,
   chopped fine (see pages 202-3)
4 oz tomato paste
1 tsp dried thyme or oregano
1 tsp ground cumin
½ tsp ground coriander

1–2 tsp salt, to taste
8–10 turns of the pepper mill
1 tbsp vinegar
1 pimento, cut into strips
   (optional but dashing)

While the beans are cooking, heat the oil in a skillet and sauté the vegetables over medium heat about 10 minutes, until they are soft and the onions clear.

Add the tomato paste to the vegetables. Stir. Turn heat to low. Add the seasonings, stir, and cook over low heat for about 10 minutes. Then stir this *sofrito* mixture into the beans.

Serves 4–6 with plain rice and fresh fruit.

Variations

☐ When you add the *sofrito* to the beans, also add the tomatoes from a 1-pound can of whole tomatoes, breaking them up with your stirring spoon as you do. If the beans are dry, add a little juice from the tomato can, but not enough to make them soupy.

☐ Add 2 or 3 tablespoons chopped fresh coriander with the seasonings. Delicious!

☐ Just before serving, stir in some chopped Mexican white cheese or Greek feta cheese.

•FRIED BLACK BEANS WITH TORTILLAS

This popular party dish is based on the Mexican classic, *frijoles refritos,* which translates as "refried beans." However, as Diane Kennedy explains in *The Cuisines of Mexico,* a more accurate translation in this case would be "well fried," because the beans are fried thoroughly, but only once.

Note: If you are using dried beans, get them started first. To save last-minute frenzy, you can cook and mash the beans ahead of time. Before frying the beans, prepare the platter and then make the sauce. When the beans are fried, heat the tortillas and serve at once.

217

The Beans

1½ cups dried black beans
1½ tsp ground cumin

1–2 tsp salt, to taste
6 tbsp oil

Cook the beans in 5 cups water, according to directions on pages 209–10, adding cumin for the cooking stage. Stir in the salt for the last 5 or 10 minutes of cooking.

Mash the beans. This can be done with a fork or potato masher, but it is easier in a food processor or blender. Include a little of the bean liquid with each batch of beans and blend about 1 cup at a time until the mixture is mushy but still a little lumpy with beans.

About 20 minutes before you are ready to eat, heat 3 table-spoons oil in a large cast-iron skillet. Cook half the beans over medium-high heat, shaking the pan back and forth every now and then to prevent sticking. The beans should begin to dry out and to harden on the bottom, but not burn. Remove to a warm plate and cover to keep warm. Add the remaining 3 table-spoons of oil to the skillet and fry the remaining beans.

Note: In *frijoles refritos,* Mexican cooks fry the beans in lard, a form of pig fat, until they are dry and crisp. This is difficult to do in lard or oil, without burning the beans. Mashed beans are still good if you fry them only until they begin to harden on the bottom. For crustier beans, turn them over and cook until the other side begins to dry.

The Platter

Arrange on a platter, as the spirit moves you:
1 medium onion, sliced thin, with the slices cut in half
1 cup shredded cheddar cheese
1 cup shredded lettuce
plus any or all of the following:

2 tsp hot chile pepper, chopped fine
½ cup ricotta cheese or sour cream

a loose cup of alfafa sprouts
¼ cup chopped nuts
1½ cups chopped fresh tomatoes
1 carrot, shredded

218

The Sauce

This makes a hot sauce, but when spread thin on tortillas and topped with the beans, it is not overwhelming. Use less chile pepper for a milder sauce, more for a fiery one.

1 cup chopped fresh tomatoes or drained canned tomatoes
2 or 3 canned serrano or jalapeño chile peppers or small fresh chiles (see pages 202–3)

1 small clove garlic, peeled and smashed with the side of a knife
1 tbsp vegetable oil
½ medium onion, chopped fine
⅛ tsp salt

Blend tomatoes, chiles, and garlic together in a blender or food processor. (If you do not have either, strain the tomatoes through a sieve, chop the chiles and garlic as fine as you can, and mix.)

Heat the oil in a small frying pan or saucepan. Add the onions and cook over medium heat until clear and soft, about 5 minutes.

Add the tomato mixture and salt and cook over medium-high heat until slightly thickened, another 5 minutes.

Cover the pot, remove from heat, and let stand until ready to serve.

The Tortillas

12 large (7") corn tortillas   oil

Buy fresh tortillas or the packaged ones sold in refrigerated cases in supermarkets or natural-food stores. Just before serving, coat a medium-sized skillet with just enough oil to cover the bottom. Fry the tortillas over medium heat for about 20 *seconds* on each side. (Too much cooking will make them too crisp to roll.) Drain on paper towel and serve.

To Serve

Everything goes on the table, in separate dishes. Then each person takes a tortilla, spreads a coat of sauce on it, adds a layer of beans, tops with the various items from the platter, then rolls up the tortilla and eats like a sandwich. This amount serves 4–6 people. For a fuller meal for 6 people, serve with rice or fresh-baked corn bread (page 209).

•TOFU-FRIED RICE

This is a good way to use leftover rice. It makes a fast one-person meal with a steamed or stir-fried vegetable. The rice should be cooked at least a day before.

2 tbsp vegetable oil
1 scallion, sliced thin
1 large mushroom, chopped
1 cup leftover cooked rice

4 oz tofu, mashed
1–2 tsp tamari or shoyu, or more
    to taste
dash sesame oil

Heat the oil in a skillet and sauté the scallions and mushrooms over medium heat for 2 or 3 minutes, until soft.

Add the rice, crumbling with your fingers to separate the grains. Fry, stirring, another 5 minutes.

Add the tofu, soy sauce, and sesame oil. Cook, stirring, another 3–5 minutes.

Variation

Instead of tofu, you can add a scrambled egg and a handful of thawed frozen peas.

•NEW-AGE STIR-FRY

In one version or another, this free adaptation of the Chinese stir-fry is a staple among American college students who do their own cooking. Like any stir-fry dish, this requires that all the vegetables be sliced and lined up within easy reach before you start cooking.

6 tbsp corn or safflower oil
2–3 cloves garlic, peeled,
    smashed, and minced
1–1½" slice fresh ginger root,
    peeled and chopped fine
    (about 1½ tbsp, chopped)
12 oz tofu, cut into 1" cubes
1 medium onion, peeled and cut
    into thin slices, with the slices
    cut in half

1 green bell pepper, cut into thin
    strips
1–2 tbsp fresh or canned chile
    pepper, chopped fine (see
    pages 202-3)
1 lb (2 stalks) broccoli,
    cut into florets, with about 3"
    of stem, sliced thin (discard
    remainder of stem, or save
    for soup)

2 cups sliced bok choy (Chinese cabbage) or fresh whole spinach leaves

¼ lb (1–1½ cups) mushrooms, sliced
1 cup mung bean sprouts
2 tsp sesame oil
2–3 tbsp tamari

Heat the oil in a wok or large skillet.

Drop in the ginger and garlic and stir for 1 minute. Add tofu and fry, stirring, for 1 or 2 minutes, until golden brown. Remove to paper towel.

Add the onions, pepper, and chile. Cook, stirring, for 2 minutes. Add the broccoli and cook, stirring, for 5 minutes.

Clear a space in the center of the pan. Add the mushrooms and bok choy and stir-fry 1 minute. Stir in the sprouts. Return the tofu to the wok. Add the sesame oil and tamari and stir. Cover and cook for 2 or 3 minutes, until the vegetables are softened but not soggy.

Serves 4–6 with brown rice.

Variations

☐ Instead of tofu, use 8 oz tempeh cut into thin shreds.
☐ Where ginger root is unavailable, powdered ginger is often used. This is a free-wheeling dish, so almost any combination of vegetables will do.

•PEANUT SAUCE WITH RICE AND BROCCOLI

This is my version of a dish once served at the Beat'n Path, a vegetarian café in Hoboken, New Jersey.

2 cups brown rice
2 stalks broccoli
3 tbsp oil
1 onion, chopped fine
1 small carrot, chopped fine
2 stalks celery with leaves, chopped fine
2 cloves garlic, crushed and minced

½ tsp ground cumin
½ tsp ground coriander
¼ tsp ground turmeric
⅛ tsp ground cayenne (hot red pepper)
½ cup apple juice
½ cup peanut butter
⅓ cup raisins
1 tbsp tamari

221

Before you begin, chop the vegetables for the sauce.

Then cook the rice in 4 cups water, as directed on page 207.

While the rice is cooking, cut the broccoli into florets about 1 inch wide at the top, with stems about 3 or 4 inches long. Steam the broccoli for about 10 minutes, until softened but not limp.

While the broccoli is steaming, cook the sauce:

Heat the oil in a medium-sized skillet. Sauté the onion, carrot, celery, and garlic over medium heat for 5 or 10 minutes until they are soft and clear and just beginning to turn golden brown.

Turn heat to low. Add the cumin, coriander, turmeric, and cayenne. Cook, stirring, about 1 minute.

Add the apple juice and stir. Add the peanut butter, stirring, until the sauce is smooth. Add the raisins, then ½ cup of water. Stir in the tamari. Cook about 10 minutes, stirring occasionally. If the sauce needs thinning, add more water.

For each serving, top a portion of rice with some broccoli and cover both with sauce.

Serves 4.

•LENTIL SOUP

1 lb (or 2 cups) dried lentils
1 bay leaf
1 large onion, chopped small
2 large green bell peppers, chopped small
2 or 3 carrots, shredded
2 large cloves garlic, minced
2 stalks celery with leaves, chopped small

1 medium potato, cut into ¼–½" cubes (optional)
1 tsp salt, or more, to taste
1 tsp dried thyme leaf
½ tsp dried sage, crumbled
½ tsp dried rosemary
8–10 turns of the pepper mill
1 16- or 20-oz can tomatoes
2–3 tbsp tomato paste
¼ cup chopped parsley

Rinse the lentils and put them in a large pot with the bay leaf and 8 cups water. Bring to a boil. Reduce heat so the lentils are not quite boiling.

Add the chopped vegetables. Add the seasonings and stir. Add the tomatoes. In the pot, break them up with a spoon.

When the lentils have cooked for 2 hours, add the tomato paste and parsley. Stir. Cook about 5 minutes and serve.

Serves 4–6 with a tossed salad and whole-wheat bread.

Variation

You can make the same soup with split peas instead of lentils.

• INDIAN LENTIL DAL

1½ cups dried lentils	1 tsp salt, or more, to taste
4 cups water	⅛–¼ tsp ground cayenne (hot
2 whole cloves garlic, peeled and	red pepper), optional
smashed flat with a broad knife	1 tsp ground turmeric
2 thin (1 × ⅛″) slices fresh	2 tbsp vegetable oil
ginger, peeled	1 tsp whole cumin seeds
1 bay leaf	1 tbsp lemon juice

Bring the water to a boil in a large heavy saucepan and add the lentils.

Add the seasonings, cover the pot, turn heat to medium low, and simmer about an hour. Add more water if needed to keep the lentils just covered.

Just before serving, heat the oil in a small frying pan and cook the cumin seeds for a few seconds until they begin to darken. Add the oil and cumin seeds to the dal with the lemon juice.

Serves 4–6 people with rice and an Indian vegetable (page 245).

Note: Indians usually make a soupier dal, using 6 cups of water for 1½ cups lentils. However, when dal and rice are the heart of the meal, we prefer a thick dal, served over the rice.

Variation

Leftover dal is delicious mixed with equal parts of cooked rice and chopped mushrooms. First, sauté the chopped mushrooms in a little oil. Then mix all three ingredients together, turn into a greased baking dish, and bake for 30 minutes at 350°F.

223

• INDIAN CHICK-PEA DAL

This recipe is adapted from Madhur Jaffrey's *Invitation to Indian Cooking*. It is a favorite of our family and guests.

3 tbsp oil
1 medium onion, chopped
2 cloves garlic, minced
1 tsp ground coriander
½ tsp ground cumin
¼ tsp ground cloves
¼ tsp ground cinnamon
¼ tsp ground nutmeg

¼ tsp ground ginger
⅛ tsp cayenne (hot red pepper),
*   optional*
1 tbsp tomato paste
¼ tsp salt
2 cups cooked chick peas (or 1
*   can)*
1 tbsp lemon juice

Heat the oil in a heavy pot or skillet.

Add the onion and garlic and cook over medium heat until just beginning to brown—about 8 or 10 minutes.

Turn heat to low and add the spices. Mix and fry, stirring, for about 2 minutes.

Add tomato paste and stir. Add salt, chick peas, and 2 tablespoons of the chick-pea cooking liquid. Stir. Stir in the lemon juice. Cover and cook 10 minutes, stirring after 5.

Serves 3 or 4 people with rice and an Indian vegetable (page 245). Or use it for a party snack with raw vegetables and cucumber raita (page 255).

• BULGUR-STUFFED PEPPERS

1 cup bulgur wheat
6 large red or green bell peppers,
*   squat and fat for stuffing*
1½ tbsp vegetable oil
1 large onion, chopped fine
2 cloves garlic, minced
½ tsp thyme leaves

½ tsp dried sage
½ tsp dried rosemary
½ tsp salt
8–10 turns of the pepper mill
1 16-oz can tomatoes, chopped
2 cups cooked chick peas
5 oz cheddar cheese, shredded

Cook the bulgur wheat in 2 cups water for 15 minutes (see page 208). Remove from heat and let sit, covered.

While the wheat is cooking, cut the tops off the peppers and remove the cores and seeds. Put the peppers upside down in a steamer and steam for 5 minutes. (Or boil them for 5 minutes.) Core and chop the pepper tops.

Heat the oil in a medium skillet and sauté the onions, garlic, and pepper tops until they are soft and the onions clear.

Add the chopped vegetables, seasonings, and tomatoes to the bulgur wheat. Stir.

Preheat oven to 350°F.

Drain the chick peas and mash with a fork, or in a blender or food processor. Stir into the bulgur-tomato mixture. Mix. Stuff mixture into the peppers.

Put the stuffed peppers in a greased baking pan. Top each one with shredded cheese. Cover with aluminum foil, tight around the edges of the pan but loose on top so the cheese won't stick. Bake 40 minutes. If the cheese is not melted after 40 minutes, remove the foil and place the pan of peppers under the broiler for about 2 minutes.

Serves 6 with bread and tossed salad. Steamed carrots also go well as a side dish.

•MINESTRONE

4 tbsp olive oil
2 large cloves garlic, minced
1 large onion, chopped small
2 medium carrots, chopped small
3 stalks celery, chopped small
2 medium potatoes, cut into ¼"
 cubes
1 large or 2 medium zucchini, cut
 into ¼" cubes
½ lb fresh green beans (or 1 pkg
 frozen), sliced thin
½ head cabbage (3 or 4 cups),
 sliced thin, then coarsely
 chopped
1 16- or 20-oz can Italian

tomatoes (or 2 cups fresh, juicy
 tomatoes, chopped)
8 cups water
1–2 tsp salt
10–12 turns of the pepper mill
½ tsp dried basil
½ tsp dried rosemary
½ tsp dried sage
¾ cup dry white beans (or 2
 cups cooked beans)
1 bay leaf
¾ cup elbow macaroni,
 preferably whole-wheat
½ cup freshly grated Parmesan
 cheese

Heat the oil in a large pot over medium-high heat. Add the garlic and onions. Cook, stirring, for 2 minutes. Add the carrots and celery. Cook, stirring occasionally, 2 or 3 minutes.

Add the potatoes, zucchini, and green beans. Cook, stirring occasionally, another 3 or 4 minutes.

Add the cabbage and stir. Add the tomatoes, breaking them into pieces with your spoon as you add them to the pot. Add the water, salt and pepper, and herbs. Bring to a boil, cover, reduce heat, and simmer for 3 hours.

While the soup is cooking, cook the beans with the bay leaf in 2½ cups water, according to the directions on pages 209-10. When the soup has cooked for 3 hours, add the cooked beans to the pot. Discard bay leaf. Bring the soup to a boil. Add the macaroni and boil gently for 15 minutes or more, until the macaroni is done.

Stir in the grated cheese and serve.

With a tossed salad, this substantial soup makes a complete meal for 6 people. Add homemade pizza (page 234) or a platter of bread and cheese for a feast for 8.

• RALPH'S MARKET PASTA AND CHICK PEAS

This recipe evolved from a lunch put together one Saturday at an excellent produce market in Hoboken, New Jersey. I happened to stop in that afternoon when the men were still talking about their delicious meal, and "Ralph's Market Pasta" is now one of our family's favorite dinners. This partial cooking and steaming might seem like an odd way to cook pasta, but the men at Ralph's tell me it's an old Italian method. They use enriched macaroni, but we have found that whole-wheat elbows work very well.

2–4 tbsp vegetable oil
1 large onion, chopped small
1 green bell pepper, chopped small
2 cloves garlic, minced
2 stalks celery with leaves, chopped small
1 or more small hot chile peppers (½ tsp or more), chopped fine (see pages 202–3)
1 large or 2 small carrots, chopped small
½ cup chopped parsley

1 small-to-medium zucchini, chopped
3 or 4 medium chopped tomatoes, or 1 16-oz can Italian tomatoes
2 cups cooked chick peas
½ tsp or more dry basil
½ tsp or more dry oregano
½ tsp or more dry rosemary
salt and pepper to taste
8 oz elbow macaroni, uncooked
½ cup freshly grated Parmesan cheese

226

Heat 2 tablespoons oil in a large cast-iron skillet. Cook the onions, peppers, garlic, celery, chiles, and carrots over moderate heat until they are soft and the onions clear, about 10 minutes. Push to the side of the skillet while you cook the zucchini and parsley.

Add more oil if necessary and cook the zucchini and parsley until zucchini is soft, about 5 minutes.

Add tomatoes, but do not yet add the juice from the can. If using canned tomatoes, break them up with a stirring spoon. Add seasonings and chick peas. Stir.

To the liquid in the tomato can add enough water to make 2½ cups. (If using fresh tomatoes, add 2½ cups water.) Add to skillet and bring to a boil.

Add the macaroni and stir it in. Cover, adjust flame so the water is just boiling, and cook for 5 minutes. (Macaroni will not be done.) Stir so that any still-hard macaroni on the top gets stirred under. Re-cover and let sit *off* flame for 20 minutes, stirring again after 10.

Serves 4 with grated Parmesan on the side and a tossed salad.

CHAPTER
27

Pasta and
Cheese Recipes

•ON COOKING PASTA

To cook pasta, make sure you have enough water. For 1 pound of spaghetti, bring 6 quarts of water to a vigorous boil. Add 1 tablespoon salt. To keep the spaghetti from sticking together, add a drop of oil to the water before dropping in the pasta. For good measure, rake the spaghetti with a long kitchen fork. Make sure the water is bubbling vigorously, then reduce the heat until the water is just boiling and cook until the pasta is done as you like it. Timing depends on shape and size. Dried white spaghetti takes about 7 to 12 minutes, whole-wheat 12 to 15. Whole-wheat spaghetti will always remain chewy and will not benefit from further cooking. Fresh pasta cooks in a few seconds, and the comparatively fresh, nondried pasta sold in some specialty groceries in about 3 minutes. (Ask when you buy it.) When the pasta is cooked, drain in a colander in the sink. Rinse, shake dry, and serve immediately.

• GARLIC SPAGHETTI WITH EGG AND CHEESE

*1 lb spaghetti**
2 cloves garlic, finely chopped
½ cup olive oil
2 eggs, beaten

½ cup freshly grated Parmesan
cheese
8 turns of the pepper mill
2 tbsp freshly chopped parsley

228

Boil the spaghetti in salted water until done to your taste. Drain through a colander in the sink and return to the cooking pot.

While the spaghetti is cooking, heat the oil in a small frying pan and sauté the garlic over very low heat, stirring, until it begins to turn a golden color (not brown). Remove from heat at once. (It will continue to cook in the hot oil.)

Pour the hot oil and garlic over the drained spaghetti and stir. Immediately, add the beaten eggs and stir well. The eggs should start to solidify around the spaghetti strands. Then add the cheese and stir well.

Transfer to a serving bowl. Add the parsley and pepper. Toss. Serves 4, with a tossed salad.

Note: Refined, white spaghetti seems to work best with this recipe.

•PESTO GENOVESE

This delicious and simple pasta dish can be enjoyed only when you can get fresh basil, in the summer and early fall. Dried basil leaves do not have the same flavor.

2 cups chopped fresh basil leaves, well packed
½ cup olive oil
2 tbsp pine nuts (pignoli) (optional but good)
2 cloves garlic, smashed and peeled

½ tsp salt
½ cup freshly grated Parmesan cheese, plus 2 or more tbsp freshly grated Romano pecorino *cheese**
1 lb fettucini noodles

To measure the basil leaves, break each leaf into 2–4 pieces and then pack into a measuring cup.

Put the basil, oil, nuts, garlic, and salt in a blender or food processor. Blend until smooth. Then, scraping with a rubber spatula, pour into a bowl and mix with the cheese.

Boil the fettucini in salted water. When cooked, mix 1 tablespoon of the cooking water into the pesto sauce. Then drain the fettucini well and pour it into a serving bowl.

Pour the pesto over the pasta, scraping with a rubber spatula. Toss and serve with wooden salad tossers.

Serves 4 with an antipasto platter or tossed salad. Or, another delicious use for pesto is to add 1 or 2 tablespoons to homemade minestrone (page 225).

Note: Many pesto recipes in American cookbooks call for Parmesan *or* Romano cheese, or any combination of the two. You can omit the Romano *pecorino,* a strong cheese made traditionally from sheep's milk, but it adds a sharp, tangy flavor that makes the sauce more interesting. In her *Classic Italian Cooking,* Marcella Hazan says that a combination of about 4 parts Parmesan to one part Romano *pecorino* comes closest to the flavor of the sheep's-milk cheese used in Genoa.

Variation

For the French *pistou,* omit the pine nuts and add 2 tablespoons tomato paste to the pesto. Use as spaghetti sauce or stir into a vegetable soup.

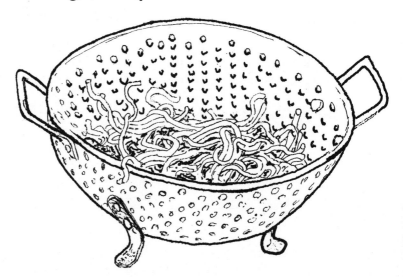

•BROCCOLI SPAGHETTI SAUCE

The secret of a rich, brownish-red spaghetti sauce is thorough, patient browning of the vegetables and tomato paste in generous amounts of oil. If you prefer, use less oil at each stage and cook the vegetables over medium heat until wilted but not browned. The sauce will still be good, but less rich.

1 bunch (2 or 3 stalks) fresh
 broccoli (about 1½ lb)
8 tbsp olive oil
2 medium onions, chopped
1 green bell pepper, chopped
2 cloves garlic, minced
1 small hot chile pepper, chopped
 fine (optional—see pages
 202–3)
1 small zucchini, chopped

1 6-oz can tomato paste
1 8-oz can tomato sauce
1 16- or 20-oz can Italian
 tomatoes
1 tsp oregano
1 tsp dried rosemary
1 tsp salt, or more, to taste
10–12 turns of the pepper mill
1 lb whole-wheat spaghetti,
 cooked

Prepare the broccoli as follows: Remove all the leaves and coarsely chop the larger leaves. Discard the tough bottom part of the stem. Slice the rest of the stem very thin and continue slicing up the stem until the tops fall into florets about 1 to 1½ inches in diameter. (Larger florets can be chopped in half.) Wash and drain.

Heat 5 tablespoons oil in a large skillet over medium-high flame. Sauté the onions, pepper, garlic, and chile for 7–8 minutes, until well browned but not burned.

Add the zucchini and cook another 5 minutes, until lightly browned. With a slotted spoon, remove the cooked vegetables to a bowl. Drain as much oil as possible back into the pan.

Reduce heat to medium. To the skillet, add 1 tablespoon oil. Add the broccoli, with leaves, and cook, stirring occasionally, for 8–10 minutes. Remove to bowl.

Return heat to medium high. (Throughout this browning operation, you might have to adjust heat up and down to keep things browning but not burning.) Add 2 tablespoons oil and then the tomato paste. Cook, stirring, about 5 minutes. The paste should turn from bright red to a dark, brownish red.

Turn heat to low. Add the tomato sauce, canned tomatoes, and seasoning. Break up the tomatoes with a wooden spoon. Stir. Return the cooked vegetables to the skillet.

Cover and cook over low heat for 1–2 hours. (Finer chopping and longer cooking makes a smooth, velvety sauce. Coarser chopping and shorter cooking makes a chewier sauce.)

Serve the sauce over spaghetti with grated cheese and a tossed salad containing chick peas. Serves 4–6.

Variations

☐ Use a head of cauliflower, cut into florets, instead of the broccoli. Or mix the two.

☐ Use 1 or 2 carrots instead of, or in addition to, the zucchini.

☐ Without the broccoli, this makes a good, basic tomato sauce for spaghetti and other Italian dishes.

• RICCO'S ZITI

This is my adaptation of the delicious ziti dish served at Ricco's Ristorante Italiano in Hoboken, New Jersey. It was demonstrated for me in the restaurant kitchen by the owner-chef, Ricco, an Italian cook from South America who looks like Paul McCartney.

1 lb ziti	*6 tbsp butter (¾ stick)*
½ cup freshly grated Parmesan cheese	*1 cup heavy cream*
	up to 1 tsp salt
1 lb mozzarella cheese	*a few turns of the pepper mill*
2 cups tomato sauce	*½ cup chopped Italian parsley*

Cook the ziti in 6 quarts boiling water for 12–15 minutes. Drain the water off through a colander. Return ziti to the pot, cover, and set on a turned-off back burner.

While the ziti is cooking, grate the Parmesan and cut the mozzarella into thin slices. Cut about ¼ of the slices into ½-inch squares.

Assemble all ingredients near the stove.

For the tomato sauce, use commercial marinara sauce or make your own sauce ahead of time according to directions for pizza sauce on pages 235–6. When the ziti is cooked, put the sauce in a small saucepan over low heat on a back burner.

Preheat the oven to 400°F.

Melt the butter in a large, heavy saucepan over medium heat. Add the cream and stir it into the butter. Add all but 2 tablespoons of the grated Parmesan and stir it in well. Add the mozzarella squares (not the slices) and keep stirring until they are melted and mixed in. Add salt and pepper and stir. (Omit or reduce salt if the mozzarella is salty.) Add the cooked ziti and stir well to coat the noodles with the cream sauce. Add all but 2 tablespoons of the chopped parsley and stir. Add the warm tomato sauce and stir it in well.

Transfer the mixture to a baking dish and top with the mozzarella slices. Place in the oven for 10 minutes until the mozzarella is completely melted but not brown. (If the cheese is not melted after 10 minutes, you can put the dish under the broiler flame for 1 or 2 minutes.) Top with the remaining 2 tablespoons each Parmesan and parsley. Serve at once.

Serves 4–6 with a tossed salad and a vegetable.

• LASAGNA

¾ lb lasagna noodles, preferably whole-wheat
1 lb mozzarella cheese
1 lb (2 cups) low-fat ricotta cheese
¾ cup freshly grated Parmesan cheese
½ cup hulled sunflower seeds

The Sauce*

4 tbsp olive oil
2 cloves garlic, minced
1 medium onion, chopped fine
1 medium carrot, chopped fine
1 stalk celery with leaves, chopped fine
½ green bell pepper, chopped fine
4 cups fresh ripe tomatoes or canned Italian tomatoes
½ tsp dried basil
½ tsp oregano

To make the sauce: Heat the oil over a medium flame in a large, heavy pan or skillet. Add the chopped vegetables and sauté for 10 minutes, until limp but not brown.

Add the tomatoes. If you are using fresh tomatoes, first drop them into boiling water for 1 minute. The skin will then peel off easily. (Use fresh tomatoes only if they are ripe and juicy.) If you are using canned tomatoes, do not yet add the juice from the can. Break the tomatoes into pieces. Add the basil and oregano.

Turn heat to very low and cook uncovered for 1 hour, adding some of the tomato juice (or water) if the sauce gets too thick to spread. This sauce can be made the night before.

To prepare the ingredients: Slice the mozzarella very thin on the slicing end of a hand grater. Grate the Parmesan. Cook the noodles in boiling water for 12 minutes. Drain in a colander.

Reserving enough tomato sauce to cover the bottom of your

baking pan, mix the remaining sauce with the ricotta. This makes the ricotta easier to spread. Stir in the seeds. Preheat the oven to 350°F.

To assemble the lasagna: Grease a baking pan with a 9-by-12-inch bottom, then cover the bottom with a thin layer of tomato sauce. Lay out noodles, slightly overlapping, to cover the pan. Cover with ⅓ of the mozzarella, then ⅓ of the ricotta-tomato sauce mixture. Make 2 more layers of noodles, mozzarella, and ricotta-tomato sauce. Top with the Parmesan. (With a larger pan, make 2 layers instead of 3.)

Bake for 40–45 minutes.

Serves 6 with a tossed salad.

Note: If you choose to use a prepared spaghetti sauce instead of making your own, use 4 cups of sauce. Mix with ricotta and proceed as directed.

• OVEN-RACK PIZZA

For the proper crispness, Italian pizza artists maintain that pizza must be baked in a brick oven. As a substitute, they suggest baking the pizza on a ceramic tile, which you can buy at a store that sells floor tiles. The tile should be preheated in the oven before the pizza is put in. Metal cookie sheets and pizza pans do not hold the heat as well and often produce pizzas with doughy crusts. If you do use a metal pan, it helps to bake the

dough for 10 minutes before adding the sauce and topping. If you choose to make pizza on a 10-inch or 12-inch tile *or* a pizza pan, simply cut this recipe in half and roll out to fit your tile or pan.

But there is another way to cook pizza. The oven-rack method suggested here is a favorite of the LaRocca family in Ann Arbor, Michigan. The dough is rolled out very thin and it does turn out crisp. The recipe makes about 12 square slices.

The Dough

1 cup warm (not hot) water
1 pkg active dry yeast
1½ cups whole-wheat flour

1½ cups unbleached white flour
⅓ cup olive oil

The Sauce

2 lb fresh ripe plum tomatoes or
   3 cups canned Italian tomatoes,
   without the juice

2 tbsp olive oil
¼ tsp dried basil
¼ tsp oregano

The Topping

¾ lb mozzarella cheese
1 small onion (optional)

1 green bell pepper (optional)
½ lb fresh mushrooms (optional)

To make the dough, drop the yeast into the water and let sit for about 5 minutes. By then the yeast should start to surge up to the surface. If it shows no activity, a drop of sugar, honey, or molasses should start it working.

Mix the flours together in a large bowl. Pour in a third of the yeast and water and mix it into the flour. Pour the oil into the remaining yeast-water mixture, then gradually stir the mixture from the cup into the dough.

When you can form a ball with the dough, remove it to a floured board or countertop and knead 5 minutes. (For kneading procedure, see the basic bread recipe on pages 205–6.) If the dough is moist and sticky, sprinkle with more whole-wheat flour as you knead. Then rinse, dry, and grease the bowl. Return

235

the dough to the bowl, cover with a cloth, and put in a warm place to rise. (An oven with a pilot light is ideal.)

While the dough is rising, prepare the sauce. Put the tomatoes in a medium frying pan with the oil, basil, and oregano. Cook uncovered over medium heat for 7 or 8 minutes. Then put a sieve over a bowl and strain the tomatoes through until only the seeds and skin are left behind. This gives you a fairly thick sauce. Be sure to scrape off the bottom of the sieve and add the scrapings to the bowl.

To prepare the topping, shred the mozzarella on a hand grater and set aside. If you wish to add the suggested vegetables, cut them into thin slices and cut the slices in half. Sauté briefly in oil until softened but not limp.

After rising for about an hour and a half, the dough should be doubled in size. This is the time to preheat the oven to 400°F. Then knead the dough for about 30 pushes and roll it out in a thin square to fit your oven rack. Tear off a sheet of aluminum foil to cover your rack. Turn up the edges of the foil. Lay the dough on the foil. Cover the dough with the tomato sauce and sprinkle evenly with the cheese and any other topping.

Pull out the lowest rack in your oven as far as it will come without tipping. With a helper so that one person stands at each side, pick up the pizza-on-foil by all four corners and place it on the rack. Return rack to oven and cook for 20 minutes.

Serve with freshly grated Parmesan cheese and dried red-pepper flakes. For a full meal for 6 people, serve with minestrone and a tossed salad.

CHAPTER
28

Egg Recipes

•BOILED EGGS

Eggs should be at room temperature before cooking. Eggs contain a small pocket of air inside the shell, and when they are heated too rapidly the air expands and cracks the shell. Either remove eggs from the refrigerator about 2 hours before cooking them, or let them sit in a saucepan of warm water for about 15 minutes, changing the water when it cools. Another way to prevent cracking is to prick the large end with a pin or needle. This allows the air to escape as it heats.

Bring to a boil enough water to completely cover the eggs. Put each egg on a spoon and place it gently into the water.

Timing depends on taste. Three minutes will make a very runny soft-boiled egg, 12 minutes a very hard-boiled egg.

•SCRAMBLED EGGS

For one serving, break 2 eggs into a bowl. Shake a little salt and pepper onto the eggs. Add 2 tablespoons milk or water and beat well. You can also beat in a little cottage cheese or ricotta and a pinch of oregano, tarragon, or thyme.

Over a medium-high flame, heat enough butter to cover a medium-sized frying pan. Pour in the beaten eggs, using a rubber spatula to scrape the bowl. When the eggs start to harden at the bottom, stir them up. Continue stirring rapidly until the eggs are no longer runny. Remove to plate at once.

• OMELETS

Everyone has a different idea about how to cook an omelet. The trick is to cook the top without burning the bottom, and to come out with a light, fluffy omelet. It may take a few tries to get the hang of omelet cooking, but I have found this method to be fast and easy.

If you are using a filling, prepare and have it ready before starting the omelet.

For best results, use a slope-sided non-stick pan.

Beat 2 eggs well with 2 tablespoons water.

Heat an 8- or 9-inch pan over a medium to medium-high flame and add 1 tablespoon butter. As soon as it melts, add the eggs. Lift a portion of the cooking eggs by sliding a spatula under an edge. Then tip the pan so that the uncooked egg flows under the raised portion. Quickly repeat this action about 90 degrees (¼ of the way around the pan) from your original lift. Move another 90 degrees and then another, until you have circled the omelet in four lift-and-tip motions. The whole process should take a total of 1 minute.

Still moving quickly, spread the filling over half the omelet while the egg is still slightly soft on top. (It will continue to cook.) Slide the spatula under the unfilled half and fold it over onto the filling. Remove from heat. With your left hand, place a plate upside-down over the omelet. Support the plate with your left hand while you hold the omelet-pan handle with your right hand. Then invert pan and plate together so that the omelet ends up on the plate. This final feat is not necessary, but it gives you a smooth, professional-looking omelet.

Suggested Fillings

☐ Shredded cheddar cheese
☐ ½ pound fresh spinach, steamed for 5 minutes, squeezed dry, and chopped
Season with ¼ teaspoon freshly grated nutmeg
☐ Leftover broccoli spaghetti sauce (page 230)
☐ Sliced fresh mushrooms, sautéed in equal parts oil and butter
☐ For a Spanish omelet, sauté in oil:
 ¼ cup chopped onion

¼ cup chopped green pepper
a few sprigs parsley, chopped
1 small clove garlic, chopped
salt and pepper to taste

Then add 1 chopped tomato, fresh or canned. Cook to heat the tomato.

• ZUCCHINI FRITTATA

This is a slow-cooking Italian version of the omelet, good for Sunday breakfast or for supper with tossed salad and bread. Frittata can be made with almost any vegetable, but zucchini works especially well.

4 tbsp olive oil
1 medium-large onion, sliced thin
  (about 1 cup sliced)
2 small zucchini, sliced thin
  (about 1½ cups sliced)
6 eggs
¼ tsp salt, or more, to taste
¼ tsp pepper, or more, to taste

2 tbsp chopped Italian parsley (In basil season, chop 1 tbsp each parsley and fresh basil leaves for a delicious frittata.)
¼ cup freshly grated Parmesan cheese
2 tbsp butter, margarine, or oil (Butter is traditionally used, but substitutes are satisfactory.)

After slicing the onion, peel or scrub the zucchini and slice them very thin on the slicing end of a hand grater (or in a food processor).

Over a medium-high flame, heat the olive oil in a large skillet. Add the onion slices and cook about 2 minutes, until clear. Add the zucchini and cook about 2 minutes, until lightly browned. Reduce heat and cook 3–5 minutes, until soft. Remove with slotted spoon and drain on paper towel.

In a large mixing bowl, beat the eggs until smooth. Add the salt, pepper, parsley, and all but 1 tablespoon of the grated Parmesan. Stir in the onions and zucchini.

To the skillet you used to fry the zucchini, add 2 tablespoons butter and melt over a medium-low flame. Pour in the egg-zucchini mixture and cook over very low heat for 15–20 minutes, until the eggs have set but are still slightly runny on top. Sprinkle with the remaining tablespoon of Parmesan and place under the broiler for 1 minute, to cook the top.

If necessary, run a spatula around the edge to separate the

omelet from the pan. Cut into 4–6 wedge-shaped pieces and remove to plates with a spatula. Leftovers can be refrigerated and eaten cold.

Variation

After cooking the onion and zucchini, add an additional 1–2 tablespoons oil to the skillet and sauté about a cup of sliced mushrooms. Drain the mushrooms on paper towel and add to the eggs with the zucchini and onion.

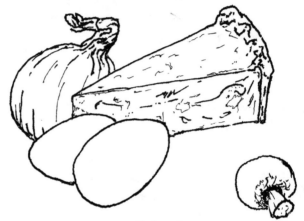

• QUICHE

1 9-inch piecrust
4 eggs
1 cup heavy cream
½ cup milk
½ tsp salt
¼ tsp nutmeg
6–8 turns of the pepper mill

1 tbsp butter
1 onion, sliced thin
1 cup imported Swiss, Gruyère,
    or Jarlsberg cheese, shredded
¼ cup fresh-grated Parmesan
    cheese

Preheat oven to 450°F.

Prick the bottom and sides of the piecrust with a fork. Bake 5 minutes. Remove from oven.

Beat the eggs. Stir the milk and cream into the eggs. Stir salt, pepper, and nutmeg into the egg-cream mixture.

Heat the butter in a small skillet and sauté the onion until clear. Sprinkle the onion over the piecrust. Spread the cheeses over the onions and then add the egg-cream mixture.

Bake 15 minutes, reduce heat to 350°F, and bake until set. (Check with a fork after 15 more minutes. If the mixture is runny or sticks to the fork, it is not done.)

240

Variations

☐ Sauté ¼ pound chopped mushrooms in butter. Add to the piecrust with the onion.

☐ Chop ½ zucchini. Sauté in butter. Add with the onion, with or without the mushrooms.

☐ Chop 1 stalk broccoli and steam 10 minutes. Add with the onion.

• EGG AND SPINACH PIE

This alternative to a traditional quiche has an interesting tart flavor and less fat.

1 8- or 9-inch piecrust
1 lb fresh spinach, without stems
2 tsp oil or butter (optional—see directions*)

3 eggs
1 cup plain yogurt

Wash the spinach well and steam for 5 minutes. Put in a colander in the sink to drain.

Preheat the oven to 450°F.

Prick the bottom and sides of the piecrust with a fork and bake 5 minutes. Remove and lower the oven temperature to 350°F.

While the piecrust is baking, beat the eggs in a large bowl. Stir in the yogurt.

Heat the oil or butter in a skillet and add the spinach. (*If you have a non-stick pan, you can omit the oil or butter.) Cook the spinach until the water emerges and evaporates, about 3-5 minutes. This ensures against a soggy bottom crust.

Spread the spinach over the piecrust and cover with the egg-yogurt mixture.

Bake until the eggs are set. (Start testing with a fork after 20 minutes. If the mixture is runny or sticks to the fork, it is not done.)

Variation

Slice and sauté 6–8 mushrooms and 2 or 3 small white onions. Add with the spinach.

• HUEVOS RANCHEROS (Mexican "Country Style" Eggs)

1 cup fresh, chopped tomatoes or
   1 cup drained canned tomatoes
1 or 2 hot chile peppers, seeded
   and coarsely chopped (see
   pages 202–3)
1 small clove garlic, smashed

½ medium onion, coarsely
   chopped
3 tbsp oil
2 tortillas
2 eggs

To make the sauce: Blend the tomatoes, chile peppers, garlic, and onion in a food processor or blender. Then heat 1 tablespoon oil in a frying pan and cook the blended ingredients over medium-high flame for about 5 minutes, until slightly thickened. This can be made ahead and reheated.

Heat 1 tablespoon oil in a medium-sized frying pan and fry the tortillas about 20 seconds on each side. Drain on paper towel.

Add another tablespoon oil if needed. Then fry the eggs in the same pan. Place them on the tortillas, cover with sauce, and eat immediately.

Vegetables and Salads – Side and Center

•HOW TO STEAM VEGETABLES

Steaming vegetables, instead of boiling them, preserves vitamins, texture, color, and taste. For three or four dollars you can buy a small steamer in the form of a collapsible stainless-steel basket, dotted with holes something like those in a colander. The sides are folded like petals in a flower and open to fit any size saucepan. Put the steamer in a saucepan containing about an inch of water. There should be enough so it won't boil away but not enough to come up past the bottom of the steamer. Bring the water to a boil, reduce heat to medium, and add your fresh or frozen vegetables. Cover. Steam from the boiling water comes up through the holes in the steamer and cooks the vegetables.

Cooking time varies according to the size of the vegetable pieces and the degree of doneness you want. In general, fresh peas, corn, and chopped zucchini will take about 5 or 6 minutes to cook. Whole green beans and sliced carrots take about 10 minutes, cabbage 15, and chopped broccoli, cauliflower, potatoes, and turnips 10-20, depending on the size of the pieces. Sliced beets take about 45 minutes. Frozen vegetables take a little less time than fresh. If the color starts to fade, the vegetables have cooked too long.

When cooking complicated vegetable dishes, it is handy to have more than one steamer.

If you can't get a steamer, boil the vegetables in a small amount of water for approximately the same time period. Save the water for soups and other vegetable dishes that call for added water. You can steam broccoli simply by standing the stalks head up in a small amount of water in a small covered saucepan.

Steamed vegetables can be served with a little lemon juice squeezed over each serving. This is especially good with leafy green vegetables such as broccoli and spinach.

•HOW TO STIR-FRY VEGETABLES

Stir-frying involves cooking vegetables over high heat in a small amount of oil, stirring constantly so they won't burn. It is important to have the oil hot before adding the vegetables, and to keep it hot while you cook. It is also essential that all the ingredients be chopped, measured out, and placed within easy reach before you begin to cook.

This method of cooking vegetables is borrowed from the Chinese, but many of the vegetables used are familiar to us as well. In addition to Chinese snow peas and Chinese cabbage, both available in many American produce markets, you can stir-fry chopped broccoli and cauliflower, whole green beans, and sliced carrots, turnips, zucchini, and acorn squash.

The Chinese wok is a cooking pan especially well suited to stir-frying. However, if you don't have a wok, you can use a heavy skillet. This should be heated before you add the oil.

To stir-fry one vegetable for one or two people, start with 1 or 2 tablespoons of oil. Then, add a small clove of garlic, peeled and minced, or a small slice of fresh ginger root, peeled and chopped fine, or both. Stir with a wooden spoon. Add the vegetables and keep stirring for 2 or 3 minutes. Then, add a dash of tamari and a dash of sesame oil.

Fast-cooking vegetables such as spinach, peas, snow peas, and bean sprouts need no further cooking. However, many vegetables will still be tough at this point. For them, cover the pan after adding the tamari and sesame oil. Turn heat to low and let the vegetables cook for another 5 minutes or so. Tougher vegetables such as broccoli, carrots, turnips, and potatoes might take longer. However, stir-fried vegetables should end up quite crisp, never limp or soggy. The Chinese say a vegetable is cooked when it reaches its height of color.

Broccoli, for example, becomes a rich bright green with a little cooking. When it begins to fade, it has cooked too long.

Stir-Fry Meal for One

You can make a complete meal for one by adding a little crumbled tofu or chopped tempeh to the vegetable. Stir in some cooked rice, or have rice on the side. To make a more interesting meal, add a few onion and green-pepper slices after the garlic and ginger, and toss in some mung bean sprouts just before adding the tamari.

•ALU-MUTTER-GOBI (Indian Mixed Vegetables)

1 small head cauliflower (about 1–1½ lb)
2 or 3 medium potatoes (about 1 lb)
6 tbsp oil
3 cloves garlic, crushed and minced
small piece ginger, about 1 by 1½ inches, peeled and chopped
1 medium onion, chopped small

1 tsp ground cumin
1 tbsp ground coriander
1 tsp turmeric
¼ tsp ground cayenne (hot red pepper), or more, to taste
1 tsp salt (optional)
1 16-oz can tomatoes
1 pkg frozen peas
3 tbsp chopped fresh coriander leaves (optional)

Cut the cauliflower into florets about 1 inch or 1½ inches across. Discard the center stem but cut stem branches into thin slices to cook with florets.

Peel the potatoes and chop into about 8 pieces each.

Heat the oil in a skillet over medium-high heat. Add the garlic, ginger, and onion. Cook for 5 minutes.

Add the cumin, coriander, turmeric, and cayenne. Stir. Add the potatoes and cauliflower and cook, stirring, about 5 minutes. Add the tomatoes and salt. Add 2 cups hot water and bring to a boil.

Reduce heat, cover skillet, and cook for about 15 minutes. Add peas and cook uncovered 5–7 minutes or more, until vegetables are soft.

Sprinkle with chopped coriander leaves and serve.

Serves 6 with dal, rice, and cucumber raita (page 255).

• MIXED-BEAN SALAD

1 cup cooked, drained kidney
   beans
1 cup cooked, drained chick peas
1 cup cooked, drained white or
   black beans
12 oz frozen lima beans, cooked
¾ lb fresh green beans, cooked
juice of 1 lemon

¼ cup vinegar
1 tsp prepared mustard
½ cup olive oil
1 medium onion, chopped fine
¼ cup parsley, chopped fine
½ tsp oregano or thyme
salt and pepper to taste

Use beans that have been cooked ahead of time and allowed to cool (see pages 209–10). Better yet, make the whole salad ahead of time and marinate for one or two days in the refrigerator.

For the dressing squeeze the lemon juice into a cup. Add the vinegar and mustard and mix. Gradually stir in the oil.

Mix the beans with the onion, parsley, and seasoning. Add the dressing and toss.

With fresh-baked corn bread (page 209), this amount makes a complete summer meal for 4. It can easily be adjusted for more or fewer people. It can also be varied to incorporate whatever cooked beans you have on hand, or whatever fresh beans happen to be in season.

• TABOULI (Middle Eastern Bulgur Salad)

1 cup bulgur wheat
3 or 4 fresh tomatoes, chopped
   small
½ peeled cucumber, chopped
   small
1 cup scallions, chopped fine

1 clove garlic, minced
½ cup fresh parsley, chopped
½ cup fresh mint, chopped*
1 tsp salt, or more, to taste
⅓ cup olive oil
⅓ cup fresh lemon juice

Put the bulgur in a bowl with 2 cups of hot water. Let sit for 2 hours. Drain well.

Add the chopped vegetables and herbs. Mix well.

Add the salt, oil, and lemon juice. Toss.

Serves 4–6 with pita bread and hummus (page 253).

246

Variation

If you are not using hummus in the same meal, add a cup of cooked chick peas to the salad.

Note: Fresh mint is the key ingredient in this recipe. Middle Eastern cooks say that without it, tabouli is not tabouli. If you can't find fresh mint, you can make a similar bulgur salad using fresh basil. Just don't call it tabouli. Bulgur salad is also worth making, but not as interesting, with plain Italian parsley.

•SALAD PLATTERS

You can serve a whole summer meal on a platter, with leaves of lettuce laid down first for a bed. Salad platters are fun to arrange and need only bread to go with them. For luxury, add a selection of cheeses. After assembling a platter, cover all ingredients with an oil and vinegar dressing (page 249).

The basic items for a salad platter include:

thin sliced onions, pushed into rings	strips of raw zucchini
thin strips of green pepper	celery strips
olives	scallions, sliced or whole
sliced mushrooms	sliced tomatoes or whole cherry tomatoes
strips of raw carrots	sliced cucumbers

By varying what you add to the basics, you can make the salad an Italian antipasto, a French salade Niçoise, or a Greek salad.

Greek salad Add sliced carrots, sliced celery, and cauliflower florets, soaked a few hours or overnight in a dressing of oil and lemon juice. In the center of the platter, use cooked or canned white beans or fava beans, tossed in oil and lemon juice. Dot with black olives. Sprinkle with small cubes of Greek feta cheese. Top with chopped fresh mint, if available.

Salade Niçoise Add fresh or frozen whole green beans, steamed for 5 minutes and cooled. In the center of the platter put a mound of cold boiled potatoes, sliced thin and mixed with parsley, salt, and pepper. Toss the potatoes separately in an oil and vinegar dressing before adding to the platter. Ring the platter with hard-boiled eggs cut into quarters. Add sliced beets, cooked and cooled. Sprinkle with thyme or tarragon. (Most salade Niçoise recipes also use tuna fish, but this can be omitted.)

Antipasto In the center of the platter, put 1 or 2 cups of cooked or canned chick peas, mixed with finely chopped parsley, onions, and garlic and tossed in oil and vinegar dressing. Add marinated artichoke hearts (available in Italian groceries or in jars in supermarkets). Add sliced provolone cheese and strips of pimento. Sprinkle with basil and oregano.

• TOSSED SALADS

Make a tossed salad interesting by mixing two or three kinds of greens. Iceberg lettuce is the type most commonly used for salads, but it is also relatively tasteless and non-nutritious. (As a rule, the darker the leaf, the higher the vitamin content.) Instead, try Boston lettuce, and mix in some leaf lettuce, endive, romaine, or escarole. All are easy to find in produce markets and supermarkets.

For a tossed salad, wash the lettuce leaves and dry them well in a salad spinner, wire basket, or colander. Then tear (do not chop) the leaves into manageable pieces.

Any of these foods are good mixed into a tossed salad:

thin green-pepper strips   *sliced cucumber*
thin-sliced onion rings   *sliced mushrooms*
shredded carrot   *thin strips of cheese*
alfalfa sprouts   *chick peas*
chopped tomatoes

Spinach Salad

A few fresh spinach leaves are good mixed in with a variety of lettuces. Or try an all-spinach salad with sliced mushrooms mixed in. Mung bean sprouts and sliced hard-boiled eggs are also good in a spinach-mushroom salad. For this, use a yogurt dressing (see below).

•DRESSINGS FOR SALADS

Basic Oil and Vinegar Dressing

2 tbsp wine vinegar
⅛ tsp salt
dash pepper

¼ tsp dry mustard or
½ tsp prepared mustard
2–6 tbsp olive oil

Beat the vinegar, salt, pepper, and mustard together in a small bowl. Then slowly beat in the oil, drop by drop. (Some like a half-and-half oil-vinegar ratio; others prefer more oil.) *Or* shake all ingredients together in a small screw-top jar.

To this basic recipe you can add ¼ teaspoon dried herbs such as thyme, basil, or oregano.

Makes up to ½ cup, enough for 4 servings of a plain tossed salad. Use more for a main-dish salad.

Yogurt-Tahini Dressing

2 tbsp lemon juice or vinegar
4 tbsp tahini

½ cup yogurt

Mix in a bowl or blender until smooth.

Tofu-Yogurt Dressing

2 oz (½ square) tofu
¼ cup tahini
¼ cup yogurt
2 tbsp oil

juice 1 lemon
1 clove garlic, smashed and
  peeled
1 tbsp prepared mustard

Mix in a blender until smooth. Add up to ¼ cup water, a little at a time, if you like a thinner dressing.

Beat'n Path Tofu Dressing

1 4-oz square tofu
¼ cup tahini
2 tbsp oil

2 tbsp cider vinegar
1 tbsp tamari

Mix in a blender until smooth. Add up to ½ cup water, a little at a time, until the dressing is the consistency you like for salad.

This dressing will keep for a few days in the refrigerator and can be used for a sandwich spread.

CHAPTER
30

Snacks, Spreads, and Sandwich Fillings

• GRANOLA

6 cups rolled oats
1 cup wheat germ
¾ cup chopped nuts (peanuts, cashews, almonds, and/or walnuts)

¾ cup seeds (sunflower, sesame, and/or pumpkin seeds)
½–¾ cup corn or safflower oil
½–¾ cup honey
1 cup raisins

Preheat the oven to 300°F.

Mix the oats, wheat germ, nuts, and seeds in a baking pan. Spread flat.

Measure ½ cup oil into a measuring cup and pour over the dry ingredients. Then measure ½ cup honey into the same cup and pour that over the dry ingredients. (The oil coating keeps the honey from sticking to the cup.) Mix thoroughly with a wooden spoon. If the grains of oats are not generally moist and sticky, add another ¼ cup each oil and honey.

Bake for 45 minutes, stirring every 15 minutes so the granola won't stick around the edges.

Turn off the oven. Stir in the raisins and return to the oven for 10 minutes until raisins are puffy.

Let cool, then store in a container with a tight-fitting lid. Have it with milk for breakfast or a snack.

Variations

☐ Add chopped dried apples and ½ teaspoon cinnamon with or instead of the raisins.
☐ Add sliced bananas for a change.
☐ Mix some granola into yogurt with bananas and honey.

• CRISPY SESAME CRACKERS

2 cups whole-wheat flour
½ cup sesame seeds
½ cup soy flour

⅓ cup corn or safflower oil
½ tsp tamari
⅔ cup water

Mix the wheat flour, soy flour, and sesame seeds. Pour the oil over the flour and mix in. Mix the tamari and water together, then mix into the flour-seed-oil mixture.

Preheat the oven to 350°F. Shape the batter into a ball, then flatten to a disk on a wooden board or countertop. With a rolling pin, roll out into a sheet ¼ inch thick. Cut the sheet into rectangles approximately 2 by 4 inches. Bake on a greased cookie sheet, about 15 minutes, until crisp.

These are good spread with tahini-miso spread (page 254).

• FILLINGS FOR PITA BREAD

A good basic filling for Middle Eastern pocket bread is chick peas and shredded greens—lettuce, cabbage, or both. The chick peas can be plain cooked or canned chick peas. Better yet, make them into hummus or falafel.

To this you can add any of the following:

bulgur wheat, cooked or soaked in water for 2 hours, or the bulgur salad tabouli (page 246)
chopped hard-boiled eggs
shredded cheese
Greek feta cheese, cubed or crumbled
sliced or cherry tomatoes

sliced onions
sliced cucumbers
shredded carrots
alfalfa sprouts
leftover bean salad (page 246)
leftover stuffed pepper filling (page 224)

Dress with a yogurt-tahini dressing (page 249).

When packing this "salad sandwich" for lunch, carry the dressing separately in a small screw-top jar such as a spice jar or baby-food jar.

•FALAFEL (Middle Eastern Chick-Pea Fritter)

1 cup cooked chick peas, drained	*¼ cup chopped parsley*
⅓ cup tahini	*salt to taste*
1 tbsp water	*dash cayenne pepper (optional)*
⅛ tsp ground cumin	*oil for deep-frying*
1 small clove garlic, minced	*flour for coating*

Mash the chick peas with a fork and mix in all other ingredients except the oil. Or, put everything but the oil and flour into a food processor and blend to a paste.

Form the mixture into 6 balls.

Heat 2 inches of oil over a medium-high flame.

Roll the balls in flour, drop into the oil, and cook until golden brown. Drain on paper towel.

Serve in pita bread with shredded lettuce and carrots and yogurt-tahini dressing (page 249).

Variations

☐ Instead of deep-frying, you can form the mixture into 2 or more round, flat patties and grill in a small frying pan that is barely coated with oil. Cook over medium-low heat for about 1 minute on each side.

☐ Or, preheat your oven to 350°F and bake the patties for 10 minutes on each side.

☐ Patties can be eaten in pita bread or with a fork. They are good smeared with yogurt, with a little fresh lemon juice and ground cumin sprinkled over the top.

•HUMMUS (Middle Eastern Chick-Pea Spread)

2 cups cooked chick peas, drained	*¼ cup olive oil*
	2 cloves garlic, minced
¼ cup freshly squeezed lemon juice	*⅓ cup tahini*

Mash the chick peas with a fork and mix in the other ingredients until smooth. Or, mix all ingredients together in a blender or food processor.

253

Uses for Hummus

☐ in pita sandwiches with shredded lettuce and carrots, yogurt dressing, alfalfa sprouts, and bulgur wheat
☐ as a spread on whole-wheat bread, or for tomato-lettuce-alfalfa-sprout sandwiches
☐ as a dip for broken-up pita bread

•SOME PACKABLE SANDWICH FILLINGS FOR WHOLE-WHEAT BREAD

All of these combinations contain a spread of one sort or another, and so do not require butter:

☐ Tahini and alfalfa sprouts
☐ Tahini and yogurt
☐ Tahini and mashed tofu, with a dash of tamari
☐ Sliced cucumber, watercress, and Beat'n Path dressing (page 250)
☐ Sliced cucumber, watercress, and yogurt
☐ Peanut butter, sliced bananas, and raisins
☐ Lettuce, sliced tomato, Beat'n Path dressing (page 250), alfalfa sprouts
☐ Tahini-miso spread (below), or tofu-miso spread (page 255), with alfalfa sprouts and lettuce
☐ Mashed cooked beans, mashed avocado, and lemon juice
☐ Low-fat ricotta, oregano, and sliced tomato
☐ Sliced cheese, sliced tomato, lettuce, and mayonnaise
☐ Egg salad: Hard-boil an egg (see page 237), cool, and peel. Mash the yolk and mix with mayonnaise and a little curry powder, salt, and pepper. Chop the egg white, mix with the yolk, and spread.

•TAHINI-MISO SPREAD

5 tbsp tahini	1 tbsp fresh-squeezed lemon juice
1 tbsp miso	

Mix until smooth.

This is good on crispy sesame crackers (page 252) or in a sandwich with shredded lettuce and alfalfa sprouts.

•TOFU-MISO SPREAD

4 oz tofu   1 tbsp tahini
1 tsp miso

Mash the tofu and mix in the other ingredients.

•CUCUMBER RAITA

A raita is a cool Indian relish, to have on the side with a spicy-hot meal. It is also good as a dip with raw vegetables.

1 cup yogurt   ⅛ tsp salt
½ cucumber, peeled and   ¼ tsp ground cumin or ground
  shredded   roasted cumin seeds (see * in
dash cayenne (hot red pepper),   recipe for Lassi, below)
  optional   dash paprika

Mix all ingredients but the paprika in a small bowl. Sprinkle with paprika.

Variation

For a non-Indian variation, omit the cumin and cayenne and add fresh chopped mint or basil leaves.

•LASSI

For an Indian summer drink, mix 1 cup yogurt and ½ peeled cucumber in a blender. Pour into a glass and stir in 1 teaspoon honey and ¼ teaspoon ground cumin.* Add an ice cube and stir.

*Note: If you can get whole cumin seeds, use them instead of ground cumin. Heat a small frying pan over medium heat. Add the cumin seeds to the dry pan and cook, shaking the pan occasionally, until the seeds begin to turn dark. This will take only 1 or 2 minutes. Then grind them to a powder, using a mortar and pestle.

Appendix

U.S. DIETARY GOALS
1. Increase carbohydrate consumption to account for 55 to 60 percent of the energy (caloric) intake.

2. Reduce overall fat consumption from approximately 40 to 30 percent of energy intake.

3. Reduce saturated fat consumption to account for about 10 percent of total energy intake; and balance that with poly-unsaturated and mono-unsaturated fats, which should account for about 10 percent of energy intake each.

4. Reduce cholesterol consumption to about 300 mg. a day.

5. Reduce sugar consumption by about 40 percent to account for about 15 percent of total energy intake.

6. Reduce salt consumption by about 50 to 85 percent to approximately 3 grams a day.

The goals are expressed graphically in Figure 1 [see page 258].

The Goals Suggest the Following Changes in Food Selection and Preparation
1. Increase consumption of fruits and vegetables and whole grains.

2. Decrease consumption of meat and increase consumption of poultry and fish.

3. Decrease consumption of foods high in fat and partially substitute poly-unsaturated fat for saturated fat.

4. Substitute non-fat milk for whole milk.

5. Decrease consumption of butterfat, eggs and other high cholesterol sources.

6. Decrease consumption of sugar and foods high in sugar content.

7. Decrease consumption of salt and foods high in salt content.

CURRENT
DIET

DIETARY
GOALS

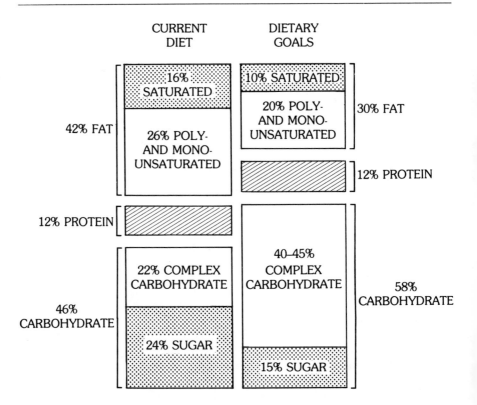

Sources for current diet: "Changes in Nutrients in the U.S. Diet Caused by Alterations in Food Intake Patterns." B. Friend. Agricultural Research Service. U.S. Department of Agriculture, 1974. Proportions of saturated versus unsaturated fats based on unpublished Agricultural Research Service data.

Reprinted from: Select Committee on Nutrition and Human Needs, U.S. Senate. *Eating in America: Dietary Goals for the United States.* 2nd ed. Cambridge: MIT Press, 1977 ($1.95).

Selected Sources
and Readings

The following bibliography includes major sources used for this book, major reviews of classic studies referred to or used for background, specific sources that require documentation, books or studies cited in the text, and suggestions for further reading. The books recommended for further reading are marked with an asterisk(*) and described in short annotations. Price information is given for paperback editions except for a few titles available only in hard cover.

For the convenience of readers seeking documentation or further information, the sources are listed in the order in which they are used or cited rather than alphabetically. Major sources are listed early in the relevant chapters.

PART 1: THE CASE AGAINST MEAT
Chapter 1, "The Age of Asparagus"

J. Leo, "How to Beat the Beef Against Meat; Parent and Teen-age Child Conflict." *Time,* vol. 114, Nov. 5, 1979, p. 112.

Janet Barkas, *The Vegetable Passion: A History of the Vegetarian State of Mind.* New York: Scribners, 1975. (Source of Hitler quote.)

Ryann Berry, Jr., *The Vegetarians.* Brookline, Mass.: Autumn Press (dist. by Random House), 1979.

Interviews with thirteen vegetarians, including Dick Gregory, Swami Satchidananda, and Helen and Scott Nearing.

Helen Nearing and Scott Nearing, *Living the Good Life.* New York: Schocken, 1970.

_____, *Continuing the Good Life.* New York: Schocken, 1979.

Dick Gregory, *Dick Gregory's Natural Diet for Folks Who Eat.* New York: Harper & Row, 1973.

National Research Council, Food and Nutrition Board, Committee on Nutritional Misinformation, "Vegetarian Diets." Washington, D.C.: National Academy Press, 1974. (Also published under the title, "Can a Vegetarian Be Well Nourished?" in *Journal of the American Medical Association,* vol. 233, no. 8, Aug. 25, 1975.)

Jean Mayer, *A Diet for Living.* New York: David McKay Co., 1975.

American Dietetic Association, "Vegetarian Position Paper." Chicago: American Dietetic Association, 1980.

Chapter 2, "Animal Rights"

* Jim Mason and Peter Singer, *Animal Factories.* New York: Crown, 1980 ($10.95).
    A strong argument against the cruelty and waste of modern meat and egg production, with photographs that support the authors' points.

Page Smith and Charles Daniel, *The Chicken Book.* New York: Little, Brown, 1975.

William Serrin, "Hog Production Swept by Agricultural Revolution." *The New York Times,* Aug. 11, 1980, p. A1.

J. Byrnes, "Raising Pigs by the Calendar at Maplewood Farm." *Hog Farm Management,* September 1976. (Source of quotation, "Forget the pig is an animal." First cited in Mason and Singer's *Animal Factories,* listed above.)

L.J. Taylor in *National Hog Farmer,* March 1978, p. 27. (Source of quotation on the breeding sow as a sausage machine. First cited in Mason and Singer's *Animal Factories,* listed above.)

Thomas Quinn, *Dairy Farm Management.* Albany: Delmar, 1980.

W.J. Miller, *Dairy Cattle Feeding and Nutrition.* New York: Academy Press, 1979.

Peter Singer, *Animal Liberation: A New Ethics for Our Treatment of Animals. New York Review,* 1975; New York: Avon, 1977.

Chapter 3, "Human Nature"

Nathaniel Altman, *Eating for Life.* Wheaton, Ill.: Quest Books, 1973.

"Research Yields Surprises About Early Human Diets." *The New York Times,* May 15, 1979, p. C1. A two-part feature including Boyce Rensberger's "Teeth Show Fruit Was the Staple" and Jane E. Brody's "Studies Suggest a Harmful Shift in Today's Menu."

Jane Goodall, *In the Shadow of Man.* Boston: Houghton Mifflin, 1971.

Richard E. Leakey and Roger Lewin, *Origins.* New York: Dutton, 1977.

_____, *People of the Lake: Mankind and Its Beginnings.* Garden City, N.Y.: Anchor Press/Doubleday, 1978.
  Both *Origins* and *People of the Lake* discuss the diets of early humans and contemporary hunting-gathering peoples.

Robert Reinhold, "New Testing on Fossil Remains Indicates Prehistoric Man Ate Balanced Diet." *New York Times,* Jan. 9, 1982, p. 11.

Chapter 4, "Why Eating Meat May Be Hazardous to Your Health"

Richard E. Leakey and Roger Lewin, *People of the Lake.* (See listing under Chapter 3, above.)
  Includes an extensive discussion of the nut-based !Kung diet.

Henry C. McGill and Glen E. Mott, "Diet and Coronary Heart Disease." Chapter 37 in Nutrition Reviews, *Present Knowledge in Nutrition,* 4th ed. New York & Washington, D.C.: The Nutrition Foundation, 1976.
  A useful survey, with bibliography, of studies linking diet and heart disease up to 1976.

Select Committee on Nutrition and Human Needs, U.S. Senate, *Dietary Goals for the U.S.—Supplemental Views.* Washington, D.C.: Government Printing Office, 1977.
  Includes extensive testimony from a variety of sources, including the meat and egg industries. Chapter 4, "Major Reports and Surveys," reviews studies on the relation between diet and heart disease.

Richard T. Silver, M.D., and Hibbard E. Williams, M.D. "The Preven-

tion of Colon Cancer." *American Journal of Medicine,* vol. 68, June 1980, p. 917.
Compact review of studies on diet and colon cancer.

R.O. West and O.B. Hayes, "Diet and Serum Cholesterol Levels: A Comparison Between Vegetarians and Non-vegetarians in a Seventh Day Adventist Group." *American Journal of Clinical Nutrition,* vol. 21, 1968, p. 853.

Roland L. Phillips, M.D., et al., "Coronary Heart Disease Mortality Among Seventh Day Adventists with Differing Dietary Habits: A Preliminary Report." *American Journal of Clinical Nutrition,* vol. 31, no. 10, October 1978, p. S191.

———, "Role of Life-Style and Dietary Habits in Risk of Cancer Among Seventh Day Adventists." *Cancer Research,* November 1975, pp. 3513 on (the entire November 1975 issue of *Cancer Research* is devoted to diet-cancer links).

D.P. Burkitt, et al., "Dietary Fiber and Disease." *Journal of the American Medical Association,* vol. 229, 1974, p. 1068.

R.B. McGandy, M.D., F.J. Stare, et al., "Dietary Regulation of Blood Cholesterol in Adolescent Males: A Pilot Study." *American Journal of Clinical Nutrition,* vol. 25, 1972, p. 61.

* Select Committee on Nutrition and Human Needs, U.S. Senate, *Eating in America: Dietary Goals for the United States,* 2nd ed. Cambridge: MIT Press, 1977 ($1.95). (Also available for $5.00 from the Government Printing Office, Washington, D.C., under the title *Dietary Goals for the United States.*)
In addition to listing the Dietary Goals, this report discusses the evidence and testimony on which they were based.

Harvey Wolinsky, "Taking Heart." *The Sciences,* February 1981.
Discusses the recent drop in American heart attack rate and probable causes.

Dietary Guidelines for Americans. A joint publication of the USDA and the Surgeon General, U.S. Department of Health and Human Services. Free during the Carter Administration, it may still be available, for $1.50, from the Government Printing Office, Washington, D.C.

Food and Nutrition Board, National Research Council, National Academy of Sciences, *Toward Healthful Diets.* Washington, D.C.: National Academy Press, 1980.

Jane E. Brody, "Experts Assail Report Declaring Curb on Cholesterol Isn't Needed." *The New York Times,* June 1, 1980, p. A1.

_____, "When Scientists Disagree Cholesterol Is in Fat City." *The New York Times,* June 1, 1980, p. C1.

Richard B. Shekelle, et al., "Diet, Serum Cholesterol and Death from Coronary Heart Disease: The Western Electric Study." *New England Journal of Medicine,* vol. 34, no. 2, Jan. 8, 1981.

Committee on Diet, Nutrition, and Cancer, National Research Council, National Academy of Sciences, "Diet, Nutrition, and Cancer." Washington, D.C.: National Academy Press, 1982.

* Patricia Hausman, *Jack Sprat's Legacy: The Science and Politics of Fat and Cholesterol.* New York: Richard Marek, 1981 ($12.95).
   By a nutritionist with the Center for Science in the Public Interest, this is especially enlightening on the politics behind government nutrition policy.

Chapter 5, "The Chemical Stew"

Samuel S. Epstein, M.D., *The Politics of Cancer,* rev. ed. Garden City, N.Y.: Anchor Press/Doubleday, 1979 ($6.95).
   A well-documented report by an authority on environmental cancer. Like the Environmental Defense Fund book listed below, this covers the science and politics of pesticides, PCB, DES, nitrites, and other food pollutants.

Environmental Defense Fund and Robert Boyle, *Malignant Neglect.* New York: Knopf, 1979.

Jacqueline Verrett and Jean Carper, *Eating May Be Hazardous to Your Health.* Garden City, N.Y.: Anchor Press/Doubleday, 1975.

National Research Council, Assembly of Life Sciences, *Health Effects of Nitrate, Nitrites and N-Nitroso Compounds.* Washington, D.C.: National Academy Press, 1981.

Bayard Webster, "Six Scientists Quit Panel in Dispute Over Livestock Drugs." *The New York Times,* Jan. 23, 1979, p. C2.

Eliot Marshall, "Antibiotics in the Barnyard." *Science,* vol. 208, April 25, 1980, p. 376.

Daniel Zwerdling, "The New Pesticide Threat." First published in the *Washington Post* in August 1973. Reprinted in *Food for People Not for Profit: A Source Book on the Food Crisis,* Catherine Lerza and

263

Michael Jacobson, eds. New York: Ballantine Books, 1975. (Source of FDA official's estimate of pesticide poisonings and deaths.)

Bayard Webster, "Nice Bugs to the Rescue as Pesticides Lose Their Zip." *The New York Times,* Sept. 23, 1979, sec. IV, p. 2.

Stephanie G. Harris and Joseph H. Highland, *Birthright Denied: The Risks and Benefits of Breast Feeding,* 3rd ed. Washington, D.C.: Environmental Defense Fund, 1981.

William E. Burrows, "Cancer Safety Controversy." *The New York Times Magazine,* March 25, 1979, pp. 82-5 on. (A report on PCBs in the environment.)

Dorothy M. Settle and Clare C. Patterson, "Lead in Albacore." *Science,* vol. 207, March 14, 1980, p. 1167.

Jean Mayer, "USDA Built-in Conflicts." Chapter 20 in *U.S. Nutrition Policies in the Seventies.* Jean Mayer, ed. San Francisco: W.H. Freeman, 1973.

Chapter 6, "The Cost of Meat"

Jim Hightower, *Hard Tomatoes, Hard Times: Report of the Agribusiness Accountability Project, Task Force on the Land Grant College Complex,* rev. ed. Cambridge: Schenkman, 1978.

————, *Eat Your Heart Out: How Food Profiteers Victimize the Consumer.* New York: Vintage, 1976 ($1.95 paperback).

Helen Guthrie, *Introductory Nutrition,* 4th ed. St Louis: Mosby, 1975.

Walter Goldschmidt, "A Tale of Two Towns." First given as testimony in 1972 Senate hearings on land monopoly in California. Reprinted in *Food for People Not for Profit,* listed under Chapter 5, above.
  Cites the author's 1946 study, "Small Business and the Community," comparing conditions in a small-farms community with those in a community with fewer, larger corporate farms.

U.S. Department of Agriculture, *A Time to Choose: Summary Report on the Structure of Agriculture.* Washington, D.C.: Government Printing Office, January 1981.

Milton Moskowitz, et al., eds. *Everybody's Business: An Almanac, The Irreverent Guide to Corporate America.* New York: Harper & Row, 1980. (Source of information on Holly Farms and other corporate data.)

John McPhee, *Giving Good Weight.* New York: Farrar, Straus & Giroux, 1979.

The title essay in this collection of McPhee's *New Yorker* pieces is a delightful report on New York City's Greenmarket.

Chapter 7, "Think of the Starving"

Frances Moore Lappé, *Diet for a Small Planet.* New York: Ballantine Books, 1971.

* _____, *Diet for a Small Planet: Tenth Anniversary Edition.* New York: Ballantine Books, 1982 ($3.50 paperback).

* _____ and Joseph Collins, *Food First: Beyond the Myth of Scarcity.* New York: Ballantine Books, 1979 ($2.95 paperback).
An eye-opening analysis of the causes and cures of world hunger.

Lester Brown, *The Twenty-Ninth Day: A World Watch Institute Book.* New York: Norton, 1978.

U.S. Presidential Commission on World Hunger, *Overcoming World Hunger: The Challenge Ahead.* Washington, D.C.: Government Printing Office, 1980.

Patricia L. Kutzner, "Eating Less in America Won't Help Poor Nations." *Hunger Notes* (a publication of World Hunger Education Service), June 1978.

E.F. Patrice Jelliffe, "The Impact of the Food Industry on the Nutritional Status of Young Children in Developing Countries." Chapter 11 in *Food and Nutrition Policy in a Changing World,* Jean Mayer and Johanna T. Dwyer, eds. New York: Oxford University Press, 1979.
A well-documented report on "commerciogenic malnutrition" resulting from bottle feeding in developing countries.

PART 2: VEGETARIAN NUTRITION: WHAT YOU NEED

For the nutrition chapters in this book I referred to hundreds of sources, including college nutrition texts, crackpot tracts I wouldn't dignify by listing, and technical studies reported in professional journals. As the authorities of last resort in the areas of nutrient requirements, deficiencies, utilization, and food sources, I relied on the following indispensable references:

Robert S. Goodhart and Maurice E. Shils, eds. *Modern Nutrition in Health and Disease,* 6th ed. Philadelphia: Lea & Febiger, 1980.
This weighty, 1,370-page reference book is a compilation of re-

views by different experts, each one a leading authority in the nutrient or nutritional topic he or she discusses.

Nutrition Reviews, *Present Knowledge in Nutrition,* 4th ed. Washington, D.C.: The Nutrition Foundation, 1976.
A more compact but also quite technical compilation, again by leading experts in the specialties they cover.

Committee on Dietary Allowances, Food and Nutrition Board, National Research Council, National Academy of Sciences, *Recommended Dietary Allowances,* 9th ed. Washington, D.C.: National Academy Press, 1980.
In this guide for practicing food professionals, the RDA committee not only recommends daily allowances for each nutrient but also explains how these amounts were arrived at. As in the other two basic sources, listed above, each chapter includes a bibliography of relevant studies.

Readers seeking reliable nutrition information in a readable form are urged to consult the following two sources:

* Jane Brody, *Jane Brody's Nutrition Book: A Lifetime Guide to Good Eating for Better Health and Weight Control.* New York: Bantam, 1982 $8.95 paperback).
By far the most comprehensive, reliable, and up-to-date nutrition guide available to the general public. The advice has value for vegetarians and nonvegetarians, and the sections on vegetarianism, animal fat, and cholesterol could make enlightening reading for parents and others who doubt the adequacy of a meatless diet. Brody's "Personal Health" column in the Wednesday *New York Times* is another excellent source of sensible nutrition advice.

* Laurel Robertson, Carol Flinders, and Bronwen Godfrey, *Laurel's Kitchen: A Handbook for Vegetarian Cookery and Nutrition.* New York: Bantam Books, 1979 ($4.50 paperback).
The most complete and reliable guide to vegetarian nutrition, with a solid variety of appealing recipes. An excellent buy.

More specific sources used or cited in Part 2 are listed below.

Chapter 11, "Carbohydrates"

Letitia Brewster and Michael F. Jacobson, Ph.D., *The Changing American Diet.* Center for Science in the Public Interest, 1755 S Street, NW, Washington, D.C. 20009. 1978, update 1982 ($4.00).
Interesting statistics on changing consumption of different foods

since 1910. (Source of information on sugar and soft drink consumption.)

"Latest Saccharin Tests Kill FDA Proposal." *Science,* vol. 208, April 11, 1980, p. 154.

John L. Hess and Karen Hess, *The Taste of America.* New York: Penguin Books, 1977.

Chapter 13, "Protein"

Frances Moore Lappé, *Diet for a Small Planet.* Listed under Chapter 7, above.

D.M. Hegsted, letter on protein quality. *American Journal of Clinical Nutrition,* vol. 30, 1977, p. 465.

Chapter 14, "Vitamins"

Linus Pauling, *Vitamin C and the Common Cold.* San Francisco: W.H. Freeman, 1970. (Reprinted in 1976 as *Vitamin C, the Common Cold, and the Flu.*)

Chapter 15, "Minerals"

The major surveys cited for iron-deficiency findings are as follows:

U.S. Department of Health, Education, and Welfare (now Health and Human Services), *Ten-State Nutrition Survey, 1968–1970.* 1973.

U.S. Department of Agriculture, *Dietary Level of Households in the United States, Spring, 1965.* Household Food Consumption Survey, 1965–66. 1968.

U.S. Department of Health, Education, and Welfare (now Health and Human Services), *Health and Nutrition Examination Survey (HANES).* 1976.

Nutrition Canada (1970–1972). Information Canada, 171 Slater St., Ottawa, Canada.

K.M. Hambidge, et al., "Zinc Nutrition of Preschool Children in the Denver Head Start Program." *American Journal of Clinical Nutrition,* vol. 29, 1976, p. 734.

Food and Agriculture Organization of the United Nations, Nutrition Division, *Calcium Requirements.* Report of a joint FAO/WHO expert committee. Rome, 1962. (Source of information on phytic acid accommodation in calcium absorption.)

PART 3: PUTTING IT TOGETHER
Chapter 17, "Food Groups"

U.S. Department of Agriculture, Human Nutrition Center, *Food.* Home & Garden Bulletin No. 228, 1980.
    The revised meal plan, issued under President Carter but withdrawn from circulation by the Reagan administration.

U.D. Register and L.M. Sonnenberg, "The Vegetarian Diet." *Journal of the American Dietetic Association,* March 1972, p. 253.

"Meal Plan for Total Vegetarians." Available free from the Department of Nutrition, School of Health, Loma Linda University, Loma Linda, Calif. 92354.

William Shurtleff and Akiko Aoyagi, *The Book of Tofu.*

_____, *The Book of Miso.*

_____, *The Book of Tempeh.*

For publishing information see listings under recommended cookbooks, below.

Chapter 18, "What You Don't Need"

Samuel S. Epstein, M.D., *The Politics of Cancer.* Listed under Chapter 5, above.

Environmental Defense Fund and Robert Boyle, *Malignant Neglect.* Listed under Chapter 5, above.

* Michael F. Jacobson, *Eaters Digest.* Garden City, N.Y.: Anchor Press/ Doubleday, 1972, updated 1976 ($5.00 paperback).
    Describes over 100 of the most commonly used additives and classifies them according to effects on health and adequacy of testing. Also available for $3.00 as an 18" × 24" poster, "Chemical Cuisine." Send to Center for Science in the Public Interest, 1755 S Street, NW, Washington, D.C. 20009.

Phyllis Lehmann, "More Than You Ever Thought You Would Know About Food Additives." *FDA Consumer,* April 1979.

Karen de Witt, "Food Law and the Carcinogen Problem." *The New York Times,* May 9, 1981, p. 20.
    Presents both sides of the current debate over scrapping or amending the Delaney clause.

Harold Hopkins, "The GRAS List Revisited." *FDA Consumer,* May 1978.

Life Sciences Research Office, Federation of American Societies for Experimental Biology, "Evaluation of GRAS Monographs (Science Literature Review)." Final report, FDA publication 223-75-2004, Washington, D.C.: Government Printing Office, 1980.

"Does Everything Cause Cancer? A Food Safety Primer." Washington, D.C.: Center for Science in the Public Interest, 1979 ($1.00).

Chapter 19, "The Search for Organic"

Luther J. Carter, "Organic Farming Becomes 'Legit.'" *Science,* July 11, 1980, vol. 209, p. 254.

Chapter 20, "Carbohydrate Power"

Jean Mayer, *Human Nutrition: Its Physiological, Medical, and Social Aspects.* Springfield, Ill.: Charles C. Thomas, 1972.
  A collection of Dr. Mayer's scholarly papers on nutrition. Includes a paper on athletic performance and diet, first published in 1959, which deals with the protein myth and the role of carbohydrates.

Bill Rodgers and Joe Concannon, *Marathoning.* New York: Simon & Schuster, 1980.

Rodger Doyle, *The Vegetarian Handbook: A Guide to Vegetarian Nutrition.* New York: Crown, 1979.
  A good general review of vegetarian nutrition. Chapter 7 discusses vegetarian athletes.

Vic Sussman, *The Vegetarian Alternative: A Guide to a Healthful and Humane Diet.* Emmaus, Pa.: Rodale Press, 1978.
  A lively and sensible argument for vegetarianism. Discusses vegetarian athletes on pp. 124-128.

Chapter 21, "Fighting Fat"

Jean Mayer, *A Diet for Living.* New York: David McKay Co., 1975.
  Addresses common concerns about diet and nutrition in an easy question-and-answer format. Chapters 7 through 9 deal specifically with nutrition and obesity, chapter 10 with underweight.

Laurel Robertson, Carol Flinders, and Bronwen Godfrey, *Laurel's Kitchen.* Listed under Part 2, above.

Theodore Berland and the Editors of *Consumer Guide, Rating the Diets.* New York: Beekman House, 1979.

Jean Mayer, *Human Nutrition.* Listed under Chapter 20, above. Includes Dr. Mayer's 1966 study of overweight adolescents.

Chapter 22, "Feeding Fido"

Richard H. Pitcairn, "Can Your Pet Be a Vegetarian?" "Healthy Pet" column, *Prevention,* October 1979, p. 132.

Terri McGinnis, *The Dog and Cat Good Food Book.* Brisbane, Calif.: Taylor & Ng (dist. by Random House), 1977.

Chapter 23, "Macrobiotics"

George Ohsawa, *Zen Macrobiotics: The Art of Rejuvenation and Longevity.* Los Angeles: The Ohsawa Foundation, 1965.

American Medical Association Council on Food and Nutrition, "Zen Macrobiotic Diets." *Journal of the American Medical Association,* Oct. 18, 1971, vol. 218, p. 397.

Frederick Stare, M.D., "This Diet Can Kill." *Ladies' Home Journal,* October 1971. Reprinted in *Reader's Digest,* February 1972.

Patricia Wells, "Macrobiotics: A Principle, Not a Diet." *The New York Times,* July 19, 1978, p. C1.

Stephen A. Appelbaum, M.D., *Out in Inner Space.* Garden City, N.Y.: Anchor Press/Doubleday, 1979.

Johanna Dwyer, M.D., reporting on nutritional deficiency in preschool macrobiotic vegan children in Boston, in *American Journal of Diseases of Children,* February 1979.

Michio Kushi, *Natural Healing Through Macrobiotics.* San Francisco: Japan Publications, 1979.

Anthony Sattilaro, M.D., and Tom Monte, *Recalled by Life: The Story of a Recovery from Cancer.* Boston: Houghton Mifflin, 1982.

Recommended Cookbooks

Brown, Edward Espe, *The Tassajara Bread Book.* Boulder: Shambhular Press, 1970 ($4.95 paperback).

A basic staff-of-life resource, with thorough, illustrated directions for all the steps in breadmaking, plus a collection of recipes for different breads, muffins, and cakes. From the head cook at Tassajara, a Zen buddhist monastery in Carmel Valley, California.

———, *Tassajara Cooking.* Boulder: Shambhular Press, 1973 ($6.95 paperback).

Purity and simplicity are among the virtues of this excellent introduction to meatless cooking with natural whole foods.

Jaffrey, Madhur, *World of the East Vegetarian Cooking.* New York: Knopf, 1981 ($17.95).

Authentic and delectable meatless specialties from the Far and Near East. Like Jaffrey's *Invitation to Indian Cooking,* listed below, this is for serious cooks who are willing to spend a little more time and effort at both shopping and cooking.

Jordan, Julie, *Wings of Life: Vegetarian Cookery.* Trumansburg, N.Y.: The Crossing Press, 1976 ($5.95 paperback).

A good starter collection of tasty recipes from the Cabbagetown Cafe, a vegetarian restaurant in Ithaca, New York.

Katzen, Mollie, *Moosewood Cookbook.* Berkeley, Calif.: Ten Speed Press, 1977 ($8.95 paperback).

Judging from their cookbooks, vegetarians in Ithaca eat well. This is an inviting collection of recipes and tips, in a hand-lettered "alternative" format, from the Moosewood Restaurant in Ithaca.

———, *Enchanted Broccoli Forest.* Berkeley, Calif.: Ten Speed Press, 1982 ($11.95 paperback).
A sequel to *Moosewood Cookbook,* bigger and more adventuresome than the first.

Lo, Kenneth H.C., *Chinese Vegetarian Cooking.* New York: Pantheon Books, 1974 ($3.95 paperback).
Directions for stir-frying, steaming, and other Chinese cooking techniques, plus recipes using noodles, bean curd, and other basic Chinese foods.

Nearing, Helen, *Simple Foods for the Good Life: An Alternative Cookbook.* New York: Delacorte Press, 1980 ($12.95).
Helen Nearing believes that no meal should take longer to cook than it does to eat. She doesn't count the time it takes to grow your own food, another of her principles. But if this philosophy appeals to you, and if wheat berries, raw oats, bran, and the like do, too, Nearing's book is for you.

Ohsawa, Lima, with Nahum Stiskin, *The Art of Just Cooking.* Brookline, Mass.: Autumn Press, 1974 ($6.50 paperback).
A leading macrobiotic cookbook, by the widow of George Ohsawa. You don't have to be macrobiotish to enjoy this pristine, Japanese-derived cuisine.

Shulman, Martha Rose, *The Vegetarian Feast.* New York: Harper & Row, 1979 ($11.95).

———, *Fast Vegetarian Feast.* New York: Dial Press, 1982 ($11.95 paperback).
The recipes in Shulman's first collection, developed at her vegetarian catering service in Texas, are delicious and creative. Her second book maintains the flair while restricting fat and salt and cutting down on cooking time.

Shurtleff, William, and Aoyagi, Akiko, *The Book of Tofu,* rev. ed. New York: Ballantine Books, 1979 ($2.95 paperback).

———, *The Book of Miso,* rev. ed. New York: Ballantine Books, 1981 ($3.50 paperback).

———, *The Book of Tempeh.* New York: Harper & Row, 1979 ($6.95 paperback).
The books that introduced soy foods to Americans, with cultural

background, instructions for making your own, and recipes for using the foods in both traditional and American dishes.

Thomas, Anna, *The Vegetarian Epicure*. New York: Vintage, 1972 ($4.95 paperback).

————, *The Vegetarian Epicure Book Two*. New York: Alfred A. Knopf, 1978 ($6.95 paperback).
Pastas, soufflés, bean soups, Mexican and Indian specialties, and other luscious offerings for sensuous vegetarians, new vegetarians, and all your meat-eating friends who think that vegetarian foods can't have pizazz.

ETHNIC COOKBOOKS
The classic ethnic cookbooks listed below are not vegetarian, but they all contain enough meatless recipes to make them worth your while —whether you want to mix up a snack, put together a many-course meal, or make your own pastas, tortillas, pita bread, or poori (one of the many Indian breads in Jaffrey's collection).

Hazan, Marcella, *The Classic Italian Cookbook*. New York, Harper Magazine Press, 1973 ($15.95).

————, *More Classic Italian Cooking*. New York: Alfred A. Knopf, 1979 ($15.95).

Jaffrey, Madhur, *An Invitation to Indian Cooking*. New York: Vintage, 1975 ($3.95 paperback).

Kennedy, Diane, *The Cuisines of Mexico*. New York: Harper & Row, 1972 ($16.95).

————, *The Tortilla Book* New York: Harper & Row, 1975 ($5.95 paperback).

Roden, Claudia, *A Book of Middle Eastern Food* New York: Vintage, 1974 ($5.95 paperback).

Index

(List of Recipes appears on page v)